Table for Eight

Table for Eight

Meagan Francis

ALPHA

A member of Penguin Group (USA) Inc.

Alpha Books

Published by the Penguin Group

Penguin Group (USA) Inc., 375 Hudson Street, New York, New York 10014, USA

Penguin Group (Canada), 90 Eglinton Avenue East, Suite 700, Toronto, Ontario M4P 2Y3, Canada (a division of Pearson Penguin Canada Inc.)

Penguin Books Ltd, 80 Strand, London WC2R 0RL, England

Penguin Ireland, 25 St. Stephen's Green, Dublin 2, Ireland (a division of Penguin Books Ltd.)

Penguin Group (Australia), 250 Camberwell Road, Camberwell, Victoria 3124, Australia (a division of Pearson Australia Group Pty. Ltd.)

Penguin Books India Pvt. Ltd., 11 Community Centre, Panchsheel Park, New Delhi—110 017, India

Penguin Group (NZ), 67 Apollo Drive, Rosedale, North Shore, Auckland 1311, New Zealand (a division of Pearson New Zealand Ltd.)

Penguin Books (South Africa) (Pty.) Ltd, 24 Sturdee Avenue, Rosebank, Johannesburg 2196, South Africa

Penguin Books Ltd., Registered Offices: 80 Strand, London WC2R 0RL, England

International Standard Book Number: 978-1-59257-673-9
Library of Congress Catalog Card Number: 2007926852

09 08 07   8   7   6   5   4   3   2   1

Interpretation of the printing code: The rightmost number of the first series of numbers is the year of the book's printing; the rightmost number of the second series of numbers is the number of the book's printing. For example, a printing code of 07-1 shows that the first printing occurred in 2007.

Printed in the United States of America

Note: This publication contains the opinions and ideas of its author. It is intended to provide helpful and informative material on the subject matter covered. It is sold with the understanding that the author and publisher are not engaged in rendering professional services in the book. If the reader requires personal assistance or advice, a competent professional should be consulted.

The author and publisher specifically disclaim any responsibility for any liability, loss, or risk, personal or otherwise, which is incurred as a consequence, directly or indirectly, of the use and application of any of the contents of this book.

Trademarks: All terms mentioned in this book that are known to be or are suspected of being trademarks or service marks have been appropriately capitalized. Alpha Books and Penguin Group (USA) Inc. cannot attest to the accuracy of this information. Use of a term in this book should not be regarded as affecting the validity of any trademark or service mark.

Most Alpha books are available at special quantity discounts for bulk purchases for sales promotions, premiums, fund-raising, or educational use. Special books, or book excerpts, can also be created to fit specific needs.

For details, write: Special Markets, Alpha Books, 375 Hudson Street, New York, NY 10014.

Contents

Introduction

When my husband and I had two kids, the world seemed specially created just for our little family. The four of us fit comfortably into nearly any passenger vehicle and even had room to spare for luggage or groceries. When traveling, we bunked down easily in hotel rooms without need for extra cots or an uncomfortable night for somebody on a hard and thinly-carpeted floor. If there were discounts for child travelers, we were always under the limit. When we went out to eat, we all fit into a booth. Three-bedroom houses or apartments were plenty big enough for us; if we had to, we could live fairly comfortably in a two-bedroom home.

When I had one child, everyone I met seemed to wonder when I'd have my second, and when I had my second, people seemed to view us as a perfectly completed set.

Then I got pregnant with my third child, and suddenly, eyebrows went up.

The comments and questions began. Parents who were struggling with one or two kids were baffled that I would be so crazy as to add another. They wondered if I was just a glutton for punishment or if I had some secret formula they didn't know about. Besides, they wondered, how could I possibly afford them all? Everyone knows kids cost hundreds of thousands of dollars!

Growing up with four siblings, I'd never really thought of a three-kid family as unusually big, but as I looked around me, I realized how few people I knew who had more than two children. When we added our fourth son last year, we were double the size of most families we know. And of course, you can imagine the reaction we got at number four: if three was weird, to many people, four was downright crazy!

In 1976, an American woman had a 36 percent chance of giving birth to four or more children in her lifetime, and about 60 percent had families of three children or more. Today, the number of women who can expect to have three or more has been cut in half to 29 percent, while those with four or more children has dwindled to 10 percent.

According to some social scientists, those numbers may be making a slow rise again. In the past year or so, big families have gotten some big press. Phrases like "three is the new two" and "four is the new three" have been tossed around in the media, indicating that more and more families may be choosing to expand beyond one or two kids.

It's true that many parents still have lots of kids for religious reasons. Catholics, Orthodox Jews, and Latter-Day Saints (sometimes called Mormons), as well as certain fundamentalist Christians, encourage large families. And Latino culture often promotes big families, which may cause an upswing in the American birth rate due to immigration.

Some social scientists point to the "at-home mom revolution" as the cause of this mini-baby-boom. For many working families, they say, the jump from two to three kids is when child care becomes unaffordable. So having more moms—and possibly, dads—willing and able to stay home makes it possible to have larger families.

And who knows—with celebrities like Angelina Jolie adopting large numbers of children from other countries, perhaps adoptive large families are the next big thing! And if you mention the fact that bigger families tend to be so because of their culture/religion? It's the elephant in the room to many people.

Of course, that doesn't mean the rest of the world has caught up yet.

Parents of larger families sometimes find it difficult to fit into a culture that's been rearranged to accommodate a family of three or four. Attitudes about what parents should provide children have shifted: it's pretty much expected that kids these days shouldn't have to share a bedroom, toys, or clothes with a sibling and many will have fully-funded college savings plans by the time they're eighteen. Fitting a family of three or more small children into today's average-size car can be nearly impossible once you factor in safety seats, while even many behemoth sport-utility vehicles only fit five comfortably (while still costing a fortune in gas!).

And it's not just the logistics, but reactions from others that big families have to deal with. While two kids usually seem completely socially acceptable—ideal, really—the birth of the third child seems to open parents up to a variety of nosy and sometimes downright rude reactions, from raised eyebrows to prying questions (my favorite: "So, uh, do you know how to use birth control?"). And when parents choose to expand to four, five, six kids, or more, they are often treated like they're crazy—or just plain stupid. Even if your family fits in where you live—for example, Utah is the one state that still averages three kids per family—you may still feel like an oddball when it comes to the expected "standard of living" that can make raising more than one or two kids trickier.

Families end up with a larger-than-average family in a variety of ways. Maybe you planned—or are still planning—to have lots of kids. Maybe you were surprised with a series of unexpected pregnancies. Or maybe you found yourself doubling—or tripling!—your family size all at once by marrying somebody with kids, adopting siblings, or giving birth to multiples. No matter how we get there, all parents with larger families face the same questions. Where will we put them all? How big a house do we really need? What kind of vehicle will accommodate all the kids without costing a fortune to run? How can we possibly give each child the attention he or she needs? And sometimes we may wonder if we are doing the right thing by bringing so many kids into the world!

This book is for anyone who's got more than the "average" number of kids, or who's curious about what it's like to have a larger family in today's smaller-family-centered society. I've spoken with a variety of parents raising as few as three—and as many as seventeen!—kids, and they've shared a wealth of wisdom, advice, tips, and encouragement that any parent can benefit from. If you already have a big family, this book is full of practical information you can use, on everything from home organization to discipline to finances. If you have a smaller family and want to see how seasoned moms run their households, deal with sibling issues, or maintain relationships with their partners—whether or not you are thinking of having a larger family yourself—I'm sure you'll find this book a useful and entertaining source of information. And if you aren't sure why anyone would do something so crazy as have three or four, five or six, or even more children, I hope to give you a window into our lives and some understanding of what make large families unique and wonderful.

Acknowledgments

Writing this book has been a learning experience! I would first like to thank the many parents who shared their tips, advice, ideas and philosophies on raising big families for this book. You are truly experts, and I know that readers will greatly benefit from your insights.

Thank you to my writing groups and to Laura Gross for support and encouragement.

Thank you to the writers at largerfamilies.com for sharing your wit and wisdom—you all are inspiring. And thanks to the greater blogging community of mothers with large and small families alike, whose insights and ideas have touched my own life and writing.

Thank you to my mom and dad for having a big family, and to my brothers and sisters for being a joy to be around. If it wasn't for all of you, I'm sure I'd have been terrified of having more than two!

Thank you to Jon, for your endless support.

And thanks to my kids, for giving me the idea to write this book in the first place. Thanks to Jacob and Isaac for helping with Owen and William a little more so that Mom could make her deadlines! And, of course, thanks to the four of you for being guinea pigs for all the ideas I gleaned while writing it.

Trademarks

How Large Is Your Table for Eight?

When you were a kid, did you ever look forward to adulthood with some very specific plans about how your life would play out? I did. I would be a singer, actress, writer, and elementary-school teacher (in no particular order). I would get married at 21, have kids at 22, and own horses. And I would have four children.

Of course, not all of my childhood dreams have come true. I'm a writer, but not a singer, actress, or schoolteacher. I don't own a single horse. I was even younger than 21 when I married and started my family. And though I did end up with the four children I wanted as a kid, back then I had no way of knowing how many factors I'd wrestle with as my family grew.

Money, for one. My parenting philosophy, which shifted a lot from baby #1 to baby #2, and then again when I added #3 and #4. My concept of "free time." My career plans. How old I wanted to be when the last kid left the nest. No matter what kind of family you always thought you wanted, life has a funny way of throwing a curveball. Maybe you never thought you wanted to have more than a couple of kids, but are now entertaining the idea of having five or six. Or maybe you're just getting your family off the ground but are pretty sure you want to have a big family. If you're trying to plan out how big—and how fast—you'll expand your family, you have a lot to consider. How closely you want to space your kids might depend on a lot of factors: your age, religious beliefs, parenting philosophies, fertility, career, finances, and more. You may want to space your children closely because you were a lot older or younger than your siblings and remember wishing you had a playmate. You might remember feeling crowded by your brothers and sisters and plan to give your own kids more breathing room. Or you may think the family spacing you grew up with was just perfect and hope to replicate it in your own family. Regardless of your plans, you want to keep some things in mind.

Your Feelings About Birth Control

Next to abstinence, hormonal birth control and natural family planning are in hot competition for the title of most effective birth control method. Many women don't want to use artificial or hormonal birth control, like the Pill, the patch, the Depo-Provera shot, condoms, or the diaphragm, for a variety of reasons. Natural family planning is noninvasive, safe, and compatible with most religious beliefs; but it takes time, forethought, and commitment.

> For more information on Natural Family Planning, try these resources: The Couple to Couple League, a nonprofit organization that teaches NFP through a Christian lens (www.ccli.org) and *Taking Charge of Your Fertility, 10th Anniversary Edition: The Definitive Guide to Natural Birth Control and Pregnancy Achievement,* by Toni Weschler, MPH (Harper Collins, 2006).

If you choose not to use birth control at all but practice what's called "ecological" breastfeeding—that is, nursing your babies around the clock without giving bottles or pacifiers—you can expect at least a 16-month spacing, because ecological breastfeeding is shown to work as an effective form of birth control until your baby is six months old—sometimes longer.

There are a lot of misconceptions in the United States about the role of breastfeeding in preventing pregnancy. However, evidence suggests that when breastfeeding is the primary source of calories for a baby's first year to year and a half of life, children tend to be spaced about two years apart. For some parents, two years won't be nearly long enough, so other forms of birth control will have to be considered. But if you're comfortable with a spacing of about a year and a half to two years or so and are planning on breastfeeding each child until at least a year (as recommended by the American Academy of Pediatrics), you may not need to worry about birth control methods at all until you feel your family is complete.

Your Personality and Preferences

Many parents of closely spaced children report that they liked never getting out of the flow of diapers, sleepless nights, and carrying little ones around. Others felt like they needed more of a "breather" after each child, particularly if they were prone to postpartum depression, had a spouse that worked long hours or traveled a lot, or were hit particularly hard by sleep deprivation.

When children are spaced closely, many parents report that the first couple of years are tough but worth it in the long run because the close siblings tend to be good friends, playing together and keeping each other occupied. On the other hand, parents of further-spaced children often report that they had more time to enjoy each baby when he or she was little and that the older children often proved to be a big help. Remember, just because kids are further apart in age doesn't mean they won't ever be friends. They may not have a lot in common when they're under your roof, but if you stay close as a family, a big-sibling/little-sibling relationship can develop into something more equal when they're both adults.

Your Career Goals

If you plan to combine work and motherhood (or fatherhood!), your line of work may dictate the way you space your kids. Will your job allow for maternity leave every three or four years when a new baby is born, or would you be better off spacing your children closely together and leaving the paid workforce—or scaling down—until after your family is complete? Is your career family-friendly? Keep in mind that the more children you have, the more likely you'll have conflicts between work and home. Finding family-friendly work is important for any parent, but it's vital for parents with lots of young kids.

mom wisdom

"Though I can't imagine telling someone else how to space their family, I'm glad we had our kids close together. I can't imagine 'starting over' with a baby when my other children were in grade school. Our way we always had someone in diapers, we always had car safety seats, we just stayed in baby/toddler mode for several continuous years. Now that's over, we're moving on and won't go back. Number four and five weren't a huge shock to the family. I joke that it was like 'throw another car seat in the van and go!'"

—Katie, mom of five, Maryland

Your Age

If you're starting your family young, you may feel like you've got all the time in the world to grow it and be in no hurry. On the other hand, maybe you'd like to have your kids in quick succession while you still have a ton of energy! Some young parents with many kids say they're glad they had them close together, because they'll be relatively young empty-nesters and able to live the freewheeling lifestyle they might have missed, only with more money than the average 20-year-olds.

If you're starting your parenting in your mid- to late-thirties or later, you have other concerns. Your chances of having multiple babies will go up but so will your chances of having fertility problems. You may feel a sense of urgency when it comes to adding kids to your family or be thinking about other options in case you find it difficult to get pregnant.

Child-Care Costs

If both parents in a family are going to be working, keep in mind that child care is very expensive for infants and then generally becomes slightly less expensive as your baby gets older, becomes a toddler, gets potty-trained, and, finally, enters preschool. If child-care costs are an issue for you, you may want to calculate how much you can afford to pay at once and space your children so you only have so many in child care at any given time. For example, to have an infant, a two-year-old, and a four-year-old in full-time child care would be a lot more expensive than an infant and a three-year-old with the next oldest in kindergarten.

mom wisdom

"We've had kids as little as 14 months apart, and as much as four years apart. In a way, the 14-month separation was easiest, since both kids were doing roughly the same things at the same time. But when they were infants, it was extremely exhausting. Which brings us to the four-year separation; in a way, that separation was equally easy since the older kids could help with their little sister. But I also had to deal with jealousy, since my then four-year-old didn't like having her position as youngest usurped by the new baby. Some people really love close spacing, while others find it really hard and prefer spacing further apart. I think a lot of it has to do with the personalities and temperaments in the family."

—Megan Baker, mom of five in Tampa, Florida

Education

Now you don't have to have everything figured out before you even start your family, but it might be a good idea to consider your beliefs and preferences when it comes to education. Will you be sending your kids to school or homeschooling? How are the public schools in your area—or would you prefer a private or religious school?

If home educating appeals to you, imagine your "perfect" home-learning environment. If your kids are closely spaced, you may be able to put them in many of the same activities, enrichment programs, and playgroups. You may also be able to easily combine lessons or pass down curriculum before you need to worry about it becoming outdated. On the other hand, if your kids are farther spaced, you might feel that you have a better opportunity to work closely with each child and get into the groove of home education before you add on another child. If your kids will be going to school, consider whether you'll enroll them in a private or parochial school and for which grades. If you plan on having your children attend a private elementary school but sending them to the public high school, for example, you may want to consider how many kids you can afford to pay tuition for at once and space them so that when one is entering the private kindergarten, another is entering the public high school. Or if you'll be sending them to a public elementary school but using a private high school, you can plan not to have more than one (or two or three or whatever you can afford) in high school at any given time. College is a trickier subject and one that a lot of people feel strongly about. We discuss college tuition and large families in more detail in the chapter on finances.

How Will I Know When to Say "When"?

Many parents base their decision of whether or not to have more kids on how easily they added the previous one to the family—if it was a particularly hard adjustment, those parents are often scared off of having another. Other parents realize that if everybody did that, many families would never go beyond one kid! Let's face it, adding a child to the family is stressful under the best of circumstances. For many parents, going from no kids to one kid pushes them to the limits of their patience and endurance, but that doesn't necessarily mean they should never take a risk of adding another. In most cases, as they learn to be kinder to themselves and develop their parenting muscles, many of those moms and dads add another child—and are happy they did so, even if that first year or so has its ups and downs.

What Do the Experts Say?

While experts don't agree on the perfect number or spacing of children—if there is such a thing!—evidence suggests that health-wise it's best for mothers and babies if children are spaced at least two years apart. This gives your body time to recover from pregnancy and birth, which is especially important if levels of important nutrients, like iron or folate, took a hit from birth or nursing. A 2003 study by the University of California showed that when women's bodies did not have a chance to replenish essential nutrients before they became pregnant again, the mother and baby entered into a sort of biological competition over available stores. And if you're planning on breastfeeding your babies through the first year or longer, as many women do, a pregnancy during that time could cause a drop in your milk supply.

Of course, there's what's optimal, and then there's real life. Though statistically babies and moms fare better when there is longer spacing between pregnancies, that doesn't mean that you or your baby are doomed to poor health if you get pregnant again soon after giving birth. Make sure to take good care of yourself by getting plenty of rest, taking a good prenatal vitamin and a food-based iron supplement (look for one at the health-food store: they're more easily absorbed than those little green pills you get from the doctor's office), getting moderate exercise, and eating a healthy diet. Chances are, both you and your baby will be just fine.

What About Sibling Rivalry?

There's mo magical age difference that will eliminate sibling rivalry—but maybe you wouldn't want to, anyway. When it comes to how kids interact, there are advantages to both closely and further-apart spacing, says Elisa Medhus, M.D., family physician, mother of five, and author of the award-winning books *Raising Everyday Heroes* (Beyond Words Publishing, 2003) and *Raising Children Who Think For Themselves* (Beyond Words Publishing, 2001). "If they're four years apart or more, the baby will have a more mature role model to follow, but the children may not have the same level of play and interaction. If they're two years apart or less, there will be more sibling rivalry, which I think is good." According to Medhus, a childhood spent squabbling—and working things out—with a sibling acts as a training ground for developing strong interpersonal skills.

I found it very difficult to go from one to two kids. I was trying to be an "ideal" mother to my first child and had a difficult time adjusting to the fact that I was not, in fact, perfect; I also had to realize that my oldest son could no longer be the central figure in my life. Suddenly, when Jacob needed help on the potty but the baby needed to eat, I was faced with a choice: whose needs were more immediate? There was a large learning curve as I tried to figure out how to relax my standards, balance the needs of two children, and take at least the most basic care of myself as well. And my oldest son, who was used to my undivided attention, had to learn to wait his turn.

But once I got that delicate juggle down with two, going from two to three kids wasn't nearly as tough, and going from three to four was by far the easiest transition. Now, though I'd like to add more kids to the family, I'm not so sure I want to be pregnant and give birth again, and we're also reevaluating our family's finances. So at this point, four is my perfect number, but I know better than to ever say "never" about having more!

Other families have other stories. For some parents, going from two to three kids—the point at which kids outnumber arms—is the biggest hurdle. Maybe a closely spaced fifth and sixth child knocks another mom for a loop. The point here is that it's not necessarily the number of kids you have that will dictate how difficult it will be to parent them. Many factors—timing, financial or other stressors, your kids' personalities, your own personality—will determine how difficult a time you have adding that third or fifth or seventh kid.

Overwhelmingly, the big-family parents I spoke to suggest that you take it one at a time when deciding how many kids will make your family complete. You may end up with a preconceived "perfect" number and still have a nagging feeling that your family isn't quite "finished." Or maybe you'll decide to throw in the childbearing towel one or two kids short of your prior target. If you're religious, your faith will probably play a big part in this decision. If you're not, perhaps your instincts will lead you. And if neither of those things give you the signal you need, you always have more pragmatic factors, like money, house size, and when you hope to retire, to help you decide!

mom wisdom

"I don't think money and space are the most important factors when deciding how many kids to have. I think it's a heart decision—it feels right. Someone told me once when I was pregnant with number three that if I didn't feel completely 100 percent done having kids, then I wasn't. If there was even a 2 percent part of me that wasn't sure, then I wasn't ready to say I was done with the whole process."

—Katie L., mom of four, North Carolina

When it comes to planning how and when your family will grow, keep in mind what they say about the best-laid plans. It's a good idea to think carefully about what kind of family arrangement you'd most like, but try to keep an open mind in case things don't go exactly as you hoped—like, say, you have twins when you were expecting one baby, or you either have trouble conceiving or get pregnant sooner than you'd planned. Life doesn't always work out the way we think it will, but surprises can be even more wonderful than what we originally had in mind.

When Pregnancy Takes You By Surprise

I was always open to having a big family, but none of my four pregnancies were planned: the timing was off on every single one. I very well remember the sinking feeling each time a double pink line emerged on the pregnancy test and another baby, not unwanted exactly, but not quite wanted *just yet*, made itself known to us. While parents of many may bristle when thoughtless strangers ask us if our pregnancies were planned, it's often because some of them weren't, and we just aren't sure what to say. How do you explain all the complicated feelings that may go along with an unintended pregnancy—fear and anger, sometimes mixed with joy and excitement—while waiting in line at the grocery store? And what if we're just confirming all those negative big-family stereotypes by admitting that not every one of our kids was perfectly planned down to the second? Maybe you never intended to have a big family. Maybe you just never expected your family to get this big. Maybe you're happy with your family's current size but live in fear of getting pregnant again.

mom wisdom

"The way I see it, what's one more? Especially when you're going from three to four, or four to five kids. At that point the family already has the minivan, the baby stuff, and so forth. It's like planning a huge, round the world vacation: you're already packed and out there to experience a once in a lifetime event, so why not stay another night and invite another friend?"

—Katie, mom of five, Maryland

In her book *Surprise Child: Finding Hope In Unexpected Pregnancy* (Waterbook Press, 2006), author Leslie Leyland Fields admits that her fifth and sixth pregnancies were the realization of one of her biggest fears. She writes that she was crushed to have to start again at the beginning, "after loving and lavishing and persevering through the infancies and toddlerhoods of three highly energetic boys and one iron-willed daughter, and while still pouring out my best energy and resources to these beloved human beings … Just as I had emerged into relative light and safety. Now another. Do it again. And then another. And not pregnancies only. Yes, the weight gain, nausea, stretch marks, sleepless nights, varicose veins, but far more, the all-night feedings, leaking breasts, fevered weeks of teething, endless laundry, perpetual exhaustion, potty training … I knew it all intimately." Fields writes that she cried in anger, numbness, and sadness, asking herself the same questions that women facing an unintended addition to an already-big family will certainly recognize: "How will I do this? How do I make it through all those interminable nights? How do we fit six kids in this house? How do we send them all to college? What will I say to the shocked faces in the grocery store? How do I find joy in this?"

If you've faced an unexpected pregnancy while building your family, Fields' words will resonate with you. And if you're still trying to find joy in an unexpected pregnancy, take heart: you are not alone. Statistically speaking, chances are good that the glowing mother down the street with the big, beautiful family didn't plan every one of her pregnancies. Even though she loves her kids to death—because once they're here, who doesn't?—that doesn't necessarily mean that she danced a jig every time she missed a period or felt that familiar twinge of nausea. No matter how much you love kids, life—and the demands of pregnancy, birth, and early parenthood—are more complicated than that. The good news is that you can get from ambivalence, or even downright anger, to acceptance, and from acceptance, to excitement. Realizing that many women—even those who seem like natural mothers—aren't always overjoyed by every pregnancy may help you make that transition. And if, over time, you can't, it's important that you talk to a counselor or health-care professional about your feelings. Having a big family is stressful to a mom's physical and emotional health and well-being, and you need to do everything you can to make sure you're healthy before a new baby comes along—for the baby, for yourself, and for the kids who are already here.

Deciding to Have a Big Family

If you're reading this because you're considering whether or not to have more than the "average" number of kids, you probably have a lot of questions: Is it responsible to have a big family? Don't I have to be some kind of superwoman Earth-mother type? Will I ever get to spend time with my husband again? What about spacing? Can I afford a big family? Do I have what it takes to parent a Table for Eight family?

What do you need? Patience. Adaptability. The ability to forgive, especially yourself. And above all, a sense of humor and perspective. When I asked parents of larger families what they felt was absolutely necessary to raise lots of kids, these traits came up again and again. But, they were quick to point out, not everybody is born with these characteristics and not everybody feels up to the task of raising a big family from the moment their first child is born. Just because you don't feel like a model of patience and organization now doesn't mean that you won't be able to adjust as your family grows. And keep in mind that, in most cases, you'll have time to grow into your family size. Most parents don't go from having no kids to having four! If you really want a big family, you can find a way to get past the obstacles that present themselves.

But it's important to be honest with yourself about whether you really want a big family. Having a lot of kids will open you up to criticism and may take your life in a different direction than you'd planned. You'll have less control over your time and money and less control over each individual child than you would with a smaller family. So make sure you don't romanticize the notion of a big, happy family before you take the time to think about whether you're up to the task.

If you're thinking of having a bunch of kids, you may be concerned about some big-family criticism or stereotypes you've heard. Consider the following frequently-asked questions and concerns from people thinking of having a large family.

Can I really afford a big family?

Notice what's conspicuously absent from the do-you-have-what-it-takes criteria listed above? A big, fat bank account. Most of the Table for Eight parents I spoke to agreed that you don't need to have lots of money to raise lots of kids. While most admitted that they make some financial sacrifices in order to raise a larger family, they were quick to point out that they're still able to pay their bills and clothe their families—there's just a difference in priorities. As Sara Newman from Tulsa, Oklahoma, so eloquently put it: "Yes, there are sacrifices, but I think I'd be making other sacrifices if we didn't have our children: self-fulfillment, lots of company, lots of love, and a support network that will last us and our children throughout our lives."

Still, it's a good idea to give your finances some consideration when you're thinking about your family size. Luckily, a lot of ways to "live well" don't include expensive toys and gadgets, brand-new cars, and a huge mortgage. Visit Chapter 8 for more tips on using money and resources wisely no matter how many kids you've got.

We're not Catholics, Mormons, or Orthodox Jews—will we be the only nonreligious parents of a big family in our community?

That's one of the biggest stereotypes the parents I spoke to encounter. Certainly, some religious beliefs encourage large families, but not all religious people have big families, and not all big families are religious. Sometimes parents are religious and have lots of kids, but they don't have lots of kids because they're religious. Big families come from all different faiths (many of which permit birth control!), and some of us aren't religious at all.

That said, big families aren't the norm these days, and you may have a hard time finding other families of more than one or two kids in your area, unless you look into religious communities. However, even that isn't a guarantee; in my sons' Catholic school, most of their friends' families are smaller than ours!

But what about overpopulation?

We've all heard about the population crisis. But many scientists have debunked the idea that overpopulation is a problem, for a number of reasons.

For starters, history has shown that as the world adds more people, resources also become more abundant, and there is plenty of food to feed everyone in the world and then some. These experts argue that hunger and poverty aren't caused by too many people but by misuse of resources and political instability.

mom wisdom

"Parents need to make sure they can handle all that comes with a big family. It is a full-time job with tons of overtime. It gets overwhelming at times. You have to be strong, have tons of patience … you have to be able to speak loudly to make your voice heard over so many other people! Your meals will never be the same. By the time you get everyone a plate of food and think it is *your* time, it is time for seconds for the gang.

Sleep? Forget it. You'll have to get up for those middle of the night vomit sessions, middle of the night nightmares, middle of the night 'just wanting to be with you'—multiplied by many children. Sick? Forget about staying in bed and resting. Your kids will get it too, and by the time one of them is getting better, the rest will be coming down with it, too.

Your world as you know it will never be the same. But if you do it right, it'll be wonderful … I love the challenges, the chaos, and all the fantastic joys that come with having a large family."

—Sheryl, mom of six in St. Louis, Missouri

Still others argue that we need to increase—or at the very least, maintain—the birth rates in order to support the elderly, who are living longer due to advanced medical science. For example, a recent report by the United States Census Bureau shows that people aged 85 and older are the fastest-growing age sector in the United States. The number of people aged 65 and older is expected to double within the next 25 years. And in some countries—for example, Germany and France—the governments are so worried about the low birth rate that they're offering parents cash incentives to have more children.

Aren't big families bad for the environment?

To be honest, the typical American way of living itself isn't great for the environment. This is true whether you're heating a 5,000 square foot house and driving around town in a gas-guzzling Hummer with one other person or five. Yes, more people do eat more food and create more waste.

However, big families have a special incentive to be good stewards of the earth. It's expensive to live a disposable lifestyle, use throwaway products, and overconsume!

Many of the larger families profiled in this book take special care to be environmentally conscious. They reuse, recycle, or do without. They teach their children to avoid waste. And it will take intelligent, motivated, and thoughtful people to create change in the world as we know it. Many of us believe that people are one of earth's greatest resources!

I read an article that said that people are having bigger families now because it's a status symbol.

I read the same thing, but I'm not sure I buy it. Sure, for some people, having a lot of kids might be a way to show off that they're able to afford it. And having more money does make it easier to have a bigger family: it's easier to raise lots of kids if you can have an at-home parent and/or afford to hire really good help. But the larger families I know definitely aren't having more kids as a status symbol! We've ended up with bigger families in a variety of ways: sometimes by chance, sometimes due to our faith, and sometimes because we just plain love kids and enjoy having a big, bustling family.

How will I be able to buy my kids all the things they need?

This question assumes that kids *need* all the things we are accustomed to providing them with in this culture. When you think about it, what do any of us really need? Food, shelter, clothing, and love are the basics. My list of needs also includes an education, laughter, joy, family, and a sense of purpose. But I don't have to spend much money to give my kids any of those things. New toys, new clothes, a big house—these are nice things I enjoy having, but they aren't really necessities.

What about experiences like travel or exposure to arts and cultural events? With careful planning, these things can be cheap or free, too. Even on a modest income, kids in big families truly don't have to go without the things they really need … and a lot of the things they really want, too. You'll find a full discussion of meeting the needs of children in Table for Eight families later in this book.

When I told a friend that I was thinking of having a big family, she said, "There are already so many unwanted children out there. Why not just adopt?"

Many large-family parents do adopt; some don't. While I think adoption is a great thing in many circumstances, it isn't something to be entered into lightly. A potential adoptive couple must take into account a lot of legal, financial, emotional, and ethical considerations; it's not as simple as "just" adopting. That said, many of the large families I know—especially the "mega" families with eight or more kids—do have adopted kids in their families.

But how will I be able to give all my kids enough attention?

It's true that I don't give my four sons the same kind of attention I gave my oldest son when he was a baby. I don't think that's a bad thing. Having more kids means that I've had to figure out what issues are really important and let go of the rest. It's also given my kids built-in playmates and a support system that will last them long past the end of my life. They know they have many different people they can turn to—Mom or Dad or one of their brothers—if they have a problem.

I know people with two kids who spend less time with them than I do with my four. And I know people with six kids who spend a lot *more* time with their kids than I do with mine! So how much time a person spends with her kids has to do with much more than just how many kids there are at home.

Being available to your kids is important, but increasingly experts are saying that a hovering, overprotective, and overinvolved parenting style doesn't do kids any favors. I spend a lot of time with my kids as a whole and one-on-one as they need it. It takes more planning and organization, and yes, we have less time to waste than some parents of smaller families might, but when it comes to love and attention, most kids in big families are not left wanting!

I told my mother-in-law that we were thinking of having four kids, and she said "They invented birth control to stop that sort of thing." I'm afraid people will think we're stupid or lazy if we have lots of kids.

Unfortunately, some people might—which is a pretty big assumption, if you ask me! Sure there are probably some parents of big families who've flunked Birth Control 101. Others have chosen not to use birth control, and still others have used the methods mentioned earlier in this chapter to space their children naturally. I personally refuse to draw a distinction between people who have large families by choice and those who end up with many kids because of birth control mishaps. People should not be punished for their fertility—all birth control fails sometimes. For some people, it fails more often than for others. For others, it was never an option to begin with. Either way, as long as the kids are loved and cared for, what difference does it make?

I can barely handle the one kid I've got. Moms with lots of kids must be saints—I don't think I'm cut out for that.

Ha. I wish I was as wonderful as some people seem to think I am! The truth is, moms and dads with lots of kids are just as diverse as the ones with one or two. Some of us are organized down to color-coded sock drawers while others just shift piles of paper from one flat surface to the next. Some of us are patient and even-tempered while others are hot-headed, with short fuses. Some of us were blessed with easy-going kids while others have to work harder to keep our brood in line. All of us have bad days where we don't think we can pick up one more toy or listen to one more whining kid. In short, we're human! We do our best, just like any other parent. You will, too; and you're likely to find that your best is really pretty good.

While raising more kids has definite challenges, families aren't a mathematical equation: having four children isn't necessarily twice as hard as having two. Six kids don't get half as much of Mom's love and time as three would. As your family grows, you will learn to let go of the "small stuff" and focus on what's really important. You'll figure out what organizational systems work for you and how to keep your house from falling in on itself. You'll discover how to give each kid the attention he or she needs without overlooking yourself or your spouse, and how to forgive yourself when you make parenting mistakes (which, by the way, are inevitable no matter how many kids you have!). Even if you don't feel up to the task of having a big family right now, if it's what you really want, you can make it work. And the wisdom other parents will share with you in this book can help—so keep reading!

Give Me Shelter:
Housing the Large Family

When I'm meeting somebody with one or two kids for the first time, they're often curious about what kind of house we live in. There seem to be two common misconceptions: one, that we're all crammed in like sardines, the other that we live in an absolutely palatial home.

On the contrary, we live in a nice-size, but very normal home with four smallish bedrooms and an office. The funny part, though, is that one of the bedrooms is rarely used, and I often feel like our house is *too* big! I expect that to change as my babies grow into little boys and my little boys amble into adolescence, but I don't ever anticipate us moving into a mansion. I couldn't afford one for one thing, don't really want to have to clean one, and I simply like knowing where everybody is in the house. Sure there are times I wish I had a third floor to retreat to for a while, but there's no doubt in my mind that a big family can get by in a regular-size space, or even a house that's on the small side if they use that space wisely.

So maybe you can't afford that 4,000-square-foot house with five bedrooms and three full baths. But plenty of larger families get by just fine in smaller houses with creativity and resourcefulness.

According to Clay Phillips, AIA, architect with Mackey Mitchell Associates in St. Louis, MO, as well as a father of four kids, Americans tend to be too fixated on square footage. "The main factor for a livable home is how the space works, not how much space there is," he asserts. Instead of focusing on how large a space is, he recommends that home-buyers and builders think about how that space flows from room to room, and from inside to outside—what architects call "permeable space." One of his pet peeves? Homes that give the largest portion of the floor space to enormous master suites. "This is a room where most people spend less than a third of their life. That may seem like a lot, but 90 percent of that time is in sleep with the lights off. What good is 300 square feet at the end of your bed if you never really use it in a meaningful way?"

Other misuses of space that Phillips notices are two-story entries and vaulted ceilings. "This is the ultimate waste of space for two reasons—it's not being used at all, and resources get wasted trying to heat and cool these spaces."

To Share Rooms or Not?

Three-bedroom homes are all over the market, but you may have noticed that houses with four, five, or more bedrooms are less available—and can be a lot more expensive. So is it okay to expect kids to share a bedroom?

Generations ago, it was generally expected that children would share bedrooms, but now some people seem to regard it as a mild form of child abuse! In my house, although we have four bedrooms, all the older boys still pile into one room together—by choice. Because they didn't seem ready for their own rooms, we turned one of the other bedrooms into a toy/game/TV room for them to use. They love it when they have friends over, and it gives them extra space during the day—while still letting them bunk up together at night.

Table for Eight parents asked their kids how they feel about sharing a bedroom with a sibling, and the responses were varied: John, seven, replied, "I don't want to share a room with my brother because he makes most of the mess and I have to clean most of it up." Rexx, six, said, "I don't want to share a room with my brother so I don't have to play with him." But it's not all bickering. John and Rexx's mom reports that the boys share a room with a bunk bed, and some nights they decide to sleep together on the bottom bunk.

Jennifer, a mom of four, reports that her sons have mixed feelings on sharing rooms. Bayne, who's twelve, doesn't like sharing with his eight-year-old brother when he doesn't clean up his messes. Eight-year-old Quillon, however, reported that he loves sharing a room with Bayne, "The best part is getting to share things, like the computer."

Six-year-old Griffon, who shares a bedroom with four-year-old Tag, doesn't appreciate his little brother taking things out while he's trying to clean up. Tag, on the other hand, loves sharing a bunk bed with his brother.

Kim, a mom of six, says that her kids are of mixed opinion. Emily, who's fourteen, says of sharing with her twelve-year-old sister, "It's not so bad. I could use a bit more closet space, though. And she needs to put her shoes away—I always trip over them." Sarah, Emily's roommate, says, "I like talking with her before we fall asleep."

Ten-year-old Paige, who shares with her eight-year-old sister Gracie, says, "It wouldn't be so bad except that she's very messy. She needs to stop messing up the closet so much." To which Gracie says, "It's nice. She mumbles in her sleep, which is funny."

Kim's five-year-old twins, Caleb and Jacob, also share a room. "I love sleeping with my buddy," Caleb reports. "He snores sometimes, though. It's funny, except when I'm really tired." "We share books before we go to sleep," says Jacob. "We can't read them, but we like to look at the pictures."

Cindy, mom of eight, paired six of her kids into three bedrooms. Her 14- and 16-year old sons Devon and Terek like being able to talk to each other before they go to bed, but Terek thinks Devon makes more than his fair share of mess. Devon, however, reports that he likes having somebody to share clean-up duties with! Eleven-year-old Laryn shares a bedroom with her two-year-old brother and says the only negative is that he wakes her up early some days.

Seven-year-old Keely and six-year-old Jaedyn, however, are "peas in a pod" and love sharing a bedroom, says Cindy. "They couldn't come up with one negative thing about sharing a room."

Are you noticing a pattern here? Older kids are mostly concerned about the mess their siblings make, while younger kids seem to love having a friend to hit the hay with every night. Cindy says that her three older boys begged to share a bedroom when they were younger and didn't complain at all until they were teenagers.

Her kids spend most of their time in the rest of the house, only really going into their bedrooms to sleep, so they don't fight over space much. "If a child wants to have some alone time, he can go to his room, and we just tell the other child to stay out for a while," says Cindy. Still, Cindy says she thinks the house—five bedrooms, 2,100 square feet—is a little too cramped for the family of ten. The family plans to eventually build on to the house, finishing the basement and adding on a bedroom in the next few years.

In her opinion, a family with eight kids needs seven bedrooms and three bathrooms: "Some children really love to share rooms, and some would like their own rooms, especially as they get older. So that size would allow for both sharing and private rooms," she says. "I think 3,500 square feet would work just fine if it was laid out well and all useable."

Other parents of teens agreed with the idea that sharing rooms usually goes over better with young kids than preteens and teens. Christina, a mother of six kids aged 17 through newborn, has four of her kids sharing: two boys aged 11 and 8 and two girls aged 4 and newborn. "The only downside is arguing over whose job it is to sweep or dust or whose dirty clothes are on the floor. My older two actually preferred to share and did on and off until they were about 11 and 8. They really do like having someone to talk to at night."

As for privacy and space issues? "Bathrooms are good places for privacy. As for space squabbles, we haven't had many—they've always shared and know how to keep their stuff separated." Christina says that an environment that promotes respect of each other and each other's things is key to avoiding squabbles over stuff and space. "Your own space doesn't have to be an entire room," she says.

While Christina says that their 2,700 square foot, four-bedroom house works, they could definitely use more space. They did find a way to add another bedroom. "We converted our unused living room into a big room for the boys. We constructed "bunkhouses" for their bed space and a closet storage system for their stuff."

Some parents reported that they planned their housing specifically so that their kids wouldn't have to share a room. "Our oldest, who is 11, is in middle school, which starts an hour later than the elementary school where her sisters go, so we felt she really needed her own room. Our 8 year old, who was the middle child for a number of years, would benefit from having her personality stamp on her own room. Our 6 year old is so bouncy and energetic she needed her own room if we wanted the peace of uneventful bedtimes. And of course, the baby needed his own room since his schedule is so different than the others' and he loves to play with his sisters anytime," says Lori, a mom of four kids aged 1 to 11.

Creating Private Space

Unfortunately, homes with more than three bedrooms can be difficult—and expensive—to come by, and in some markets houses with four or more bedrooms are practically unavailable. If you're having a hard time finding a house with a separate bedroom for each child and it's important to you that each child has his own space, consider these tips:

Rethink the idea of what makes a space a "bedroom." Does your house have a den, a family room, or even a large walk-in closet that you can convert into a bedroom? If your house is big on square footage but doesn't have a lot of rooms, you might be able to create more space for sleeping and privacy.

Finish a basement or an attic. This can be a relatively inexpensive process that could add a whole floor's worth of living space to your house.

Create separate rooms the Brady Bunch way. String up a curtain, erect a panel or large bookcase, or find some other way to divide a bigger bedroom into two.

Play musical rooms. If you've got, say, four bedrooms for five kids, maybe an easy-going younger child—who probably doesn't care so much about privacy yet—can "float" from room to room, staying with one sibling for a month at a time while the others get some breathing room.

Regardless of how you or your kids feel about sharing their space, in some houses there's just no alternative. So perhaps these tips will help your children co-abide peacefully!

Provide kids with space to keep their own things. In space-challenged rooms, an under-the-bed box for each child might do the job. A dresser drawer, plastic bin, or shelf for each child may also work.

Check out stores, like Ikea, for storage systems you can build to fit your family's needs. For kids very worried about siblings getting into their treasures, consider a sturdy box with a lock.

Teach kids to respect one another's property. In our house, most of the toys are for common use, but a few belong specifically to one child. While we emphasize taking care of toys and books regardless of who they belong to, we tell our sons that it's even more important to return something in the same shape as you found it when it doesn't belong to you. If a child breaks a sibling's possession, he's responsible for helping to replace it. An older child might do chores to earn the money, while a young child might just go along for the trip to replace the item so that he understands that material goods don't just reproduce themselves!

Teach kids to care for their own things. In our family, each child has certain prized possessions that we help him keep safe by providing him with a place to put them. At the same time, the boys have learned that it's not reasonable to expect that a special toy left lying on the floor will escape the clutches of a younger brother. They're learning that, if they really want to keep something in good shape, it's their responsibility to put it away on the "up high" shelf on top of their wardrobe.

Consider turning your biggest bedroom into a rec room. It's easier for kids to share bedrooms if their bigger toys, books, game systems, etc., are kept elsewhere. In some families, bedrooms are strictly for sleeping while the "living" goes on elsewhere in the house.

Come up with ways for each kid to get private time alone. This is especially important as kids get older. If it truly doesn't seem like there's any extra space for this, maybe you can schedule time for older kids to hang out in your bedroom or another quiet area of the house. Or you can make an emergency "private place" that kids can use as needed. This doesn't have to be an entire room—maybe a comfy chair in a corner of the house that doesn't see as much action could work.

Think carefully about which children you put together. It might seem obvious to put the kids together who are closest in age or the ones who play together the most. But by day's end, it's possible that playmate siblings are ready for a break, and sibs close in age might have conflict-prone personalities. In some families, the older kids might prefer to bunk with the baby of the family.

Consider co-sleeping. In many households, a baby doesn't need his own room for a year or more, instead bunking with Mom and Dad. This arrangement can save space and make night waking more convenient for you.

Bathrooms

Perhaps even more important than the number of bedrooms in your house is the number of bathrooms. Before I had a big family, I was perplexed by real estate listings that describe four-bedroom homes with five bathrooms—why would a family ever need more bathrooms than bedrooms? But now I can see why it could be a nice touch. After all, you can pile a lot of kids into a bedroom to sleep, but usually only one person can use a toilet at a time!

You might try these tips for making your bathroom or bathrooms as efficient as possible:

Jack and Jill. If you're buying or rebuilding, consider a Jack and Jill bathroom, which connects two bedrooms with a bathroom in the middle. If you go this route, two sinks and plenty of counter space definitely help make it more useable. Or you can have a bathroom with a door that divides the shower from the toilets. Some bathrooms have two interior doors, with a toilet/sink on either end and a bathtub/shower in the middle. This feature can help the morning rush to get ready flow better, because a kid can be primping or using the toilet on either side while another kid is taking a bath or shower.

If your bathroom isn't multifunctional, insist that bathrooms be used for using the toilet, brushing teeth, and showering or bathing only. Everyone in the family must brush hair, use hairdryers and curling irons, and apply lotion, makeup, and other after-bath toiletries in her own bedroom.

Take a tip from college dorm life, and use personal totes. To save space and keep siblings out of one another's special shampoos and soaps, give each child a plastic tote to carry his or her special toiletries, razors, shower puffs, etc.

Give each child a hook in his or her own room to hang wet towels on. That way the bathroom won't be overtaken by wet towels, and each towel will get a lot more life—saving you from endless laundry.

Another option is building an additional bathroom on to your current home. Adding a bath can be relatively inexpensive and will almost definitely make your home more attractive to buyers if you want to sell in the future. Even if you don't have enough space or cash to build a full bath with shower or tub, a half bath with a toilet and sink will ease some of the strain! Look at home remodeling websites and books for ideas and instructions.

mom wisdom

"Privacy usually isn't a problem for my family because we have so many boys! The kids will usually shower together (except for my daughter, obviously); one will be in the shower while the other is there talking to him. The rules we have in place are:

- If you are in the bathroom, the door must be shut.
- Before you enter anyone else's bedroom or a closed bathroom door, you must first knock and ask permission to enter. My husband and I make sure we do this, too.
- Do not walk around naked or in just underwear if you are over the age of three.

—Amy, mom of six, Texas

Smart Strategies for Buying or Building On

If you're in the market for a new house or considering moving out of a too-small one, look past what's on the surface and think about the home's potential. If you or your spouse are at all handy—or willing to learn—you can save some money by buying a house that needs some work but has more room for your family to grow in. A full basement can be finished into extra bedrooms or recreation space. A large attic or loft room can be divided into two or more private areas. If your lot is large, you can expand the house out into the yard, or you can build a "mother-in-law" apartment above the garage for an older child (or your mother-in-law!).

If you're building a new house, think square—the more standard the house's shape, the less expensive it will probably be to build.

Architect Clay Phillips advises multi-functional thinking. "Avoid thinking of rooms as single-use spaces," he says. "For example, a formal dining room will get little to no action during a family week (even in large families). How else can that space be utilized?" Phillips recalls a hotel he visited in Toronto that was an inspiring example of how space can be well-utilized. "The room where I stayed, including the bathroom and shower, separated from the sleeping space by a glass wall, filled a 12" × 10" space. The entire room was designed with a number of fold-down and pull-out items that could be put up and out of the way when not needed." Phillips admits that fold-away beds and tables might not please every person's aesthetic senses but says anyone could learn from its use of sparse space.

For instance, Christina and her husband, who have six kids, converted the double garage into a rec room for the toys, ping pong table, and play equipment. "We have an elaborate floor-to-ceiling storage system on hinges, with clear bins and labels, to accommodate toys and storage." Christina likes this setup better than a finished basement because it's right off the kitchen, meaning that even the youngest kids can play without being too far from her sight.

Don't Neglect the Outdoors

But Christina's house just wouldn't be the same without her ⅔ acre yard, which she says is the "key to life as we know it!" The yard is used for climbing trees, playing sports, entertaining friends, and family football games.

If you're living in, or looking to buy a house that seems on the small side, don't underestimate the importance of an inviting and useable back yard. With some forethought and planning, you can make your yard into an extension of your house, even if it's not huge. Some things to consider as you're planning your outdoor living space:

Fences. A fenced-in yard can mean the difference between you getting to do some gardening or relaxing in your yard when it's nice out, or constantly running after toddlers as they make a break for the street. Privacy fences aren't for everyone, but they can help you relax a little if it means your kids can run freer in the yard without worrying that their antics will annoy a cranky neighbor.

Playthings. Be wary of trampolines and pools: they can be very dangerous for children, and with lots of kids, there are bound to be times when a few of them are out of your sight. A small climbing structure meant for small children to use is a safer option; just make sure the ground beneath is well-padded.

Pets. It's convenient to let your pet roam free in your fenced yard, but not so convenient if it means the kids can never go outside for fear of stepping in a not-so-special surprise. It takes some extra effort and time to get your animals used to pooping in a specific area of the yard, but the effort is well worth it. Or you can take an extra minute or two to hit the yard with a pooper-scooper daily so it doesn't, well, pile up. "Our dog kept 'going' all over the yard, and finally the kids didn't even want to play out there because they kept stepping in it," says Megan, mom of five. "We made it my two oldest sons' jobs to go out in the yard immediately after school and use the pooper scooper. Strangely, they think this is a really fun chore, so it works out."

Seating, eating, and shade. With lots of kids, you're going to be spending lots of time outside with them, so why not make it comfortable? Invest in some lounge chairs, maybe a gazebo, and a picnic table or two for easy, low-fuss summer dinners. I absolutely love eating outside—you never have to sweep up afterward!

Consider closets. Nothing separates good and bad design like closet space. With a big family, you need plenty of places to stash clothing, coats and shoes, a multitude of towels and bed linens, board games, toys, extra food, and all those breakables you won't be using for at least ten years. Sure you can make do without closets by purchasing wardrobes and other storage solutions, but isn't it easier to keep it all behind closed doors with built-in closets?

Mud rooms, hall closets, and entryways. I've learned from experience that a pretty corner coat rack is no match for six sets of winter coats, snowpants, spring jackets, rain coats, windbreakers … well, you get the picture. Few decorative hook systems can really match the coat-hanging needs of a big family, so unless you want your living room scattered with outerwear, a house with a mud room, entryway, or some other off-the-beaten-path place for coats, gloves, hats, and boots is a must. If your home doesn't have a mud room, entryway, or hall closet, you may want to train your kids to carry all their stuff to their own rooms, or perhaps create a place in the basement set up for this purpose.

Keep Your Lifestyle in Mind

If you have two floors, pay close attention to what rooms you're putting above other rooms. For instance, if your bedroom is on the first floor, does it make sense to put the playroom right above you so that you're treated to the sounds of thundering feet—especially if you're trying to get the baby to sleep? If you spend a lot of time in your kitchen, it makes sense for it to be an area that looks into the backyard or play room, so your little ones can be close by as you prepare meals. Or if you work from home while a sitter watches your kids in the house, you may need to make sure your office is as far away as possible from the busiest area of the house.

Also look at things like laundry and utility rooms. Laundry chutes and first-floor laundry rooms can make your life easier if you don't like going up and down stairs with heavy baskets. If you've ever thought that your life would be that much easier if you could do two loads of laundry at once, you might want to consider wiring your laundry room to accommodate two washers and two dryers. Consider your lifestyle as you try to figure out how to make the best use of the space you have or look at new homes.

If you're sick of laundry going moldy in the washing machine while you're busy with the kids, you may want to consider a washer-dryer combo. Cons: they're expensive and it can take a long time for a combo unit to complete a cycle. Pros: they're energy-efficient, you don't have to worry about switching loads, and you'll never have to rewash the musty-smelling clothes you forgot about overnight.

Urban Living with a Big Family

As I write this, my family is in the middle of a move to Chicago from our current town of about 3,000 people. Needless to say, it's a bit of a culture shock, and I ran into several snags while finding a new home. Here are some things to keep in mind if you're planning to move to a city with your big family, or are already a city-dweller planning to have a big family:

Schools. In many large urban areas, the public education system can be very competitive, meaning you'll need to start thinking about where your kids will be going way before they're kindergarten aged. What does this mean for a big family? If you plan to pursue selective-enrollment schools that operate either on a lottery basis or require that your children meet some criteria like academic achievement, there's no guarantee that all your kids will get into the same school. You could face a lot of driving around in the morning once all your kids are school-aged. In most cities, kids can automatically go to their neighborhood school, which is a lot less driving and hassle. If that option appeals to you make sure your new neighborhood has a good school.

If you plan to send your kids to a private school or homeschool them, however, it doesn't matter so much exactly where you live, or whether your new home falls into any particular school's boundaries. This may mean that you can get away with a less-expensive house payment or rent, because a lot of times, houses near more "desirable" schools cost a lot more.

Housing discrimination. If you've been told that you have "too many" children to rent a house or apartment, you may have been the victim of housing discrimination. The Equal Housing Opportunity Act makes it illegal for potential landlords to discriminate against you based on your family status, which may include your family's size. But as frustrating as it can be to be denied housing because you have a big family, housing discrimination isn't always easy to prove.

First of all, it's important to look into the occupancy laws in your area. While you may have heard the generic standard of "two residents per bedroom," this is not set in stone—it may depend on factors like the size of the bedrooms or the home overall. Sometimes the rule is "two per bedroom, plus one" meaning that a family of seven could live in a three-bedroom home. And there may be rules that allow you to have a baby under a year old in a bedroom with two other people, but not an older child. If you think you've been unfairly denied housing based on your family's size, you can file a complaint here: www.hud.gov/complaints/housediscrim.cfm.

One way to avoid this kind of discrimination altogether is to be proactive in your house search. Instead of looking at rental ads, showing up for tours, and filling out applications only to be turned down once the land-lord saw how many kids I had, I decided to post a "home wanted" ad on www.craigslist.org. I laid out my family situation, and then my requests: first floor (so I didn't have to cart kids up flights of stairs or worry that my kids' running feet were disturbing downstairs neighbors), fenced yard, two bathrooms, close to a park, etc., and my price range. I received many responses, and ended up signing a lease on a great two-floor apartment with plenty of space, a park a block away, and a fenced yard. My landlady is a lovely woman who'd lived in our unit with her three children and could vouch for how family-friendly the place is. And as it turns out, our new home is in a heavily Orthodox Jewish neighborhood, meaning there are lots of other big families around, too.

Neighbors

Living in a city, it's much harder to find single-family housing, so chances are good that you'll be living in some kind of attached housing like an apartment building, duplex, or townhouse. This means you'll have close-by neighbors who might not appreciate living near a lot of kids, or have children you'd rather your kids didn't associate with. For a lot of people this is just a reality of city living, but if the idea bothers you, you may want to hold out for areas that offer single-family homes you can afford.

Neighborhoods

If you're considering moving to a city you aren't already very familiar with, it's a good idea to rent for a while and see if what you thought you wanted is what you really want. For example, you might think you want to live in a less concentrated area, but then wish you were closer to public transportation. On the flip side, you might think you want to live right by the train, but then find that the sound keeps you up all night! Hipper areas, with lots of nightlife or restaurants, may be more congested, making parking difficult, but could be more walkable, meaning you'll need your car less often. You won't really know what it's like to cart all your kids around any particular neighborhood until you live there for a while, so plan to spend some time experimenting before you settle in for good.

How the Bigger Half Lives

Most of the parents I interviewed agreed that a home is what you make of it. Even the most humble spaces can work for a bigger family if you keep them neat, don't accumulate too much stuff, find creative ways to store things, and use your space wisely. Read the following profiles of big families who live in very ordinary-size homes to see how they feel about decor, where they buy furniture, and how they make the most of the space they have.

For some people, creating a homey, warm, attractive living space—no matter how many family members or how little the house—just seems to come naturally. And then there's the rest of us. For those of us who struggle with making the most of our homes, architect and father of four Clay Phillips offers these final words of advice:

"Good design is simple, really. Just remember a few key elements:

"Appropriate scale: You're a human, you live in a house, therefore the house should be human sized, not rhinoceros sized.

"'Lineuperism': Line up that thing with this thing so that the two different things begin to relate—try to coordinate the pieces of your house just like you coordinate colors.

"Quality matters: Choose quality materials over cheap materials. Nicer quality materials make everyone happy. If you don't believe me, pour yourself a nice cup of coffee and compare it to a cup of used mop water. You like the coffee, it makes you happy. The mop water? Not so good."

Words to live by—and create a living room by. Now that you've been inspired, check out these resources for more tips and information:

- **www.notsobighouse.com**   Website of Sarah Susanka, FAIA—architect, best-selling author, and advocate for better, not bigger home design. The site features articles and resources for getting a lot out of a littler space, and even offers "not-so-big" house plans for sale.

- **www.hgtv.com**   It's got everything: décor to design to tips for do-it-yourself home projects, remodeling, and buying or selling your home.

- **www.houseplans.com**   Ogle tens of thousands of home layouts! The site allows you to search plans by number of bedrooms, bathrooms, garage stalls and other criteria, as you figure out what kind of house would best suit your lifestyle and budget.

Table for Eight Profile

Sheryl Coulter, St. Louis, Missouri
Six kids, ages 15, 9, 8, 5, 4, and 4

Housing Stats: Suburban home, 1,800 sq. feet, 3 bedrooms, 2 baths

Future Plans: The basement is in the process of being remodeled into two more bedrooms, a bathroom, a playroom, and a family room.

Furniture Finds: My furniture consists of, "I just got a new couch, would you like our old one?" Everything gets broken eventually anyway, so we buy nearly all our décor second-hand.

Space-saving Strategy: Anything that can function as two things works. A chest can hold a pile of blankets and give seating for three, or sometimes it is a bed! All our couches are used for sitting, sleeping, and jumping on.

Table for Eight Profile

Jackie Lee, Vero Beach, Florida
Eight kids ranging from 21 to 3

House Specs: Small-town, 2,500 sq. feet, 4 bedrooms, 3 baths

Bedroom-Sharing Status: Two oldest boys share, two girls share, and four youngest boys share. A total of three kids' bedrooms.

Pros: They have to learn to get along with each other.

Cons: Rooms often get really messy.

Squabble Busters: We haven't really had space squabbles, just the issue of little ones getting into bigger ones' stuff. We've solved this by putting things up on shelves. The kids like having roommates—for my oldest, I offered to put a sofa bed in the living room and make that his, but he wanted to share a room with his brother. The two girls would probably not mind having separate rooms just because theirs is the smallest. If it was bigger and they had more use for their stuff, they probably wouldn't care.

The small living room/piano room/parlor off the front door has been the nursery for the last two babies. I put the portacrib in the corner, where it's not really visible from the door, and I have a comfortable rocking armchair in there, and that's where I nursed when they were little. The last four babies have all had a portacrib instead of a regular crib—it makes traveling very easy because their familiar bed is always with them.

Minimum House Size: Two to four kids per bedroom is perfectly sufficient. Having roommates requires kids to learn to get along with others and to edit possessions so as to have enough room for stuff. 2,500 square feet is more than adequate for us, though again, I wish I could take square footage from our bathroom and put it in their bedrooms. We have the smallest house and the largest family on the block. We live in a rich retirement area, and every time we see real estate ads trumpeting some 6,000 square-foot mansion, we joke: "Wow, they must have a lot of kids!"

Décor Strategy: How my house is decorated is very important to me because I spend most of my time here. I like to read decorating magazines, but not to excess because they tend to make me dissatisfied with what I have if I read them too much. With kids and dogs, I've learned a few essentials: furniture should be a tough, neutral, textured fabric that doesn't show stains; knick-knacks and fragile lamps on tables don't cut it; and keeping the entry to the house clean and uncluttered makes a good first impression.

How To Make Small Spaces Look Bigger: Declutter, declutter, declutter! Scale furniture arrangements to the size of the room. I like to line pictures up on the wall at the same height—makes the room look neater. Make sure rugs and window treatments don't overpower—keep them in scale with the size of the room.

Space-Saving Philosophy: Fight envy. Bloom where you are planted—limits are what spark creativity. Pray, plan, and most importantly, make the best of what you have. Even your dream house will never be perfect. The house is a stage—but the plan going on inside it is what gives it life.

Table for Eight Profile

Katie Lewis, Raleigh, North Carolina
Four kids

House Specs: Bungalow, 1,733 sq. feet, 3 bedrooms, 2.5 baths

Future Plans: Way down the line we'd like to add a two-car garage with a bonus room over it and screen in our deck. My husband just built a shed, but a garage to put the dogs in (we have four) in the winter and the cars would be a great help. The bonus room would simple be a play/school room so my dining room can go back to being used for dining!

Bedroom-Sharing Status: One room has my two daughters and the other is for my two sons. The age difference (nine and two) between the girls is probably the greatest challenge. But we have made the dining room a den of sorts, and most toys stay there except the ones they agree on—dolls, books, Barbies, etc.

Avoiding Space Squabbles: We try to give Kaitlin [their oldest daughter] her own time in her room, but the kids really play in the main parts of the house anyway. Closet organizers divide the closet right down the middle, and bookshelves keep everyone's books separated. They really have been great about sharing the space, but that will probably change as they get older.

Minimum House Size: I think we could be comfortable in the square footage we have; it's just a matter of getting rid of the things we don't use. We seem to accumulate so many *things* and they take up space. Plus, it seems like toys are getting bigger and bigger. It's hard to arrange all the toys so we are sorting through and paring down.

Décor Strategy: We love Craigslist. We got a couch in perfect shape for $75, a free leather recliner, and an entertainment center for $50. The living room looked completely different in two days—and we were able to sell the stuff we had for $200, so we actually made money!

Whenever I want something "new" I check places like Craigslist. org or the ReUse Center first. I know that if we saved, we could buy brand-new furniture at the furniture stores, but I figure with three kids under three, why bother! I look for things that are durable and cheap.

Other great spots to pick things up are auctions (www.auctionzip. com is a great locator). We got an antique dresser for my daughters for $35 and one for our room for $60. Also try your county surplus sales. We picked up an entire school library set of desks/counters/cabinets for $20 and redid the "den" with them. It holds our board games, our rabbit cage, and our computer, and has two built-in desks to work on. Plus, we'll be able to sell it to recoup our money later.

Storage Strategies: I find storage items in unusual places—trunks as coffee tables for blanket/game storage, baskets on shelves to hold things. My biggest space saver is a shelving unit with baskets in it for the front hall shoe clutter.

Space-Saving Philosophy: Get rid of what you don't need. We have found so much usable space by getting rid of things that serve no purpose in our day-to-day lives.

Table for Eight Profile

Kimberly R., Indiana
Six children ages 14, 12, 10, 8, 5, and 5

House Stats: Suburban house, 2,650 sq. feet, 4 bedrooms, 3 baths

Bedroom-Sharing Status: Fourteen- and twelve-year-old girls share, ten- and eight-year-old girls share, and five-year-old twin boys share.

Squabble Busters: Each bedroom in our house has a walk-in closet, which is a blessing. In the closet, each child has a hope chest. They can keep their treasures in there, away from grabbing fingers. If someone needs some quiet space, they can go to their room and put a little handmade sign on the door that says, "Give me 30, please." This cannot be abused. If it isn't possible to use their bedroom, they can use my room or another part of the house. I understand the need for quiet time.

Creative Space-Savers: For us, the formal living room was wasted space. It was a big room with pretty furniture that was never used. We decided to make the living room our main family room, with couches, chairs, and the TV. The original family room, which was on the small side, is now a dining room complete with a fireplace.

We have two tables, one that seats six and one that seats ten. So now we have two tables in pretty close proximity, but it works out beautifully! When we entertain or have big family dinners, we are all together. It also gives us extra space for homeschooling.

Furniture Philosophy: We start with high quality, new furniture. It lasts so much longer. Yes, it's more expensive in the beginning, but I think it saves money in the long run. I do buy real wood pieces at thrift shops or garage sales—things like end tables, desks, bookcases. I like to restore them.

Décor Strategy: I believe that our homes are a reflection of us. I like things to be comfortable, but pretty. You can have both with a large family. Decluttering and fresh paint makes anything look better!

Making the Most of Your Home: Be proud of what you have, and it will show. Even the smallest, most humble treasure can shine.

Keeping the Household Running

No matter the size or state of your home, chances are it could be cleaner or more organized—or both! In my house, I often feel like I could do nothing but carry stacks of papers, toys, clothes, and dishes back to their original places from morning until night, and at the end of the day, the house would still look as though it had been hit by a bomb fashioned from Lego pieces.

Of course, it doesn't help that I'm highly distractible when it comes to housecleaning. I'll wander into a room with a specific objective—say, dusting the piano—but then promptly forget it when I see that the dining room table needs to be cleared off. As I'm taking the stack of papers from the dining room table to my desk, I notice a dirty sock on the floor, so I put down the papers to pick up the sock and … well, you get the idea.

My husband's almost the exact opposite. He's such a perfectionist and so single-minded in his homemaking tasks that he can spend an hour of precious pre-visitor preparation time rearranging the wires behind the television set.

Between the two of us, we are pretty housekeeping-challenged. So I was especially interested in hearing from other parents of Table for Eight families—particularly parents of *really* big families—to find out how they keep everything running smoothly—or at least, how they keep the house from falling down around their ears.

Get a Guru

Many of largerfamilies.com's readers swear by the "FlyLady" program for turning an out-of-control home into a pleasant place to live. FlyLady acts as a sort of e-mail based personal cleaning coach. The e-mails walk you through the process of decluttering your house and keeping it that way, by reminding you to perform certain tasks each day—for instance, the 27-Fling Boogie, where you pick 27 pieces of clutter in your home to toss. FlyLady doesn't take a lot of time out of your day, and if you're easily sidetracked and have a hard time figuring out what tasks to do next, the reminders landing in your inbox can be valuable. On the flip side, if you don't like being told what to do, you might find the e-mailed directions instructing you to shine your sink or put up your shoes annoying. Still, signing up for the list is free, and if it's not your cup of tea, you can always unsubscribe, so there's no harm in trying it out. For more information, check out www.flylady.net.

Another great resource is Large Family Logistics, a Christian-inspired site that advises moms to divide housework into days, the way our grandmothers and great-grandmothers likely did; for instance, do laundry on Mondays, errands on Tuesdays, etc. Check it out at www.largefamilylogistics.net.

Controlling Clutter

No matter what system you choose, most experts seem to agree that eliminating, or at least reducing, clutter is the key to keeping a pleasant, neat home. But when you've got lots of kids, each generating his own stacks of toys, books, schoolwork, artwork, and various other odds and ends, clutter can quickly become overwhelming.

When it comes to keeping your house neat and organized, a little preparation goes a *long* way. Don't wait until your home is overrun by stuff and you're trying to crawl out from under a pile of unneeded papers before you take charge.

Different systems will vary in their approach, but most include the following steps for getting your home under control and out of clutter's clutches:

Purge. Room by room, figure out what needs to stay and what can go. Think about your personality before you do this. Are you prone to throwing or giving away perfectly good items that you'll need later simply because you aren't sure what to do with them? Or are you on the other end of the spectrum, hanging on to every scrap of paper and ball of lint because it might come in handy "someday"? Either way, it's time to get a grip. Get a marker, two boxes, and a trash bag. One box is for stuff you'll give away; one is for stuff you'll put away; and, of course, the trash bag is for stuff you'll throw away—right away. Once the "put away" items are boxed, label them and take them directly to the basement, attic, or wherever you'll be storing them. Once the "give away" items are boxed, give them away— right away! Put them in your car, and drive directly to the Salvation Army, or walk to your computer and immediately list them on Freecycle.org. Whatever you're going to do with them, just do it quickly, before you find yourself picking through the box, removing items one by one!

Prepare. Go into each room with a piece of paper and a pencil and take careful notes. What storage items would make the room more functional? Is there a place to put everything that goes in the room? Lining the walls with simple shelves with baskets or plastic bins can be an inexpensive way to get stuff off the floor and tables and into a place of its own. Ask your kids for their input. Because you'll be expecting them to do a fair amount of the work of keeping their stuff out of your way, it makes sense to get them involved in planning how to make it happen.

Purchase. If at all possible, buy all the stuff you'll need to make your house functional in one trip; making a million trips to the store isn't a smart use of time or gas money! For inexpensive storage options, try a local discount store like Sam's Club or Costco; or IKEA, a store that sells value-priced furniture, home-organization systems, and more (check it out on the web at www.ikea.com). You can also look for plastic dish tubs, storage bins, and baskets at dollar stores, thrift stores, and yard sales.

Toys

One benefit of closely-spaced kids is that you may be able to get away with one communal area for toys if they're all playing with the same kinds of things at the same time. But this doesn't always work if you've got a mix of older kids, whose toys tend to have choke-prone little bits and pieces, and chew-happy babies or toddlers. Here are some ideas for storing toys so they stay off your living-room floor:

Buy a variety of buckets or tubs in a different color for each child. Once or twice a day, give each child his bucket or bin and send him around the house to fill it with his toys. Do this right before bed so you'll wake up to a toy-free living area in the morning. Once filled, the toy bins can go in a predetermined place, or each kid can pick a spot in his or her bedroom to store it. Toddlers and even babies can do this chore if they have help, and it'll get them into the habit of picking up after themselves when they're old enough.

If toys aren't divisible by child in your family, try doing it by room. Maybe you've got a lot of communal toys that are stored in a variety of places—bath toys in the bathroom, board games in the living room, etc. If this is the case, make sure each room has adequate, easy-to-access storage: a drawer, a bin, or maybe a piece of furniture with a hidden storage unit—and assign each child a room to declutter at different times of the day.

mom wisdom

"My older kids have really outgrown most toys, and the younger ones just use what the older ones no longer want. They get a new item for birthdays and we give each child three gifts for Christmas. We figure if it was good enough for Jesus to get three gifts on the first Christmas, it's good enough for us! I try to go through toys twice a year and give or throw away anything that is in triplicate, broken, or outgrown by everyone. I also give the children a choice as to whether they want to sell whatever they don't want or need in a garage sale (and keep that money). They get to pick out just enough toys to keep in their bedrooms, usually in a box in the closet or a toy box in the room. I have a rule that toys *have* to be kept in the bedrooms, or it would be utter chaos around here. With that many kids, I'd constantly be stepping on army guys or Legos. I keep a big Tupperware container of toys in the garage, and every now and then we swap things out. It's like Christmas to them all over again—they haven't seen those toys in a long while, so it's like they are new to them again!"

—Amy, mom of six, Texas

Toy-overload is one problem that's best nipped at the bud. A few well-made, simple, open-ended toys will last longer, wear better, and provide much more imaginative play than boxes and bins full of the latest plastic fad. And keep in mind that some toys—like those that come in Happy Meals—are really made to be disposable. I long ago stopped feeling guilty about tossing them into the trash after an hour or two of play instead of putting them into the toy box, where they were usually never played with again.

Schoolwork

I homeschooled my kids for a year, and now they're enrolled in school. In both scenarios, our house was completely overrun with paper. When we homeschooled, half-finished art projects, worksheets, and papers were everywhere. Now that the boys are in school, they each dump a backpack full of finished art projects, worksheets, notes from the teacher, permission slips, and fundraising reminders on the table each day. These tips will help keep the onslaught of paper under control:

Search and destroy. This is my method of choice. I look at what's in the boys' backpacks the minute they walk in the door, before they've had a chance to get involved in some other activity and before I've had the chance to get tired and cranky! I flip through the paperwork and make three piles: trash/recycling, deal with now, and deal with later. The "deal with now" pile might contain homework and notes that I need to follow up on right away. The "deal with later" pile might have the school-year calendar, a permission slip for a far-off event, or a fundraiser order form. I have one drawer in my dining room that's set aside specifically for school correspondence, and I go through it every night to make sure I'm not missing anything.

Once in a while, my sorting might include a fourth pile: keepsakes. But I only keep items that really show off my child's personality or growth, which means I save very few worksheets or cookie-cutter art projects—unless my child really made it his own! The keepsakes go in a separate drawer in my office. At the end of each school year, I sort through the drawer and put each child's keepsakes in a manila envelope labeled with his name and the school year; these go in a waterproof tub in the basement.

The office approach. Another system that might work for you is the "inbox" arrangement: each child gets his own in-tray or drawer, the kind you'd find at an office-supply store, somewhere in the main area of the house. When each child gets home from school, she's responsible for removing all the paperwork from her backpack and placing it into her tray or drawer. You can then go through each child's drawer at your leisure (ha!).

The organized homeschooler. One really nice thing about homeschooling is that, to some extent, you can keep the output of unnecessary paper under control.

- Use scrap paper within an inch of its life. Instead of letting your kids scribble on one side, then tossing or recycling, treat paper like a precious commodity and you'll be less likely to end up with an overload. "We are very careful about using paper sparingly, both to go easy on our budget and the planet, and also to keep it from piling up," says Holly, a homeschooling mom of four kids. When her older kids have finished filling out a worksheet, Holly has them use the backside for practicing handwriting or doing math problems. When there's no room left for that, Holly passes the piece of paper on to her four-year-old daughter, who's only too happy to "do school" by coloring all over her brothers' papers. The upshot? Not a single bit of white space gets wasted.

- Take a tip from the 1800's schoolroom, and use small chalkboards for working mathematical problems and practicing handwriting. There's no waste! You can also use dry-erase boards or a drawing toy like the Aqua-Doodle, which lets you draw over and over again on a special material using a water-based pen.

- Some of your children's work can be done on the computer—and stay there saved as files. To avoid "computer clutter," give each child his or her own folder and if applicable, create sub-folders for each subject. Major projects that require several documents or drafts each may warrant yet another sub-folder. To keep the files from taking over your hard drive, go through the folders every couple of months or so to delete documents you don't need anymore. Kristi, mom of five, deletes unneeded files each school semester, but says she has a hard time permanently trashing some of them: "I always think they might come in handy one day for another assignment, or that I might want to keep them for posterity," she says. Her clutter-busting solution? Each year gets its own folder, and each child gets a sub-folder within it, where Kristi stores anything she thinks they might need later. Because text documents take up very little room on an average-size hard drive, she doesn't really worry about them taking up too much memory; and because all the sub-folders are hidden inside one folder, it looks neat and tidy on her desktop. "I figure if I ever really need one of those files, I can find it easily enough using the computer's search function," she says.

- Keep a shredding machine in your "school" area. Shredding paper is more fun than just throwing it away or tossing it into the recycling box, and the shreddings can be used for padding boxes. If you end up with a surplus of shredded paper, list it on Freecycle.org, a website that allows you to connect with other people who might want whatever you've got to give away (and don't think "but nobody would want shredded paper"—believe me, plenty of people will take it if it's there!) Or see if a friend who mails a lot of packages or a local business would like it.

- No matter how good you are at conserving, homeschooling is going to create some paper! Creating a space for your books and papers—whether it's a whole room, a closet, or even just a shelf or file cabinet—can help you keep it under control and will also keep you from running all over the house looking for "school stuff."

Artwork

Nobody wants to throw away her precious child's artistic efforts, but let's face it—there's just nowhere to keep 100 crayon drawings of stick figures. In our house, we only keep artwork when it's very special to the child or when it really demonstrates her own unique artistic sensibility (i.e., we usually toss those cookie-cutter pictures made from precut shapes and cotton balls). Sometimes, even special projects become too numerous to keep. If your house is overrun by artwork, one option is to scan artwork to a graphic file on the computer or take a picture of the creation. You can then take the pictures and put them in a folder on the computer or in a scrapbook for you or your child to keep.

mom wisdom

"In our house, artwork goes on top of my china cabinet, which is out of sight. If the kids don't ask about the piece of art for six months, it goes out with the trash. If they do ask about it, it goes on the fridge or on cork boards in their room. I also have a scrapbook pile where I put things that I want to keep. When the pile gets too big, we have a 'put things in your scrapbook' evening."

—Kim, mom of six, Maryland

Hand-Me-Downs

Organizing hand-me-downs is one of the hardest tasks as far as I'm concerned. Even with four boys who were all born in roughly the same season, different brands' sizes fit differently, so the same kid might be wearing 24 month clothes from one store at the same time he's wearing 3T from another. And I often find that clothes stored in the attic or basement get "lost" and aren't available when I need them for the next child. Here are some systems other moms with lots of kids use to keep track of their hand-me-downs—and make sure that the clothes they buy earn their keep:

Keep it moving. "When the kids outgrow things, I toss them into a box in their closet. Once a month, I sort the clothes out of the box into the right bag in the attic. The girls' clothes that my youngest daughter has outgrown are going to consignment sales since we won't need them anymore. I've put a few aside for friends and for her when she gets older, since she might like to pass them on to her own kids, but really, very few stick around—we just don't have the storage space for them. I'll do the same with the youngest boys' clothes as he outgrows them, too."—Katie Lewis, mom of five.

Have a try-on-a-thon. "I store off-season items in storage bins. When the season changes, we have a 'try-on-a-thon.' What fits, we keep; what doesn't, we donate."—Carla, mom of four, Maryland

The musical closet system. "We put clothing into boxes with the size written on it. As my oldest child outgrows his current clothing, it gets thrown into a box in his closet. When the box is full, it gets moved into the next child's closet as his 'next size.' Shoes migrate to the closet where they will fit the next child if they are in good shape. Having lots of hand-me-downs, I have noticed that sometimes my children have more pants than they ever need in any one size. So I will take a few extra pair and put them in the box even before they are too small—this way I know the next child will get a few pair that aren't quite as worn!"—Shannon, mom of four in Oregon

> Ziploc now makes giant waterproof storage bags. You can label them, fit them into smaller spaces than a huge tub might fit, and best of all—you can see what's inside them.

Systems That Work

The best-laid plans for decluttering and cleaning will only work if you have a system that works for your family. Some moms of many have their housekeeping systems down to a science, and I've collected a few innovative tips for you:

Marie's Laundry System

"My all-time triumph is my laundry system. I used to have a 'hamper' for dirty clothes, and when I had time (usually after it was overflowing miserably) I would sort. But the piles of whites, darks, etc., would get overrun by new dirty laundry before I got to those loads, and I'd have to start over." Finally, the answer to Marie's large-family laundry woes came to her: color-coded baskets. "Now we have a white basket for light colors, a bright-colored basket for bright colors, a dark basket for dark colors, and a different one for towels. When we had all eight kids at home, we also had a basket for heavy things like sweats and jeans, and another for khaki, yellow, and brown. Everyone was responsible for sorting their own laundry for a while, but they weren't getting it right, so I added a hamper where everyone could place dirty clothes and I or one of the older kids would sort it each day. When a basket was full, I'd do that load. I'd do a load or two every day, but it wasn't overwhelming."—Marie, mom of eight, Illinois

Color-coded hangers. "Each boy has his own color hanger. Everything dries on the line on its color hanger, so anyone can put away dry clothes and know exactly where they go. Since socks shrink when washed or dried, I label them with a 1, 2, 3, or 4 for my first, second, third, or fourth-born."—Lisa, mom of four, Pennsylvania

Pass the basket and clean as you go. "I love having a basket that sits at the bottom of the stairs. As things are found downstairs that do not belong there, they are placed in the basket. The kids have all been instructed that when they pass the basket, they must see if any items belong to them and take them up with them. I clean my bathroom once a week, usually on Sunday morning. Just before I take my shower, I spray it with household cleaner and scrub it. That way when my shower is over, I simply dry it out and it is sparkling clean. Then, my morning routine consists of thinking to myself that everything I touch needs to be cleaned when I am done. So when I brush my teeth, I clean the entire sink and surrounding area when I am done. Then I continue to pick up and wipe things down on the way out of the bathroom. This routine of picking up and cleaning up as I go stays with me most of the time, which is probably the only reason I can keep my house clean on a daily basis."—Wendy, mom of five, Texas

Kim's Laundry System

Here's how Kim, a mom of six in Illinois, tames the laundry monster:

Consistency is key: "In order for any system to work, you have to work it. Inevitably, life will throw a wrench into your skills from time to time, but the key is to stay on track so you can swerve around the wrench."

Kids can sort: "In the laundry room, there are several baskets on the floor. They are marked as such: whites, darks, lights, linens, delicates, and miscellaneous, for 'Mom where do I put this shirt? It has too many colors!' Everyone is responsible for getting their clothing into the appropriate basket before bed each night, and when one of the dirty baskets has enough for a full load, I wash it. I do linens on Saturday. I only use white towels, sheets, and other linens—this makes my life so much easier."

Don't let it pile up: "I do, on average, two loads of laundry a day, with the exception of Sunday. When the dryer is done, I do not pile the clothes into a basket and dump it on a bed. Instead, I fold the clothes as I take them out of the dryer. As I fold them, I place the clean clothes in a basket for each family member. It takes far less time to do it this way!"

Kids can put away, too: "Before dinner, the person with the 'put away' chore (for that day) is responsible for putting away all of the clean/folded clothes. It is a quick chore since the folding and sorting is already done. Then that child puts the empty baskets back in the laundry room, ready for the following day."

Let socks be homeless: "Socks are the thorn in my side. Like linens, we only have white socks, with the exception of my husband's work socks. When socks come out of the dryer, they are tossed into a sock basket, unmatched. They stay there until someone needs a pair. It isn't the neatest system, but it works for us."

The Tools You Need

When I asked Table of Eight moms what products they felt were must-haves, a few came up again and again:

- **White vinegar**. It's safe, nontoxic (which means the kids can use it, too!) and cheap, and it has hundreds of household uses from making windows and sinks sparkle to keeping laundry soft.
- **Baking soda**. It's cheap and safe, and can be used for deodorizing the carpet or fridge and scrubbing the sink or tub.
- **Lavender essential oil.** It has natural antimicrobial properties and smells nice, too, so it makes a nice alternative to overpowering disinfectant.
- **Good spray bottles.** Use them for mixing up your own cleaning solutions. For making your own safe and effective cleaning supplies, check out www.betterbasics.com.
- **Old toothbrushes.** Use these for spot-treating stains.
- **Mr. Clean Magic Erasers.** I don't know how they do it, but these things really do work like magic to remove crayon and pen marks from walls and other surfaces.
- **A good feather or micro-fiber duster.**
- **Swiffer and Swiffer Wet Jet**. Need I say more?

- **Disposable Clorox or Windex wipes.** These are great for last-minute clean-up, like when company's on its way!
- **A good vacuum cleaner.** One that works well is a worthwhile investment. Check out Consumer Reports to see which brands and models offer the best value.

Getting the Kids on Board

In a big family, cultivating a sense of teamwork is key to keeping everything running smoothly. It's best to start early when you can, because attitudes about housework and a child's role in keeping the household running are formed young.

"My six-year-old folds towels, puts her laundry away, and puts napkins on the table," says Marie Little, mom of eight in Illinois. "My eleven-year-old can wash dishes, mow the lawn, and put away his laundry. I have a dish schedule which is based on everyone's availability. If they're working a part-time job, they only have to do one day a week, but they have to contribute to the household finances. However much my insurance bill goes up when I add them as a driver, that's how much they pay me each month. They don't get driving privileges until they have a job. If they aren't willing to share their paycheck, I don't share my cars."

But Marie knows it's not enough to just expect kids to start doing the work, you have to start them young. "From the time my kids were walking, I started giving them little jobs to do," she says. And even now, she says, sometimes she has to assign a consequence—like a lost privilege—to keep the kids following through on their assigned tasks.

"My personal philosophy is pretty simple: this is a family, therefore everyone pitches in," says Bonny, a mom of five kids in Minnesota. "My kids were expected to be picking up toys, etc., around age three or so. We've always just done it together. By the time they were two and a half or three, they wanted to be doing whatever I was doing, anyway. My four-year-old twins and seven-year-old can wipe down surfaces, pick up, sort laundry, wash floors, and my older kids can do pretty much anything with regard to household chores." As for how she motivates her kids, Bonny says that the older two know that responsibilities come before privileges: "When the doorbell or phone rings and a friend wants to get together or they want 'screen time' on the TV or computer, they're going to want to be able to do that. If they slack off on their responsibilities, they may very well miss out on something. The younger kids don't seem to need any motivation, other than keeping them from being sidetracked. When we're doing things together, that doesn't seem to happen as easily."

"My five-year-old and four-year-old are very good at picking up their toys, and the two-year-old has begun to pitch in," says Laura Wells, mom of four in Virginia. "We try to make it a before-bed thing, and since it's such a habit and we're all doing it together, they rarely complain. We have containers for every different category of toy, and everyone knows where each thing goes. Another thing they are expected to do is clear their dishes from the table and bring them to the kitchen counter. The five-year-old has a self-imposed chore of preparing everyone's tooth-brushes and nighttime water cups (they get a small drink before bed)." As for when she'll begin introducing more specific chores, Laura says she isn't sure—but it'll be earlier than her own parents did. "They waited until I was twelve years old, and I rebelled against it for years."

Some families find it helpful to set up a "household headquarters" with a calendar, peg board or corkboard, dry-erase board, and a chore list for keeping track of who is expected to do what—and when.

Sick of store-bought planners and calendars that only have room for four or five family members total?

- Go high-tech! Create a family schedule at www.google.com/calendar. The calendar is color-coded for each member, and you can easily add and change events and print out copies to post on the fridge or corkboard.
- www.lotsofkids.com offers a chore-chart maker you can customize to your family's size and print from your computer

---

Parents may find that they need to write things down, too. Whether you use a day planner, a big calendar, or a Palm Pilot, get everything out of your head and down in writing as soon as you can, advises Katie, mom of five in Maryland. "As soon as the baseball game schedule is in my hands, I write it down both in my day planner and the kitchen calendar. If one of the kids has a field trip or book report due, I write it down. Even though I know soccer practice is always Thursday at 6 P.M., I write it down anyway. I used to write down how often my preemie twins ate and had wet diapers. If we're out of toilet paper or I need to make a trip to the bank, I write it down. Honestly, I've written 'take a shower' on my day planner to do list more often than I'd like to admit." Katie says her husband has taken to telling her to write important things down so she won't forget. "Sometimes that stings, but really, if I don't write it down, I'll forget to vacuum the van," she laughs. "There's just too much going on when you have a larger family, so the more I can get out of my brain, the better."

Once your household is running smoothly enough, you may find that you take on more of a supervisory role than a working role: "I personally spend no regular amount of time on housework, yard work, or home maintenance," says Ramona Edwards, a mom of eleven whose kids follow a detailed chore chart each week. "Rather, my time is spent supervising and organizing our 'work force' and following up on the jobs they're doing. My kids keep the household running. Our philosophy is that everyone in the family should work for the good of the group, in addition to taking care of themselves." Ramona says that she didn't start this early enough with her oldest kids, and that it shows. "They are the hardest to motivate."

Think Ramona's approach and high expectations are too harsh? Keep in mind that 100 years ago, this type of cooperation was expected from kids. Did they have less happy childhoods than the kids of today? I would argue not. A teamwork approach helps a child learn to be a part of something bigger than himself; to put the needs of others before his immediate wishes. It teaches him some important lessons: self-discipline, selflessness, and delayed gratification. And though some big families get a bad rap for making their kids run the household, the truth is that, unless their lives are seriously over-scheduled, most kids have plenty of time on their hands. Even with chores, they have plenty of time for play and imagination. In fact, many kids will find a way to incorporate imagination and creativity into their work. And doing housework together can be a great way to catch up with your kids and spend that quality time we all hear so much about, while working together on a common goal.

In the Western world, we've become used to a picture of family life that includes kids who rule the roost and parents who bend over backward to keep everything smooth, happy, and fun for them. But that doesn't mean that it's the only, or even the best, way of doing things. Increasingly, experts are reporting that our current culture that tends to coddle kids and expect very little of them does more to hurt than help. Kids need to feel they are useful and have something to offer and contribute. They need to know they have an important place within the family. Not only that, but kids who grow up learning how to do their own laundry, cook, and manage their time will be at a distinct advantage when they go off to college or get their own place for the first time.

It's not easy to motivate the masses or raise kids who understand just how much work it takes to run a household. Sometimes, it seems like it would be easier just to do everything ourselves—or even easier to earn the money to hire somebody else to do it! But getting your children involved is worth the effort. So roll up your sleeves and start today. Your friends and family may raise their eyebrows, but one day they'll be able to see the proof in the pudding—in capable, responsible young adults who can confidently do a load of laundry and clear the table without being asked.

Additional Resources

- **www.lotsofkids.com** This site features resources like tips and advice on organization and household management, chore charts, reviews of calendars and other organizers, and much more—all aimed at families with lots of kids.
- **www.tonsofkids.net** Check out the "Tons of Kids" message board community to find out how other parents of large families keep everything running smoothly.
- **www.thenewhomemaker.com** is the modern mom's answer to making a home, featuring advice on everything from cleaning to cooking and raising kids.

Getting Around:
Transporting Your Table
for Eight

When I finally got around to installing the car seat for my soon-to-be-third baby into my Saturn XLS a few years ago, I experienced a moment of panic.

My older sons, at six and four, were still sitting in booster seats. According to my state's laws, my oldest son didn't absolutely have to use a booster, but safety guidelines recommended one through the age of eight. And even with only two car seats, cramming three kids into the back of the car was going to be a difficult—if not impossible—task.

We made do, uncomfortably, for a while by putting one adult in the back with two boosters while the rear-facing carseat went up front in the passenger seat (with the airbag turned off). This arrangement was not only uncomfortable and inconvenient but not particularly safe, because even without an airbag, the back seat is best for kids. We received a handed-down and much-appreciated minivan as a gift from my husband's parents before number four came along, which was quite a lucky score—there's no way to cram a family of six into an average family sedan nowadays, unless one person walks or rides in the trunk!

It's at times like this that some Table for Eight parents think back fondly to the highway boats you may remember from your childhood. Those wide, long bench-seated wonders often had six seat belts and a roomy trunk. Of course, they also had a bad reputation as gas-guzzlers.

When I was a kid, a lot of families I knew had station wagons with an extra row of seats in the back—or if not, all that extra room for a kid or two to lie down in. But with what we know now about child-safety seats and seatbelts, kids rolling around in the car is no longer a responsible option, and most station wagons now offer seating for only five people.

And nowadays, even many "big" vehicles—like many SUV models—don't carry more than five passengers comfortably—and that's assuming that most of them are past the car seat or booster stage. Many families are concerned about gas mileage, expense, and pollution, and may not relish the idea of driving a vehicle the size of a bus. So what's a family with four, five, six, or more kids to do? What kind of gas mileage, pricing, and features can you expect from vehicles meant to carry the bigger-than-average family?

Rides for a Table for Eight

Here's a look at your four basic choices, plus a suggestion, for transporting a big family.

Wagons, sedans, and crossovers. Remember that back row of seats in your family's wood-panel station wagon? They aren't as common as they once were, but you can still find station wagons and new wagon-SUV "crossovers"—vehicles that are built on a station wagon or minivan frame but feature SUV styling and space—that seat six or seven passengers. For example, the Ford Freestyle, which looks like a cross between an SUV and a minivan, features a third-row seat that can also fold flat into the floor. The Mazda CX-9 looks like a stylish station wagon, but seats seven and features plenty of cargo space and easy access to the back row of seats. And both Volvo and Mercedes make station wagons with an optional extra row of seats in the back.

Minivans. The soccer-mom icon is still an economical and roomy choice for families of up to eight people. For a new, mid-size minivan you can expect to spend from about $20,000 (for a basic model) to $40,000 or more for a tricked-out luxury family-mobile. They are generally less expensive to insure and maintain than SUVs and use less gas, too: you can do better than 20 mpg on the highway with many newer minivan models. Minivans may include features like easy-to-adjust seats, side and rear doors that open and shut at the press of a button, storage containers, and heat and air conditioning controls in the far back seats.

Some also allow you to remove or fold down back seating on those rare occasions that you've got more cargo than kids in the vehicle. Minivans are also considered very safe and often come equipped with safety features like side airbags. While most minivans feature two seats in the front, two captain's chairs in the middle, and a bench seat in the back, a few, like the Toyota Sienna and the Honda Pilot, offer bench seats in the middle, too, which could allow a family of eight adequate—if not entirely comfortable—seating.

SUV. Sport-utility vehicles have come a long way from the functional and rugged off-road autos of the past. But just because a car has huge tires and sucks up a bunch of gas doesn't mean it's got ample room for a large family. And even "compact" and "crossover" SUVs, which may only seat four or five people comfortably, often have pretty dismal gas mileage—some as low as *15 or 16 MPG.*

But some SUVs seem made just for big families. The GMC Yukon, Ford Excursion, and Chevy Suburban, for example, can hold up to nine passengers. But you'll pay for this super-capacity in a large car payment and horrible gas mileage; and they usually cost more to insure. They can be more difficult for little kids to climb up into because they're higher off the ground than a wagon or minivan. And some SUVs are also more prone to roll-over accidents because their center of gravity is higher than the typical vehicle.

Really big vans. Families with more than six kids may need to really think outside the box when it comes to getting around! Seating at least seven but up to fifteen passengers, the full-size van is the answer for many mega families. They're also a good option if your family has to haul a lot of heavy items around. They aren't too expensive, generally costing in the mid-20K to upper-30K range. On the downside, they tend to be clunky, don't offer a lot of options, and guzzle gas like it's diet soda. If you're going with a full-size van, it's probably a good idea to have a second, smaller car to use when you won't have all the kids with you.

Two or more smaller cars. If you don't often need to take all the kids out with only one driver, you may find it more economical to purchase two smaller, more fuel-efficient vehicles instead of one large one.

This is especially true if you live in an area with good public transportation, if your community is very walker-friendly, or if you have several drivers in the home or older teens who could stay home with younger siblings while you run a quick errand. For longer trips when you want everyone to ride together, you could consider renting or borrowing a larger vehicle.

Or you can have one small car for getting around town alone or with just a few of the kids at a time, and one family vehicle for trips that include everyone. This is also a good option for those parents who can't bear the thought of not owning at least one "fun" car. Scott, a father of five kids in New Jersey, says that his Subaru WRX is his compromise between practicality and fun. "It only seats five people, but I can still use it to drive to and from work, or to take the older kids to school or on an errand." For trips with the whole family, Scott says, he doesn't mind driving the "Mom-Mobile"—the family's seven-seater Dodge Caravan—when he has to, but when he doesn't have the whole crew with him, he doesn't see the point in driving something so big, and, well, boring. "Having a big family means a lot of sacrifices, but I like that I can still drive fast once in a while," he says.

mom wisdom

"When we added the sixth child to the family, we considered buying a Suburban or some other car that would seat eight. But then we realized there was just no reason to buy a huge new vehicle to cart our family around, when we could easily split our outings into smaller groups. So instead we bought two small family vehicles for less money than one big SUV would have cost. Since we have teens, it works really well: sometimes our 17-year-old will take her younger brother to swimming practice, or I might leave a few of the kids home with my 15-year-old when I go grocery shopping. We have an old full-size van we could use in a pinch, but we rarely drive it."

—Sandra, mom of six, Cleveland, Ohio

Car-Purchasing Tips

Think about the interior. Many people with kids swear by leather or a synthetic leather-like material because it wipes up easily and won't soak in stains from malfunctioning sippy cups and over-squeezed juice boxes. If you do go with a fabric interior, you might want to invest in a fabric protection spray, like Scotchguard. If you're really concerned about the upholstery, you can purchase mats specially made to go under your child's car seat to protect it from dents made by the safety seat or messes made by the child. It's important to make sure any mat you use "grips" the safety seat and doesn't allow it to slip or slide around. If you aren't sure whether the mat is really safe to use with your child's safety seat, take it to the police station and ask for an evaluation.

Make sure you can grow into it. If you're planning on your car being an investment that will last several years, make sure there will still be enough leg and cargo space when your babies and preschoolers grow up into big kids and preteens. Also keep in mind that if you're planning on handing down the car to a future driver in the family, you'll want the vehicle to be easy to handle for safety's sake.

Take into consideration which features are just fluff and which would actually make your life easier. If you travel a lot, a built-in DVD player could make long trips that much more bearable for your kids, and, therefore, for you. For running around town, you could much appreciate doors that open and shut at the press of a button on your key ring—especially when you've got your arms full of kids and groceries.

mom wisdom

"The saving grace in our van has been the CD player—we always have kids' music playing. When traveling a long distance, the portable DVD players are a lifesaver. Other tips for happy driving: always have a snack bag packed. You never know how long you are going to be gone (something always comes up) and who is going to get hungry or thirsty. I have a bag of books that always stays in the car. There are several handheld games that stay in, as well. And of course, a fully-stocked diaper bag is in there, too!"

—Lisa, mom of four, Pennsylvania

The Environmentally-Conscious Family

If you're worried about greenhouse gasses—or just want to save money at the pump—you may wonder if it's possible to cart your big family around at all.

No matter how you slice it, any vehicle that's big enough to transport a family of six or more safely and comfortably is going to use some gas. But that doesn't mean there's nothing you can do to reduce your family's transportation footprint on the earth. Try these tips for increasing your car's fuel efficiency:

Accelerate and decelerate smoothly, and maintain a steady speed whenever possible. Smooth driving not only uses less gas, but it's also better for your brakes, too (not to mention safer).

Forget the warm-up. If you're letting your car run for ten minutes on winter mornings to "warm up" the engine, you can stop; the fuel-injected engines in modern cars don't need more than thirty seconds or so of running the engine before they're ready to go, and even older engines only need a few minutes at most. Most of the warming up actually occurs while the car is in motion; idling for a long time in your driveway just wastes gas. Dress warmly and, unless it's dangerously cold, get the kids in the car before you start it. Driving will help the car's heating system get working—and if you're like me, you may find that getting all the kids buckled in is enough to make you work up a sweat, even in wintry temperatures.

Maintain your car according to the owner's manual. Replace fluids, filters, and oil regularly, and keep your tires properly inflated. Keeping your car maintained will help your car run more efficiently and use less gas. It'll also help your car last longer, save you money on repairs, and make your drive safer.

Use your air conditioning only when you really need it. That's not always easy when you've got a row full of sweaty kids begging you to blast the AC, but air conditioning can make an already gas-guzzling vehicle even thirstier. When you're running errands in town on not-so-stifling days, try airing out the car the old-fashioned way: by rolling down windows. Don't do this on the highway, however: research shows that vehicles get better gas mileage with the windows closed when traveling at highway speeds. If you're taking a long trip on a hot day, try running the AC on a low level while you're on the highway, but turn it off and roll down the windows if you get stuck in bumper-to-bumper traffic.

Don't "top off" your gas when you're filling up. I know, I know—it's annoying to have $24.88 in gas when you like those nice round numbers, but overfilling the gas tank can result in spilled gas.

Unload the trunk. Unnecessary weight in the car makes your engine work harder, especially during the winter months. Don't leave heavy items in the trunk when you aren't using them.

Plan your errands ahead of time, and consolidate trips when you can. Seems obvious, huh? But when I really gave this some thought, I realized that I was taking at least four or five unnecessary trips across town every week. Even though the time it takes me to get from my house to the grocery store is negligible, combining my trip to the library with grocery shopping and then swinging by to pick up my son from preschool is a lot easier on my gas budget—not to mention the environment—than if I made three trips to do the same things. Over time, little differences add up.

Start a carpool. With a big family, carpooling isn't always feasible, but if you can leave some kids at home with a teen sibling or your spouse, you may find that you've got room for taking an extra kid or two to an after-school activity in exchange for another parent picking up your child the next time around.

If you have, or can find, a vehicle that takes diesel fuel, you may be able to make your own biodiesel—that is, fuel made from plant material. You can find out more about biodiesel at www. veggievan.org or http://biodieselamerica.org.

Thinking of going hybrid? Your options are limited. As I'm writing this, the only hybrid model available that seats seven people is the Toyota Highlander, which gets 27 miles to the gallon on the highway and 31-32 in the city, and sports a price tag of about $32,000-$36,000. The majority of the other hybrids only seat four or five people, but hopefully over time hybrid models will become a feasible option for Table for Eight families.

Seating Solutions

Nothing is more aggravating than five hours of "Mom, he *touched* me!" When it comes to surviving road trips, how many kids are in the car matters less than how they're arranged. These tips might help keep your big family happy even on long road trips.

Rearrange the pain. Instead of craning around in your seat to cheer up a cranky baby every few minutes, why not put your youngest child next to the family instigator—you know, the kid who's most likely to start bickering and fights on a normal trip—and give him or her the job of keeping the baby entertained, picking up dropped toys, etc.? You might find that the job will keep your child from being bored, which will, in turn, keep him from picking on his siblings. Plus, it'll put physical space between the instigator and the other kids who are old enough to fight with him!

Stop every so often and let older kids pick a new place to sit. This method works for Gina, mom of five in upstate New York, who says that when the mood starts getting tense on long trips, she finds that mixing up the seating can help diffuse bickering. "We go to a rest stop, and I let the kids get out and stretch their legs, or run around in the grass for a minute if it's nice out. Then I let the kids choose new seats, one by one, making sure that each child gets a chance at getting his 'first pick' at some point during the trip." Of course, letting a child who's still in a safety seat pick a new place to sit—and then having to uninstall and reinstall the seat several times—could be a total pain, so this tip works best for bigger kids.

mom wisdom

"I have a one-year-old, a three-year-old, and a five-year-old, all still in car seats, plus my older kids aged eight and ten. I have my three-year-old and five-year-old in the two captain's chairs in the middle, and my ten-year-old is responsible for getting the one-year-old into his car seat—we gave him very careful instructions—between the two biggest kids in the far back. That keeps the two older kids from bickering during the trip, and it keeps the youngest from fussing—he loves to listen to them talk."

—Sarah, mom of five, Kentucky

Put younger kids between older kids. Not only is it nearly impossible to buckle in two bulky car seats side-by-side, but splitting up the babies has other benefits as well: the older kids can help keep the little ones entertained and are less likely to bicker than sibs close in age (of course, this advice goes out the window if your two-year-old and ten-year-old fight a lot!).

Out and About

I remember the first time I went somewhere alone with four children. With an infant, a two-year-old who is still likely to bolt into traffic if given the opportunity, and two older kids who were generally self-sufficient but still likely to do something careless or need help, I remember feeling completely overwhelmed. With just one of me and only two hands, how was I ever going to manage four small kids?

Getting Out the Door

Before you can go anywhere, you've first got to get out the front door. This alone can be enough to make even a seasoned parent start to sweat. Katie, a mom of five, including twins, in Maryland, says that when she wants to go somewhere with all her kids, she does it in stages. "First, everyone gets dressed. Then, everyone eats breakfast, or whatever meal we're on. Then we make sure hair is brushed, faces clean, and everyone has gone to the bathroom. Next, shoes and jackets (if necessary). It's easier for me to have everyone doing things at the same time so I'm not finding socks for someone while another is trying to find a library book and then library book finder needs socks a few minutes later." After she makes sure all the kids are presentable and ready to go, Katie does an equipment check: "I look to make sure we have everything extra that needs to go out the door with us like backpacks or soccer balls. I double-check that we have everything as we buckle into the van. And then I always make a trip back into the house for something," she laughs. As time goes by, she says the kids have caught on to her organized style of getting out the door—and they respond faster. "My kids can move pretty fast through these things on their own now. I think years of them hearing me say, 'Okay, put your shirt on now, go potty now, get your shoes on now!' has helped."

I have a similar system, only mine includes about six trips into the house once all the kids are buckled in. I find that if I try to gather things together while I'm also getting the kids ready, chances are good Owen, the toddler, will strip off his jacket while I'm trying to find my keys; William, my three-year-old, will wander upstairs while I'm getting the jacket back on Owen, and Jacob and Isaac, my older sons, will lose interest entirely and disappear into the yard. To keep everyone under control, I buckle them all into the car when they're ready, then run back and forth between the house and the car to finish loading it up. Because my van is only steps from my front door, I feel safe doing this as long as the older kids are in the van with the little ones so they can let me know if anyone needs me. However, we'll be moving to a big city soon, and I'll be parking on the street—so I won't feel as safe with this method. I got this tip from Carla, a mom of four who lives in a walk-up apartment building in Chicago: "I gather up all the stuff we'll need before I even start to get the kids ready, and we put it all into one of those folding shopping carts like old people use," she says. "Then, the kids and I all walk to the car together, with one of the kids pushing the cart. When I keep the back of my minivan clean enough, I can just stick the whole cart back there without folding it back up." Sounds like a plan I might have to try.

Carting the Kids Around

Unfortunately, you don't always have an option of sticking your entire family in an enormous stroller—especially if some of your kids are school-age. But bigger families still find ways to shop and go to festivals, fairs, concerts, and even restaurants. So how do they do it?

Multi-seat strollers. You can buy double, triple, and even quadruple-passenger strollers that will accommodate infants and toddlers from regular baby-goods stores. These work well if your children are close in age or multiples, but the quarters would be a little cramped for older children, and there is often a per-seat weight limit that would accommodate only infants and toddlers. A quad stroller can cost up to $500 or more. If you go this route, try to keep in mind what you'll be using the stroller for and what features you'll need. With side-by-side strollers, you'll have a harder time navigating crowds and making it through narrow doors, but with the in-line kind, by the time you get the front of the stroller through a door, it might be closing on you!

Daycare strollers. Check out catalogs and online stores aimed at child-care providers, which offer strollers and buggies that carry up to six kids and often can fit older preschoolers, too.

Strollers with a jump seat. If you have a baby and a preschool-age child, consider a stroller with a platform on the back. They tend to be less bulky and easier to fold up than multiple-seat buggies but offer a platform where older kids can sit or stand. This is a good choice if you have a baby and an older child who walks some of the time but may occasionally need to grab a ride. One model to look for is the Baby Trend Sit-N-Stand.

Slings, front packs, and backpacks. Wearing your baby on your body gives you a convenient, hands-free way to carry her. These carriers make walking in crowds a breeze. The only downside is you have no place to stash bags, diapers, and drinks, and if your carrier isn't the right type for you (or if you aren't used to wearing one), you may end up with a sore back or shoulders. When you get your carrier, try it out a few times on short jaunts before you venture out for a day trip.

Wagons. Wagons are still an easy, convenient way to tote kids around. You can fit a few at once, or let an older child pull the wagon so your hands are free for smaller kids. Pulling a heavy wagon can be hard on the back after a while, so this is probably a better choice for transporting kids someplace where you're doing a lot of stopping and standing, like a fair, outdoor concert, or festival; rather than when you have to cover a lot of ground quickly. You can also use the wagon to haul your stuff and let older kids take turns pulling it, which is a good way to keep them occupied and keep their hands off one another.

Restraints. Yeah, I hear what you're saying—kids aren't dogs! Once upon a time, I held firm to the idea that putting a child on a harness or wrist leash was cruel. Then I had a kid who liked to run away while I was busy with groceries or an in-arms baby, and I got over it. If you want to use a child "leash," ignore the stares and glares and remind yourself that safety is the most important thing. Your two-year-old will get over the humiliation of being tethered to Mom with three feet of nylon more easily than he'll get over an encounter with an unfriendly dog or a busy street.

Mix it up. Unless you've got a family full of multiples or very closely spaced children, chances are good that you've got a fairly wide range of ages in your family—some reliable walkers, maybe a child who can walk but sometimes gets tired or wanders, and some littler ones who need to be carried or pushed. The parents I surveyed reported using some of these combinations:

- Mom with a sling, Dad with a backpack, taking turns with a stroller
- Dad with a double stroller, Mom slinging two kids (one on each hip)
- An older child pushing a single-seat stroller while Mom pushes a double stroller
- Babies in slings, with a wagon for a preschooler and the diaper bag
- Two older kids taking turns holding a preschooler's hand, with a baby and a toddler in a double stroller

After you've read the tips in this chapter, check out these resources for more information on vehicles and equipment that can help you get your big family around town in style … and relative comfort:

- Check out www.showeryourbaby.com or www.daycaremall.com for a selection of double, triple, quadruple, and even six-seater strollers!
- Did you know you can carry two babies in slings at a time? For double-slinging directions and other advice on choosing and using a baby carrier, check out The Mamatoto Project at www.wearyourbaby.com.
- For information on buying a fuel-efficient vehicle and how you can help conserve gas check out www.fueleconomy.gov, a site maintained by the U.S. Department of Energy.
- To compare prices, features, fuel economy, and more on vehicles, visit www.edmunds.com.

If you're still adding to your family, think about quality when investing in items like baby carriers and strollers. It can be hard to plunk down more money up front, but you'll save over time by purchasing durable items that can stand the test of time and many kids! Buying used is always a good idea—when a piece of equipment has already seen some action, you can really see how it'll hold up over time—and you can get a high-quality model at a more affordable price.

Working It Out: Having a Career and a Big Family

Just in case you were under the impression that big families all have a full-time at-home parent, think again; in plenty of larger families, both parents work at least some of the time. Because child-care prices for more than one or two kids can approach astronomical heights, you may be wondering how they afford it—not to mention how they manage to balance a career and many children. This chapter shows you how other parents of lots of kids find childcare that fits their family—and their budget, find flexible work options, finish their education, and balance life and work—even with a big family.

Working 9-5

If you and your spouse both work traditional office hours, you probably know well the feeling of trying to herd a bunch of children out the door in the morning and then get them all back home at night.

Let the kids bathe the night before and sleep in their clothes. Well, why not? As long as they aren't wearing scratchy wool sweaters or belted trousers or something uncomfortable like that, taking care of the bathing and dressing the night before will save you a ton of time in the morning. And if they do wear clothes that aren't conducive to good sleep, you can at least put them to bed in the underwear and undershirt they'll wear in the morning, and put their clean clothes near the bed. Anything that shaves off a few minutes here and there will add up to a much calmer and less hurried morning for you.

Something's Gotta Give

Supermom really is a myth, and the idea that we can have a fulfilling job, a clean house, happy kids, and a home-cooked meal on the table every night is unrealistic for any mother. Add in lots of kids to keep happy and fed and it becomes downright impossible. Write down a detailed list of everything you feel like you "should" do in a day, and then delegate a few of them to somebody else—like your spouse, your kids, or hired help—and see what happens. Hint: don't even *think* about giving up sleep! You need that to be a good parent and a productive worker.

Find Child Care That Goes the Extra Mile

When you've got a lot of kids—each with a lot of needs—and a limited amount of time with them, how can you possibly fit it all in? One way is to look for a child-care arrangement that helps meet those needs so that when you get home from work, you can focus on relaxing with your kids. For example, an increasing number of child-care centers offer extra enrichment programs, like ballet or karate, and many provide help with homework. Though of course you'll want to keep an eye on what your child is learning in school, if they come home with a jump-start on their work it can make your evening a lot less stressful. Or maybe you can hire a nanny who will take care of some of the after-school run-around, or pay her a little bit more each hour to handle light housework, start dinner, or run errands. Finding multifunctional child care will cost you a little more, but you may find that having extra help saves you in the long run: if you're less harried when you get home, you may be less likely to resort to pizza or fast food as a last-minute meal plan. Plus, depending on how many children you have, hiring a nanny—or even a nanny and some part-time cleaning help—could very well be less expensive than paying an individual hourly cost for each of them to go to child care.

Make Sure Your Company Is Family-Friendly

Parents, especially mothers, with a lot of children face serious obstacles in the workplace (see "The Mommy Tax," later). For instance—if one of your kids gets sick, it's likely to be much more than a two-day affair as it spreads from child to child to child to child. Research shows that it's best for your health and well-being if you take at least three months off after having each baby—and when you're planning for a big family, that time can really add up. If you'll be breastfeeding your babies—best for their health and a huge boon to your budget—you'll really need a supportive workplace where you can find time and space to either pump or nurse your baby during the day.

If your current employer isn't family-friendly, looking for a job elsewhere might seem impractical or even impossible. But you'll save yourself a lot of stress if you look for employers that offer family-friendly company policies like on-site or company-sponsored childcare, flexible schedule options, ample sick time, the ability to telecommute or work from home when necessary, back-up child care for sick days, and policies that support breastfeeding employees.

Even if you can't leave your current job, check out Working Mother's list of the top 100 Best Companies for Mothers at www.workingmother. com. It might give you some ideas for policies and strategies that you can suggest to your boss.

Eat Together

I've said it before, but eating dinner together is one of the single most important and meaningful things you can do with your family. It provides your kids with a sense of continuity and routine, and gives you all an opportunity to sit down and face each other, day after day. In a big family, it's so easy sometimes for the quieter kids to slip through the cracks or for little problems to go unnoticed until they become big problems. A family meal forces everyone to show up, talk to each other, and be accounted for.

Be Open to Nontraditional Arrangements

Say you're the man of the house, and you work in a great family-friendly company … while your wife works 60-70 hour weeks with little flexibility or vacation time. It may seem unnatural because we're so used to moms handling the lion's share of domestic tasks and child-related care, but shouldn't you take over the doctor's and dentist's visits, join the PTA, and take Susie to ballet practice? "My wife works as a lawyer, and I'm a software developer," says Scott, a father of four in Phoenix, Arizona. "I have a lot of flexibility in my job, and she basically has none. But for the first few years after we had kids we really tried to make our family life fit that traditional pattern: if a child was sick she'd stay home and then have to work all evening and night to make up for it, while I probably could easily have taken the time off and then just absorbed it by working a little extra each day the following week. When we added our fourth child, everything came to a head and my wife completely freaked out because she couldn't do it all. I agreed to take a much more central role in the kids' lives, which actually, I had wanted to do anyway. And I started arranging things like back-up child care and grocery shopping, too. That left my wife able to focus on her job when she's at work, and to just hang out with us when she's at home, without having to stress out over everything."

The Mommy Tax

If your family isn't complete yet, you need to be aware of the costs—both seen and unseen—that having more children may have on your career. Though many companies offer short-term disability insurance or paid maternity leave up to six weeks postpartum and beyond, and the Family and Medical Leave Act entitles employees at qualifying companies up to 12 weeks unpaid leave, that doesn't mean your career will emerge unscathed. The much-publicized "mommy track," in which mothers move in and out of the workplace in order to have babies or care for small children, often results in lower pay and fewer promotions. A 2005 report called "Getting a Job: Is There a Motherhood Penalty?" by Shelley J. Correll at the Department of Sociology at Cornell University, found that women with children may actually face a more difficult time getting hired at all, even when they are well-qualified for a job, and when they are hired, are often offered lower starting wages—and that the more children they have the worse the problem is. In fact, the report refers to the lowered salary as a "per-child wage penalty." In the book *The Motherhood Manifesto: What America's Moms Want—And What To Do About It* (Nation Books, 2006), authors Joan Blades and Kristin Rowe-Finkbeiner call this discrimination toward mothers "the maternal wall."

9-5 and Beyond

What do you think of when you hear the phrase "working mom"? Let me guess—that tired old image of supermom in a power suit, dropping the kids off at a daycare center while she leaves for her 9-5 job in an office downtown, making presentations to corporate bigwigs, and hauling out her industrial-strength breast pump at lunch?

That's the cliché, but we all know that in reality, families find all kinds of ways—some traditional and some extremely unconventional—to make work, well, *work* for them. There's the 9-5 Monday through Friday option, which most of us are already pretty familiar with, but it doesn't always make financial sense to work a traditional job when you've got a houseful of kids. Child-care costs can be prohibitive, and if you're growing your family, you may be pregnant or caring for a newborn every year or two.

Maybe you've decided you won't go back to work until your youngest starts school, but if you plan on reentering the workforce, it's probably a good idea to have something to add to your resume in the meanwhile—particularly if you plan to be out of the workforce with young children for many years. If you're homeschooling, you may have children in the house for the next 18—or more—years!

If you want or need to work, you can think outside the 9-5, Monday-Friday mold. Consider these flexible ways you can build a resumé, pursue your passions, and/or reach your financial goals.

Flexible Schedules

If a 9-5 job won't work for you, you may have options. Increasingly, employers are exploring the idea of offering flex-time (employees work a set number of hours per week, but with flexible schedules), job-shares (two or more employees share a single job), reduced and part-time schedules, and four-day workweeks as a way to accommodate workers with family responsibilities. Or you may have the option of working in the office 3-4 days and at home 1-2 days.

These can be especially helpful for parents of many for a few reasons: first, the ability to reduce the number of hours all your kids are in child care will equal major savings for your family. Second, it allows you to work around the varied school, after-school, and child-care schedules that can become more complicated the more children you have. For example, if one of your kids gets out of school at 3:00 and then you have to drive across town to pick up another child at 3:30, and have a third child to ballet practice by 4:00, the ability to work a 7-3 shift rather than 9-5 makes all the difference in the world. Also, when you've got several school-aged children, chances are good you'll have to deal with many conflicting performances, meetings, and conferences. Having a flexible work schedule won't solve those problems, but it will make them a lot easier to work around.

Working part-time on the weekend or evenings, when your partner is home with the kids, is another option. Many couples trade off shifts with the kids—a workable option if you don't mind foregoing some of your time together while the kids are small.

"Not getting to have dinner together every night as a family was a bummer at first, but the unexpected benefit was that my husband became a lot more confident at parenting the kids alone," says Terry, mother of six children in Springfield, Illinois, who recently took on a retail management job that requires her to be out of the house two or three evenings a week and working a shift every other weekend. "The kids seem closer to Dad now, and he doesn't always pass off discipline and housekeeping tasks to me like he used to." And, says Terry, her income allowed her husband to pass up a promotion that would have required him to spend a lot more hours at work. "His job is already stressful, and it would have been really hard on him and us if he'd had to spend even more time in the office," says Terry. "I feel like we have a nice balance."

Be a Do-Gooder

Volunteer activities can provide valuable experience and help build a resume for paid work down the road. If you aren't already experienced in an area you hope to find work in later, volunteering can be a great way to build skills and learn "on the job."

To find volunteer opportunities, look around your community: your church or religious community; arts groups; your child's school, sports team, or club; hospitals and humanitarian organizations—all probably have needs and will appreciate your help.

But if you're not sure what the best volunteer positions for you might be, it may help to first identify where your strengths lie and what kind of experience you'd like to highlight on a resumé when you start looking for paid work. For example, if you're hoping to develop and emphasize your communication skills, you could volunteer to write or edit the newsletter for a nonprofit organization you admire. If it's technical skills you hope to stress, maybe your child's school could use help maintaining the computer system or setting up a network. Heading up committees of all types is a good way to draw attention to leadership skills.

mom wisdom

"I work one day a week at my kids' school doing development and marketing. Instead of pay, I get a reduced tuition rate (our kids attend our local parish school). I fit my work around my household responsibilities and shuttling kids around. As I do work for my children's school, I try to fit things in around their schedule: during nap times and after they go to bed. If I have a meeting, I have set up playdates or hired a baby-sitter on occasion so I can meet without interruptions. If it's really important, my husband has even taken time away from his work to help out. Usually though, my kids just come with me. You get me and my entourage!"

—Tricia, mom of five, Washington

Hang out a Shingle

Do you love cosmetics, candy, or computer parts? Maybe you can turn that enthusiasm into an at-home business and mix your passion with profit.

Some professions are especially well-suited to a home office. Writing is one. (I'm typing this chapter on my laptop, in bed, with my baby curled up next to me and my older kids running in and out of the room.) Graphic design, proofreading, editing, and data entry can be done from a computer in any area of your house.

If you're a crafter, herbalist, soapmaker, or seamstress, you can also try selling your wares at local fairs and flea markets or set up shop online. The Internet may also offer an opportunity for broad exposure for your home-based business, relatively inexpensively. Many mothers put homemaking experience and skills to use, providing child-care or cleaning services.

The Work-At-Home Reality

I can tell what you're thinking: "Okay, but what's it *really* like to be an at-home working mom with a bunch of kids? Is it possible to come off as a professional when there's a sippy cup on your desk and a baby bouncing on your knee?"

Sometimes, working at home as the mom of many can be relatively easy, as when the children are napping on schedule or going through one of those rare phases where they play harmoniously together in their bedrooms instead of crawling around under our feet yanking out the printer paper. But just when you start to get used to it, your toddler starts that must-sit-on-Mom-constantly phase or your older kids decide they're unable to play quietly for the ten minutes it takes to complete a client phone call. On those days, calling or e-mailing a fellow working-at-home-mom friend for commiseration can give you a sense of perspective and remind you that this, too, shall pass. If you want more information on working from home or want to meet other moms who work at home, check out www.wahm.com. Besides helpful information and advice, wahm.com has message boards that can help you make connections with other working-at-home parents.

For in-depth information and support for starting a specific home-based business or working as a freelancer or consultant from home, get some books that will walk you through the basics and then seek support from others in the same boat (check out the appendix for a list of resources).

A Day in the Life of a Work-At-Home Mom

Carmen, a mom of five kids in Washington state, and her husband both work from home; he's a tax accountant, while she assembles entities like corporations and partnerships. Carmen also homeschools her kids. How does she do it all?

"I work from about 4:30 A.M. to 11 A.M. in the office, and then home-school the kids and complete my homemaker duties in the afternoon/evenings. I do most of my work before anyone else gets up, so I can get a lot done without any interruptions. By the time the three-year-old gets up, the others are ready to be awakened. They take care of her for the first two hours, and then I'm with the kids the rest of the day."

mom wisdom

"I do my work while my older children are in school and my younger two are napping. When I meet clients face to face, I usually choose a nice restaurant or café and bring my laptop with me to show them the work that I've done. My husband and I trade child care when the other needs quiet time—I'll watch the kids while he's on an important call, or he'll watch the kids while I go to a meeting."

—Megan, mom of five and web developer, Florida

Here's Carmen's schedule:

"Mondays: work 5 A.M. to 11 A.M., then lunch. After lunch I make a weekly menu and grocery list, try to run any necessary errands, have dinner, and then the kids have karate from 7 P.M. to 9 P.M.

"Tuesdays: work 5 A.M. to 11 A.M., then lunch. After lunch I clean Zone 1 (kitchen, kitchen bathroom, dining room, family room.) Then we have dinner, and I have volunteer work from 6 P.M. to 9 P.M.

"Wednesdays: work 5 A.M. to 11 A.M., then lunch. After lunch I do the grocery shopping: Costco and a regular grocery store. We have dinner, and then church services in the evening.

"Thursdays: work 5 A.M. to 11 A.M., then lunch. After lunch I clean Zone 2 (master bedroom, master bathroom, upstairs office/work room, formal living room, entry, halls, laundry room, Dad's bedroom, Dad's bathroom.) We have dinner, and then the kids have karate from 7 P.M. to 9 P.M.

"Fridays: work 5 A.M. to 11 A.M., then lunch. After lunch I work on Zone 3 (downstairs office, halls, library, boys' room, boys' bathroom, guest room). We have dinner, and then I take the evening off.

"Saturdays: work 5 A.M. to 11 A.M., then lunch. Saturdays we often spend watching our 14-year-old son compete in cross-country competitions, track competitions, or whatever else is happening."

Continuing Your Education

Returning to school sounds expensive and time-consuming, right? But with the growing popularity of Internet-based courses, going to college has become more and more accessible for adults with family and job responsibilities. Many community colleges offer some or all of the coursework required for an associate's degree online, and some universities offer bachelors' and masters' programs entirely online as well. Best yet, many of these programs function just like standard university classes would—which means your diploma will be indistinguishable from that of a traditional student's and you may qualify for financial aid.

Sarah, a mom of four children under the age of seven, found the "virtual college" experience a perfect fit for her situation. "I just divorced last year, and I really needed to get some education—I don't have much of a resumé," says the student in Lansing, Michigan. "But child care for that many kids would have been impossible for me to afford. Plus, my kids are little, and I didn't relish the idea of putting them all in daycare while I went to school." Sarah was able to complete almost all of the initial coursework for a computer science degree online and is looking forward to transferring to a four-year university next year—where she'll also take her classes over the Internet. "I qualified for enough financial aid that I only had to get a very part-time job, and I work on my schoolwork during naps, early in the morning, and when the kids are with their dad. I feel like I not only gained four years of being with my kids most of the time—by the time I'm done with my degree, my youngest will be starting kindergarten—but also, I'm going to come out way ahead in the end, with a degree I can use to support my family."

Amy, mom of five in Cleveland, Ohio, decided to pursue online classes after her youngest child was born and found that the flexible nature of Internet classes fit in perfectly with her busy life. "I did most of my coursework while the kids were asleep or entertained with something else. I completed my entire associate's degree online," says Amy, who is now working toward a bachelor's degree in business management online.

Finding an exclusively virtual program in your chosen field may require some research. Although more and more colleges are offering entire programs online, the degree you want might not be an option locally, meaning you may have to find an out-of-state school. For instance, when I attended college online, I was able to get most of my basic courses taken care of here in town, through the distance education department of my local community college. But when it came time to transfer to complete my upper-level courses, I had to look harder, finally settling on a university two states away that had several degree completion programs offered entirely online. I live five hours from the college campus, which worked out fine because I never had to set foot on it!

Be careful when you're doing your college search to distinguish the diploma mills from respected institutions of higher learning. Many nonaccredited "universities" lurk on the web. A good rule of thumb: if your potential school's web address ends in .edu, it is likely an accredited college or university. If it ends in .org or .com, watch out—the "degree" you earn may be virtually useless in your chosen field or for transfer to another school. If in doubt, check the school's accreditation status. There are six regional accrediting agencies that are widely respected and accepted by other academic institutions—an important factor to consider if you plan to transfer schools, attend graduate school, or go into a field in which the respectability of your alma mater is important.

The six regional accrediting bodies are:

Middle State Association of Colleges and Schools
www.msache.org

New England Association of Schools and Colleges
www.neasc.org

North Central Association of Colleges and Schools
www.ncacihe.org

Northwest Association of Schools and Colleges
www.cocnasc.org

Southern Association of Colleges and Schools
www.sacs.org

Western Association of Schools and Colleges
www.wascweb.org

Even if the college you're considering is accredited, it can't hurt to do an extensive search on it to make sure it's got a good academic reputation. College is expensive and time-consuming, so you want to make sure your education will be credible to future employers or if you want to move on to graduate school.

mom wisdom

Shirley, mom of five kids, is completing her education through an online program geared toward working adults. "I completed almost all of my college education after having my fifth child. I went back for an associates degree in nursing when the kids were six months, two years, four years, eight years, and fourteen years old. Two years after I graduated, I started my bachelor's degree program in nursing. Three months after I earned my bachelor's degree in nursing, I entered a graduate program for my masters in nursing." Not all of these programs are legitimate, however, and even some "accredited" online universities have a bad reputation in the academic world.

Remember: while online learning is a flexible method of earning college credit, most courses are not self-paced. Although you can do the work at a time that is convenient for you, you'll have plenty of deadlines and, sometimes, group projects to coordinate. Learning online can be lonely, because you'll be interacting with a remote professor and faceless fellow students over a modem rather than face-to-face. You'll need to be organized, independent, and motivated. And while you don't have to be a computer geek, a basic understanding of the Internet, e-mail and message boards, and the ability to communicate clearly in writing are definite necessities for success.

You'll also need to meet certain technology requirements. First, you must own a reasonably new computer that is hooked up to the Internet or have regular use of one. Also, certain courses may require that you own or purchase specific computer software. Check the technology and software requirements for your intended classes before the semester starts to avoid unwelcome surprises! And remember, financial aid may cover the costs of computer software and Internet access, as these are school-related expenses.

To get started, check with your local community college or university and see which programs and classes are offered in your area. My local community college offers a collaborative service with other community colleges in the state—if they don't have a class you need, you can sign up to take the class through the other school in the collaborative without going through the school's application process. If there's nothing close by, look outside your area—some schools offer special tuition rates for their out-of-state virtual students.

But you don't think Internet classes are for you? Weekend or evening classes may also be an option. Investigate your local community college or university, or check to see if another university in your state offers a satellite campus near your home—they often offer flexible programs for returning adult students with families.

Finding Child Care

Let's face it, good child-care is expensive, and it gets more expensive the more children you have. If you need full-time care, look into home day-cares as an option. They are often less expensive in general than child-care centers, and because they don't divide children by age, you may find that they charge the same flat fee whether your child is three months old or three years old, whereas center care usually charges a lot more for infants and non-potty-trained toddlers than older kids.

Of course, home daycares have limits on how many kids they can take at a time, so chances are good one home daycare won't be an option for your whole family. And because your children are already around a large multi-aged group every day at home, you might prefer to have them in a center, where they'll have more opportunity to interact with kids their same age. Also, elementary schools often have child-care centers on campus, which can allow you to keep all or most of your kids in one place, with one drop-off and pick-up point … making life a lot more convenient.

If you only need a few hours of child care each week, you may be in for an unpleasant surprise—part-time daycare can be more expensive on a per-hour basis and harder to find than full-time. Care providers are often forced to charge a premium for part-time slots, because they have no guarantee they'll find another child to fill the hours left vacant by your schedule; and because they may be trying to fit you in around another part-timer, the available hours could be limited. Call around; some daycares specialize in flexible and part-time schedules and may be happy to accommodate yours.

If you need care for more than one or two of your kids, an in-home sitter may be a better—and possibly, less expensive—option. If you have a college or university nearby, consider advertising in the school paper or at the career center—child development or elementary education majors are often on the lookout for an opportunity to work with children. Another option is to find a retired "grandmother" type who's looking for something to fill her time. Many older people relish the chance to hang around with little kids, and can make very good baby-sitters. And if you can find a retiree who raised a big family too, so much the better!

Are you working from home? A mother's helper might fit the bill if you just need somebody to distract the kids so you can concentrate for a while. Because you'll be in the house, you may be comfortable with a young teen or preteen—ask around your neighborhood or church congregation for recommendations, or call the local junior high or high school and ask if they keep a baby-sitter registry.

However, keep in mind that a preteen or young teen—or even an older teen!—might be intimidated and overwhelmed by caring for a big family. It might be a good idea to hire two at a time so that they have more control over the group. To keep things simple, split the kids into two groups and put each mother's helper in charge of those specific kids. And make sure to be upfront with your babysitter or mom's helper about payment, right off the bat. A lot of sitters get paid more based on how many children they're caring for, which is fair, to a certain extent … unless it means you end up paying a thirteen-year-old $20 an hour to watch your six kids, several of whom might be old enough not to need much care, anyway. Sit down ahead of time with the babysitter and negotiate her fees so there's no awkwardness or hard feelings later.

If you have friends with kids, you can swap care or start a baby-sitting co-op. There are many ways to organize a co-op, but one of the simplest ways is to start each member of the co-op out with a certain amount of "baby-sitting money," which she then uses to "pay" for child care. For instance, one dollar in play money could represent one hour of care for one child. Limiting the amount of money each member starts with is a good way to ensure fairness—as soon as one mom's money is all gone, she'll have to "earn" more by reciprocating. This can be difficult when there's a huge difference between your family's size and your friends' families. For example, is the hour your friend spends watching your four children worth four hours of watching her one child? I think there's a balance to be found: yes, it's more difficult in some ways to watch four children as opposed to one, but your time is as valuable as anyone else's. It also depends on the kids' ages: bigger kids eat more and might make more messes, but you actually might work harder caring for your friend's one small baby than she would watching four older, more self-sufficient kids.

You'll probably have to negotiate to come to an arrangement that's fair to all parties if you swap care or use a baby-sitting co-op with moms of smaller families. Or you may just want to seek out other big families to swap care with. I don't mind at all babysitting lots of kids at once, because I'm already used to the noise and chaos, and it gives all my kids something to do!

A nanny share is another part-time option. Many good professional nannies are looking for full-time employment, with a hefty full-time price tag. But if you can coordinate with another family so that the nanny spends part of her week or day with you and the rest with the other family, you can save a lot of money. Again, if the other family is a lot smaller than yours, you'll probably have to do some negotiating to figure out how to split the fee. Talk to the potential nanny about how much more she would generally charge, say, a family of five as compared to a family of two, and then see if she'll wiggle on that amount. That will give you an idea of her per-hour rate for your family and allow you to split the total fee fairly with the other family.

Enlisting older kids to help can be an option as well. Carmen, who described her work schedule earlier, relies on her bigger kids to help out with the little ones while she works. "At one point I was going nuts, trying to homeschool the kids, do the housekeeping and the cooking and the errands," in addition to her full-time job. "I sat down in total frustration and looked out the window ... and there were three of my children, totally bored. I had an epiphany—Eureka! There is my work force. My kids are a valuable resource that allows me to do much more than I would be able to do without them." As part of their regular chores, Carmen's older kids baby-sit her three-year-old for two hours a day while she works. "There is a balance—fun things with work. But the kids do learn early on that privileges have to be balanced with responsibilities. We don't allow privileges without suitable responsibilities." For more information on potential pitfalls of enlisting older kids as baby sitters—and how you can avoid them—visit Chapter 10.

The Work-Family Balance

I spoke with some Table for Eight parents to find out how they make their own lives work.

"I think that it is absolutely possible to balance work and a large family. Being a fulfilled and educated working adult makes me a better mother because I am happy and confident and doing something I find meaningful. It's not the same for everyone, but in my situation, my husband and I find that balance is something we have committed to. We consciously try to keep a good sense of humor and make sure our kids know that they are our absolute first priority, no matter what. Everything else just kind of falls into place."—Jennifer, mom of five, Arizona

"Balancing work and kids is very difficult, but I continue to try. I don't think the balancing is any easier if you have one child or six … it's all a full-time job. I keep buying new organizer calendars in the quest for organization and balance!"—Michelle, mom of four, Colorado

"Do what you can, when you can. Make the most of the opportunities you have, whether it's with your kids or your work. Remember that you're only human and that the dishes will still be there tomorrow, no one will die if the rug isn't vacuumed, but you could wake up tomorrow and your little boy may have decided that he's too old to snuggle in your lap and be read to."—Jennifer, mom of four, Indiana

Though working and child-care issues can be more and more complicated the bigger your family gets, having a lot of kids also gives you a team of consultants who will let you know when things aren't going well. Have regular family meetings to discuss schedules and activities, to point out where things aren't getting done and where your kids or spouse may need to take on more responsibility, and to make sure everybody in the family has a voice. Making sure that running the family is truly a team effort is the first step to a balance that works.

6

Feeding Your Flock

When you have a big family, ordering pizza from the cheapest chain—even with a coupon—can become an expensive affair, especially if your brood includes hungry teenagers. And supplying healthy meals three meals a day, every day, may seem like more than your budget can bear.

In addition to these concerns, today's generation of parents has a few distinct obstacles when it comes to putting budget-friendly and crowd-pleasing meals on the table. Many of us had two working parents who might not have had time to show us the ropes when it came to shopping for groceries and planning and preparing meals. Unlike generations past, many of us didn't grow up in the kitchen, learning at our own mothers' aprons. And even if we do have the cooking skills to avoid living on convenience foods and becoming familiar faces at the nearest drive-thru, we may not have a clue how to stock a pantry or grocery shop for a big family without breaking the bank.

So how can a Table for Eight parent keep everyone fed: healthily, inexpensively, and relatively happily?

As it turns out, there are many ways to feed a large family. From cooking just once a month to buying in bulk to doubling and tripling recipes, parents of lots of kids offer up a variety of tips and techniques to help you serve up big-family-friendly fare—without going to the poorhouse or spending most of your time in the kitchen. Planning ahead is important; if you give your meal shopping, preparation, and cooking some thought before you ever pick up a pan, you'll save time, money, and work.

Stock Your Pantry

If you have the right staples on hand, you can whip together a meal without too much thought. But trying to plan your pantry can be intimidating. What do you really need to have on hand?

How you stock your pantry will depend a lot on the types of foods you cook the most, but it's always a good idea to have a baseline. Other parents of big broods make sure to keep some of these items on hand at all times:

Baking Supplies:

Flour

Sugar—white, brown, powdered

Salt

Baking soda

Baking powder

Bread crumbs

Vanilla extract

Spices

Cornmeal

Instant yeast

Vinegar (White is cheap and versatile, good for cooking and cleaning. You may also want to stock up on apple cider vinegar and specialty vinegars for certain recipes.)

Powdered milk or buttermilk (Powdered is cheaper than fresh for cooking and lasts a good long while.)

Condensed milk

Honey

Oils (Canola and olive are two healthy choices.)

Brown rice syrup, stevia—healthier alternative to white sugar

Pasta, Legumes, and Nuts

A variety of pasta

Dried noodles

Canned or dried beans (Dried are cheaper but take longer to make.)

A variety of nuts

Soups, Sauces, and Sandwich Spreads

Canned broth and soups

Bullion

Spaghetti sauce—unless you prefer to make your own

Peanut Butter

Tuna

Salsa

Jelly

Fruits and Veggies

Dried and canned fruit

Potatoes

Onions

Applesauce

Tomatoes—whole, diced, paste, and sauce

Canned fruit

Olives

Extra dressings and condiments (If your family goes through a lot of ketchup or salad dressing, for example, it's always a good idea to have spare bottles on hand!)

Grains

Oatmeal (You might want to have a few different kinds; steel-cut and classic oats are the healthiest, but instant can make a quick and easy breakfast for those on-the-run days.)

Other cereal grains—quinoa, millet, barley, etc.

Pancake mix—store-bought or homemade.

Rice (Brown is the healthiest; jasmine rice can spice up a meal with a dash of Asian flavor, and short-grain white is quickest to make.)

Popcorn (It's easy to make in large batches on the stovetop, and a lot cheaper and better-tasting than the microwave variety or other salty snacks.)

Cake, muffin, and biscuit mixes (If you buy these on sale, they can be as inexpensive as cooking from scratch and can save the day in a pinch.)

Cereals

Other things you may want to add to your regular shopping list:

Freezer

Boneless, skinless chicken breasts

Veggies

Ground beef

Juices

Other meats

Berries (If you pick these yourself, freeze them on a cookie sheet before you put them in a bag. That way they won't stick together.)

Bread (It freezes nicely, so you can buy a bunch when it's on mega-sale.)

mom wisdom

"If you're starting from scratch with your pantry, you need to be patient. Pick the five to ten things you think you'd use the most and add them to the grocery list. Do this at every shopping trip until you have everything on your pantry list. With a complete pantry, you'll find that you can cook just about anything from scratch with ease. Add a good cookbook—Fannie Farmer is great for all cooks, beginning to advanced—and you can kiss canned soups, boxed meals, and frozen convenience foods good-bye!"

—Kim, mom of six, Indiana

Perishables

Milk

Eggs

Cheese—sliced for sandwiches and block or shredded for cooking

Breakfast meats

Sandwich meats

Tofu or meat alternatives

Yogurt (Buy large containers of plain or vanilla-flavored and then let family members add fresh fruit or berries to their own liking.)

Butter

Fresh seasonal vegetables, fruits, and berries

Convenience Foods

Sure, it's cheaper and usually healthier to cook from scratch. But some convenience foods are relatively healthy, and if it means the difference between eating at home and hitting the drive-thru, worth the investment. These convenience foods are worth keeping around:

Preroasted chicken strips (Put them on salads, in pasta, in fajitas …)

Frozen burritos (These are a great on-the-go meal, especially for busy teens.)

Hot-pocket type sandwiches

Frozen waffles

Frozen bread dough

Boxed and bagged meals—Hamburger Helper, macaroni and cheese, boxed pasta, frozen skillet meals with pasta, meat and veggies all in the bag.

Keeping Track of All That Food

After you've decided what foods you need to have on hand at all times, devise a system for keeping track of it all. This will help you be more efficient in your meal planning and grocery shopping, because you'll know exactly what you need from each trip to the store and can cut out both unnecessary trips and unnecessary calls to the pizza delivery line because you think you're "out" of everything! It'll also allow you to plan your shopping ahead of time, coordinating sales and coupons and saving you money.

Here are a few ways you can stay on top of the food in your house:

Make a list, and tape it to the inside of your pantry door or on your fridge. When you're almost out of any item, make a check mark next to it on the list. When you go shopping, transfer the items from the checklist to your shopping list. I've included a pantry list you can copy and use at your own home at the end of this chapter. A dry-erase board also works well for this.

Pantry List

Use the suggested pantry items above as a starting point, but feel free to substitute items your family prefers. To make sure you don't run out of anything, purchase replacements as soon as you're down to one jar, box, bottle, or can left.

Item		Quantity Remaining

Keep your fridge and pantry organized. That way it will be easy to tell what's missing and what's getting low. Line up your canned goods in rows by brand or type, or label your shelves if that helps.

Get technical. Use a spreadsheet program like Microsoft Excel to keep track of what foods you are running low on and what you need to purchase. This is also an easy and effective way to track sales, record prices per ounce, and keep on track with your budget, because the program does the math for you. If you aren't computer-savvy, this might be a good project for a technically-inclined spouse or teenager.

Buy in quantity. Grains, lentils, cereals, and baking supplies you can often buy in large quantities at health-food stores, shopping clubs, like Sam's Club or Costco, or in the bulk section of your regular grocery store. Transfer the bulk items to buckets, bins, or canisters and label each one clearly. Or put packages in see-through plastic containers with pouring spouts. That way you can easily see what's in each container and when you're getting low. In many stores you can bring your own container from home and refill it at the store, creating less waste. At some food co-ops and health food stores, you can get a discount for bringing your own container, too.

Money-Saving Ideas

Yes, it can cost a lot to feed a houseful of growing kids, but it doesn't have to break your budget. Shopping sales, using coupons, and avoiding restaurant and take-out fare in favor of home-cooked meals are all great ways to save money, but here are a few other tips:

Take a calculator along when you shop. This is a great way to keep track of how much money worth of food you've got in your cart so far and gives you a quick and easy way to calculate whether Brand A or Brand B is a better deal.

Pay in cash. Decide ahead of time what you'll spend, and only bring that amount along. Force yourself to stay within your budget—you'd be surprised how creative you can get when you know you can't spend more than what you have in your purse!

Buy a deep freeze. It's an investment, but when items like frozen meat go on sale, you'll be able to stock up and save down the road.

De-emphasize meat. If meat takes center stage in your meals, consider rethinking its importance. In many countries, meat is treated as a garnish, not the main meal. Doctors generally agree that this can be a much healthier way to eat than the standard American dinner in which meat takes center stage. It's generally cheaper and quicker to cook meatless or meat-light meals, too, and cleanup can be much easier.

mom wisdom

"Filler foods like starches really help to stretch a meal. Corn, rice, beans/legumes, and pasta are all cheap and help give you a bit more bang for your buck. We also buy from local produce farmers as much as possible. Not only is the produce organic and fresh off the field, but it's usually cheaper, too. We also buy shelf-stable products in bulk for our pantry, like canned fruits and veggies."

—Megan, mom of five, Tampa, Florida

Cereal: Getting the Most Bang for Your Buck

The cereal aisle practically gives me hives. How is it that a box of puffed-up, artificially flavored sugar can cost more per ounce than high-quality cheese? And have you noticed that the minute you bring home a box of "sugar" cereal, the kids are all over it like vultures?

These tips I've culled from my own cereal-buying trials and errors and advice from other parents of big families.

Stick to generics. I know, I know, some of them don't taste anything like their brand-name counterparts. But some generics are almost indistinguishable from the familiar brands, and others are getting better. Figure out which ones come in close, and slowly mix them in with your regular cereal in higher and higher proportions. Soon your family will be eating generics without noticing the difference. (If you absolutely can't give up your own brand-name Sugar Coated Crappies, consider hiding a box for yourself and getting your kids used to the cheaper off-brands. Mom's prerogative!)

Look for density. Yes, a small box of grape-nuts or shredded wheat can be pricey. But each spoonful of a dense, whole-grain cereal or one with nuts, seeds, or dried fruits packs a lot more nutritional value than the puffed-up variety that is mostly air. It doesn't take a lot of shredded wheat to fill me up, but I can easily eat four bowls of puffed rice cereal in one sitting. (And that's just wrong.)

Shop sales and coupons religiously. It's best if you can use them together. Give yourself an upper limit on what you'll spend on cereal, and don't go over it. If your favorite cereal ever dips below that amount, buy every box in sight—with all those preservatives, unopened boxes of most varieties last forever, and it's worth making the storage space for it.

mom wisdom

"We keep a special area, completely separate from our other food and household items, that's for emergency times only. We call it the 'bird flu' area just so the kids know where to take things when I'm stocking it. That way we have supplies in case something happens where we can't go into town for an extended period of time. Around here, we have had snowstorms that have kept us housebound for five or more days. I rotate the food items in this area so things stay fresh. We also have things like extra toilet paper, paper towels, matches, toothpaste, diapers, and wipes, in this area."

—Jill, mom of four, Texas

Meal Planning for Table for Eight Families

If there's one thing accomplished—and busy—home cooks seem to agree on, it's that planning out your meals ahead of time is an absolute must. If you aren't sure what's going to be for dinner on Tuesday, it will be only too easy to find yourself hungry, cranky, and calling the pizza delivery place at 6:00 that night! Meal planning not only helps keep you on track for the week's meals—because you know what you're going to make days in advance, you can gather ingredients together when you get a chance, and you'll make sure to start preparing in time—but also gives you a guideline when you're creating your shopping lists.

Some families plan out every meal—breakfast, lunch, dinner, and even snacks—a week or more in advance. In my house, we plan only dinners and choose from a list of easy options for breakfast (eggs, pancakes, cereal), lunch (soup, sandwiches, salads), and snacks (fruit, nuts, cheese, and crackers).

At the end of this chapter you'll find several checklists and forms you can copy and use while creating your own meal plan.

Get the Kids on Board

When it comes to shopping and cooking, consider your bigger kids part of the work force. And train them young; even small tots can set the table or put away silverware. As your kids get older, they can cut up veggies, stir pots, and prepare side dishes. And of course, there's after-meal cleanup: clearing the table, scraping plates, scrubbing pots and pans, loading the dishwasher. When kids grow up cooking, they are comfortable in the kitchen, plus they learn cooking and preparation skills that will serve them well as adults. And when kids have a chance to cook, they often feel a greater sense of ownership over the meals they help prepare—meaning they're less likely to complain about having to eat their peas. This is particularly important in a big family, because when you've got a lot of kids, complaints about what's on the table can eat up most of your meal time.

mom wisdom

"It's important that all my kids know how to cook when they leave home. Even the little kids can help in the kitchen by cracking eggs in a bowl, pouring in ingredients that are pre-measured. Our older kids all have to learn one meal from start to finish by themselves every couple of months."

—Cindy, mom of eight, Colorado

Dealing with Picky Eaters

All families have at least one kid who won't eat anything. And if you have a large family, chances are you'll have two or three—at least. So how can you get your kids to eat without turning into a short-order cook?

There are several approaches to this time-worn dilemma, and none is necessarily the "right" or "wrong" way. Like anything else, how you deal with picky eaters will probably have a lot to do with how you were raised as well as what your personal beliefs and values are. To some parents, providing eating experiences that are positive and pleasurable for everyone involved takes precedence, even if that often means the meals they put blood, sweat, and spices into go uneaten. Others feel that it's important for children to learn to eat things they don't like and that it's impolite to refuse food that's served, so kids are required to clear their plates—even if it's something dreaded, like Brussels sprouts. Other parents take a more middle-of-the-road approach. Here's how some of the parents I surveyed handle mealtime pickiness:

Serve at least one crowd pleaser at each meal. "I try to have at least one thing on the table that everyone will like. I don't make special alternatives, but there is always a snack or meal just around the corner, so nobody seems to go hungry—unless they want to. Also the kids are welcome to eat a fruit or veggie any time of the day."—Bonny, mom of five, Minnesota.

Offer a simple alternative. "My kids are picky eaters, so I generally make a main meal and then either reserve some parts 'plain' for the pickies or offer one simple alternative like sandwiches or eggs. I want to make sure everyone eats, and I'm fine with offering one or more easy alternatives, but I won't make six different meals to meet that goal."—Amanda, mom of five, Michigan.

Avoid food fights. "If I know that someone really doesn't like something, say, cauliflower, I will make sure there is another choice on the table that evening as well. But I won't make another whole meal. Having said that, we do not make food a battleground in this house. There is always something on the table that appeals to the person—and they are left to make their own choices and listen to their own body."—Kim, mom of six from Indiana

Allow for growing independence. "I give everyone the same, but as they get older (facing independence), I allow them to offer me another choice that they can prepare themselves."—Amanda, mom to 17 in Iowa.

Stay away from force-feeding. "At lunch they can ask for anything within reason, and they will get it. At supper everyone eats the same food (except our allergic child), unless it's on their 'can't force it down' list. That person can have something else. My kids each have one or two things they just can't stand, so we don't force them to eat that particular food if I fix it for the rest of the family. If we have something new, everyone has to try it."—Cindy, mom of eight, Colorado

Clean Up As You Go

Who wants to face a disgusting kitchen after a meal? The easiest way to deal with this situation is to clean up as you cook; or better yet, enlist a kid to wipe up spills, rinse pots and mixing bowls, and put them into the dishwasher or in the sink to soak as you work.

With lots of kids, you'll have lots of dishes after each meal. That means you might have to load the dishwasher (if you have one) several times each day. It's a good idea to have one or two of your kids attack the dishwasher in the early afternoon—maybe right after school—so that it's open when you start preparing dinner. Then you can just scrape or rinse and load up the dishes as you're done with them.

Sometimes, despite your best efforts, the dirty dishes will start to pile up until it seems impossible to dig out. When this happens, it's time to "reboot the kitchen," says Robin Elise Weiss, mom of seven and author. In her family, this "reboot" means they use paper plates and throwaway cups until they can get on top of the dishes again. "We do this when the dishes have gotten away from us and one more meal would send us over the edge," she says.

Another common theme in big families: over-use of cups. I'm not sure how it happens that in our family of six, there might be at any given time 12 cups in use on the counter. After a while, they all start to get shoved together and nobody can tell whose is whose, so they get a new one, and then another new one, and then another new one … nothing is quite as disheartening as cramming the dishwasher as full as I can and then realizing that half of it is cups.

One solution is to give each child his or her own cup that he/she can use throughout the day. Each child can get a cup with a different cartoon character, or one that's in a different color, or you can write their name on the cup with a permanent marker—those cheapie take-home plastic cups you get from restaurants are great for this purpose. If different-colored cups offend your aesthetic sensibilities at the table, use regular glasses during dinner and leave the plastic cups for all-day use. If the kids are just drinking water out of them, it's no biggie if they don't make it into the after-dinner dishwasher load.

Maximize Your Time

Prepare meals that give maximum satisfaction for minimum fuss. Soups may seem time-consuming, for example, but for a lot of that time they're just simmering away on the stovetop. And soups freeze beautifully and actually taste better the second or third time you heat them up.

mom wisdom

"When I am chopping foods, I keep a bowl beside me for the ends and things that will go in the garbage. That way I am making only one trip to the trash can. My kitchen is long and narrow so that saves me time."

—Carly, mom of four, Ohio

Take It Easy

Not *all* home-cooked meals have to include a main meat dish or complicated sauces. Pasta and sauce, sandwiches and salads, and rice and beans are all healthy, well-balanced meals that are inexpensive, quick to prepare, and won't leave a huge mess behind.

Prep Multiple Meals at Once

Never chop, mince, or dice garlic for only one meal when you can just as easily cut up enough for three and refrigerate the rest for later. To make this work well, it helps to have a system of containers with airtight lids that you can label. The same sentiment goes for rice, beans, or pasta—you can always cook more than you need today, then refrigerate the extra for later this week, whether you end up using it for lunches or another dinner. Think creatively when it comes to using leftover food; for instance, the bones from a roast chicken can make stock for tomorrow's soup, or you can shred leftover meat into fajitas or barbecue sandwiches.

You can cook twice or three times the amount of food you need for a meal and freeze the extra portions. Or you can take it an extra step. Some families take the idea of cooking and shopping in large quantities very seriously—doing a major shopping trip, and often a major cooking session, just once a month. In order to make once-a-month cooking (OAMC), also called "freezer cooking," and shopping work with a big family, you'll need lots of cupboard, refrigerator, and freezer space; a day or so that you can set aside just for all the preparing, cooking, and portioning you'll have to do; plus plenty of containers for storing meals once you've prepared them.

If you simply don't have space for all that food, you can modify OAMC, cooking once every two weeks or just once a week. But the nice thing about doing it once monthly is that after you put in the work prepping all those meals, you'll have a freezer stocked with dinners for a whole month. Since it doesn't take much more time to chop up ten onions than it does to chop just one, OAMC is one way to take advantage of economy of time.

If you want to give OAMC a stab, you'll have to take some things into account. Pay special attention to the way you store your foods in the freezer, and make sure you have appropriate containers that will ward off freezer burn. You'll also need a lot of freezer space—probably a separate freezer from your main fridge. Some OAMC enthusiasts buddy up with a friend to do the shopping, prepping, and cooking. To find out more about freezer cooking, check out these resources: www.30daygourmet.com or www.dinnersinthefreezer.com.

Even if cooking once a month doesn't work for you, you may still find it helpful to limit your big grocery shopping trips to once monthly. At the very least, try to find ways to reduce the number of trips you make to the store. At the end of this chapter, you'll find resources for planning your meals and shopping trips and staying on budget.

Actually Getting the Shopping Done

Grocery and meal planning is all well and good, but it won't help as much as it could if you can't make it through the store without pulling your hair out. Can you take all your kids along on a big shopping trip? Many parents do, but it's generally easier to concentrate on the task at hand if you leave some of them at home with one spouse or a teen sibling.

If you have or want to take all your kids to the store, it's a good idea to bring a snack along for toddlers and to give older kids a job. Even if you're pushing a cart, older kids can carry a handled basket and be in charge of selecting certain items. This will help keep their hands off items you don't want and, more importantly, off of each other.

Some stores provide carts with plenty of seating space for kids. Those carts can be bulky and difficult to push, but think of it as a sanity-saver as well as a great way to get some exercise! Also some grocery stores now offer tot-drop areas where you can let your kids play, supervised, while you shop. Bless them.

You can also trade off with a friend, watching her kids while she shops and letting her watch yours while you shop.

You might even try trading a kid or two while you're shopping, because many children are better behaved when they're with anyone besides their own parents, especially in public!

Packing School Lunches

Few things can strike fear into a mother's heart as much as the midnight realization that she's got a bunch of kids to send off to school in the morning—and nothing to put in their lunchboxes.

Sure, she *could* pay $2.25 per kid for some salty, greasy mystery meat and limp, canned vegetables in the hot lunch line. But we're talking about eating healthy and economical food here!

First, let me give you some tips regarding packaging. I avoid soft-sided, insulated lunchboxes if at all possible. Yes, they're everywhere, and yes, a lot of schools no longer allow hard plastic boxes. But vinyl lunch containers can be nearly impossible to clean, and mine all get a funky odor within weeks. Some vinyl lunchboxes contain lead that can leach out onto your child's hands or food. Here are a few alternatives that you may find more convenient:

The old standby. a classic brown bag. If you can get your kids to fold them and bring them back every day, you can probably get from a few days' to a week's use out of each bag. Yes, it will create some waste, but certainly not as much as throwing away a Styrofoam tray every single day, which is what happens at some schools.

Canvas lunch sacks. They're basic; they're machine-washable; and if you buy them from an environmentally-conscious retailer like Ecobags. com, they're made from recycled materials. Your kids can decorate their own with permanent marker, and when they get gross, you can just toss them in the wash.

Japanese-style Bento boxes. They come with small compartments and containers, so you can pack a meal of nutritious appetizers like hummus and pita, carrots and dip, nuts and seeds, and cut-up fruit or berries in place of the typical sandwich and apple. You can find Bento boxes at www.laptoplunches.com.

Now, let's talk about the food that goes into those lunch containers:

Prepare everything in advance. Have the kids help you portion out veggies, dips, mixes, etc., once a week or every couple of days, and keep them on their own shelf in the fridge. Then your kids can "pack" their own lunches by grabbing an assortment of foods that appeal to them each morning. If you've provided mostly healthy options, you can feel good about letting them pick without having to hover.

Be proactive. The minute my kids walk in the door from school, they are to take their lunch boxes to the kitchen, put the reusable containers into the sink or dishwasher, and dump any trash. This saves me from the horror of having to deal with it right before bed or first thing in the morning.

Save any extra plastic silverware, salt, and ketchup packets, and reusable containers with lids when you get takeout food. They often come in handy when you're packing school lunches.

Look for alternative sources of protein power. I'm always concerned about making sure my kids' lunches have enough protein. My usual answer is a peanut butter sandwich, but that isn't an option if your kids don't like peanut butter, or can't have peanut products at school because of an allergic classmate. Seeds and nuts are great alternative sources of protein. Homemade granola, trail mix, or other seed-nut combinations are an inexpensive way to make a bunch of lunches with staying power.

If you're like me, the best way to learn about feeding a big family is to see how other moms do it. Here, I've profiled three moms of lots of kids to see how they save money, plan their menus, do their shopping, and cook healthy meals for their families.

Table for Eight Profile: Bare-Bones Budgeting

With five growing kids—including one teenage boy—and a busy life as a homeschooling mom with a part-time job, Bonny of Minneapolis, Minnesota, manages to stick close to $150 a month on groceries. After you scrape your lower jaw off the floor, check out how she does it.

Table for Eight Profile: Bare-Bones Budgeting

"Planning my menus around the sales flyer (which I can access online, if I don't get a Sunday paper or haven't been to the store to grab one) really is what saves me. We buy very little that is not on sale, stocking up on what is on sale. For instance, 24 oz. packages of chicken thighs and drummies were $1.00 apiece this week.

"I plan one week, ideally two weeks, of dinner menus at a time, based around the sale sheet and what is already in the freezer and pantry. This is probably my biggest money- and time-saver. I don't always have each meal on the assigned day (except for pizza on Thursdays), and I fill in the main dish with whatever veggies or salad I have on hand.

"I double recipes frequently, freezing half. I rarely buy meat that is over $2.00 per pound. I use the store coupons often, combined with manufacturer coupons when I have them. I am not religious about clipping coupons, but sometimes you can get something for practically free between the two.

"I buy most things at the regular grocery store, but get a few things elsewhere. For instance, I get spaghetti sauce and applesauce at a discount store and organic oats for 89 cents a pound at the health food store. And yes, I'm aware of the contradiction!"

Table for Eight Profile: Businesslike and Brief

Between her home business and homeschooling, Carmen, mom of five in Washington state simply doesn't have time for drawn-out shopping trips. So what is her solution? Treat it like a business—highlighter pens and all. Here's how Carmen keeps track of her busy family's food.

"When I go to any of the stores, I always take a yellow highlighter and a pen. I keep the menu/grocery list (visit the end of this chapter to see Carmen's grocery list) on a clip board, and set it on my purse in the basket. When I add an item to my basket, I fold the list in half so I see the back and write in pen the amount of the item, rounded up to the next dollar amount.

"Then, on the front of the list, I highlight over that item. I can see very quickly the items I haven't yet gotten into my basket. I can 'do' Costco in about 20 minutes, the grocery store in about 15, and the food co-op in 5. Then I'm usually done for the week. It takes longer driving to and from, getting in/out of the vehicle, and wait-ing in the check out line than the actual shopping.

"To best do my job, I always wear something with front pockets. I carry my pen, highlighter, lip balm, cell phone, buying-club card, and grocery card in my pockets. I make sure everyone going with me is good to go—warm, rested, fed, that they've gone to the bathroom. I wear comfortable shoes. Essentially, I take it very seriously, and treat it as a job. I look for ways to make the process more efficient."

Following, you'll find a pantry-planning checklist, shopping list, and a menu-planning form to copy and use yourself. Or use them as examples to create your own on your computer. Either way, using the tips and resources in this chapter, you will be well on your way to creating a healthy, affordable Table For Eight.

Table for Eight Profile: Practical and Prepared

Kim, a mom of six in Indiana, spends $520 or less per month on food and household products. And that includes food and sup-plies for her three pets! Here's how she does it: "My two biggest budget-savers are meal planning and list-making. I shop for two weeks' worth of meals each time, planned according to specials or in-season produce. For instance, if fish is on sale, we have fish a bit more than usual. I plan all three meals for each day. I cook complete meals and don't rely on prepackaged foods. I keep a well-stocked pantry and have an inventory sheet on the inside of the pantry door. If something gets used, we mark it off, and I add it to the shopping list. I do the same thing with the big freezer in our garage. When something is on sale that we use often, like tomato sauce, I stock up. We aren't big milk drinkers, so we save a bundle right there! We go through on average 1½ gallons a week, mostly on cereal or for cooking.

"For meat, I am lucky enough to live near a large Amish commu-nity. I get fresh, free range chicken (cut up or whole) for $1.29 a pound. I also get my cheese from their little shop, as well as most of my eggs ($1.50 for 18). In the summer, I get most of our produce from their stands or my own garden. I can, dry, or freeze the sur-plus, which comes in handy in the fall/winter. I also buy the bags of skinless, boneless chicken breasts when they are buy-one, get-one-free at the store, about every six weeks. I buy four bags (and get four free). When meat is on sale, I stock up. I use my Food

Saver vacuum packager for freezer protection. This summer, my husband Jeff and I are going to go in with another family and purchase a side of beef and pig. The meat is locally raised, free range. It is fairly priced and will store beautifully. If that sounds like something you would like to try, check out your County Extension office (usually connected to a college). Here's an example of a week's worth of menus:

"Monday
Breakfast: oatmeal
Lunch: turkey roll-ups, pears
Dinner: tilapia, couscous, peas/carrots (JELL-O for dessert)

"Tuesday
Breakfast: yogurt, bananas, berries, toast
Lunch: chicken salad sandwiches
Dinner: turkey burgers, sweet potato fries, green beans (pudding for dessert)

"Wednesday
Breakfast: scrambled eggs
Lunch: grilled cheese, grapes
Dinner: spaghetti (sauce made the day before), salad (no planned dessert—church night)

"Thursday
Breakfast: cereal
Lunch: leftover spaghetti
Dinner: grilled chicken, brown rice, salad (cookies or fruit for dessert)

"Friday
Breakfast: cream of wheat
Lunch: chicken noodle soup (in freezer)
Dinner: tacos, beans, fruit salad (sherbet for dessert)

"Saturday
Breakfast: pancakes
Lunch: leftovers from Thursday/Friday
Dinner: salmon, roasted red potatoes, spinach (popsicles for dessert)

"Sunday
Breakfast: cereal
Lunch: eat out after church
Dinner: beef stew, salad (strawberry shortcake for dessert)

"I do not purchase prepackaged items. That saves a ton of money and is much healthier for you. I rarely use coupons since most of them are for things we don't eat.

"When I make spaghetti sauce, I triple my recipe and freeze it in meal-size portions. Same thing for casseroles, soups, and so forth.

"Snack foods consist of popcorn, pretzels, fruit, granola, and cookies (we bake a batch each week). I do not make a habit of buying soda or sugary junk food. For the occasional treat—sure. However, once it is gone, it is gone. It is not a regular staple in the pantry. We buy bread at the bread store (Aunt Millie's) once a month. It's not day-old bread but overstock from the morning delivery. I can get six loaves of good wheat bread (3 grams of fiber per slice) for $3.00—that's 50 cents a loaf! I usually walk out with 30 loaves of bread (and lots of strange stares!). I keep three loaves at a time in the pantry (it goes fast around here) and the rest in the fridge or freezer.

"It may all seem like a lot of work, but really, it isn't. You find your groove and stick to a pattern. It is second nature to me now. With some careful planning, you can save a lot of money.

"Food, while important, yummy, and sustaining, shouldn't take up a large percentage of the monthly income—especially when you consider where the food eventually ends up."

Kim blogs about her family at www.livingafulllife.blogspot.com.

Co-op or Health-Food Store	Discount Store/Buying Club	Grocery Store

	Main	Needed Groceries				
	Dish/Sides					
		Meat	Produce	Frozen	Canned	Other
Sunday						
Monday						
Tuesday						
Wednesday						
Thursday						
Friday						
Saturday						

Meal Ideas

Sunday	
Monday	
Tuesday	
Wednesday	
Thursday	
Friday	
Saturday	

Money, Money, Money

"How can you afford them all?"

Every Table for Eight parent has been asked this question at one time or another, and sometimes we ask ourselves the same question. There are a lot of theories about how much it costs to raise a child—perhaps you've heard the popular $200,000-and-up-per-kid figure. But do those numbers really add up? And if it costs $200,000 to raise one child, does each subsequent child also cost $200,000, for a total of $800,000 for four kids, or—gulp—a million for five?

"No way," say parents of many. Though everyone I interviewed admitted that kids can definitely be expensive to raise, most felt that once you've adjusted for having a bigger-than-average family—by buying a larger house or car, for example—you can save a lot of money by making lifestyle changes and spending conscientiously. "As our income has not increased at the rate of our family, we've learned many tricks on budgeting and living within our means—lessons worth learning, no matter a family's size or income bracket," says Bonny, mom of five, from Minneapolis.

Sara, a mom of four with another on the way, from Oklahoma agrees. "I think we have become less interested in material things out of necessity, but that just frees up more income to do what's important. I can't help but roll my eyes at the things mothers are pressured to buy out of the fear their children will be stunted somehow if they don't."

On the other hand, most agreed that raising a big family will require some financial belt-tightening unless the parents happen to be wealthy. As we've already learned, once you get to four or five kids, you may need a larger home or a bigger vehicle than you could get by with before—which will probably increase your living costs. And eventually, many hand-me-downs—whether toys or clothes—will begin to fall apart and need to be replaced. So while it might not be exponentially more expensive to have a big family, it still pays to adopt money-saving strategies. And raising your kids to be shrewd and thoughtful consumers can only help in the long run.

Wants vs. Needs

Do you want it, or do you *need* it? Most of us are good at recognizing the difference between a "need" and a "want," if we're honest with ourselves. Kids aren't always as good at this unless we are careful to teach and model values that place people, experiences, and relationships well above "stuff" on the chain of importance. So how can you help your kids recognize the difference between wants and needs … and remind yourself, as well? Here are some tried-and-true methods:

Don't view shopping as recreation. Stay out of Target, Wal-Mart, and other big-box type stores, where you can easily drop hundreds of dollars on things you didn't even know you needed. If you need something from one of these stores, plan your shopping trip just before you have an appointment to be somewhere, so you don't have time to meander the aisles. Or shop while you're tired or hungry, so that you're not in the mood to linger. (But don't shop for groceries while hungry—it could have the exact opposite of your desired effect!)

Put yourself on pause. Give yourself a 72-hour or longer waiting period before dropping a considerable amount of money on anything. You may be able to find the item cheaper elsewhere, or you might realize you don't really want or need it that badly.

Stay away from credit. Debt is an epidemic in this country, and given the high interest rates on credit cards, you'll be paying for that purchase for a good long while to come if you carry a balance from month to month.

Don't watch too much TV. Especially stay away from shows that make you feel dissatisfied with your own lot in life. It's fun to watch home-decorating programs if they give you ideas for how to give your own house an inexpensive boost, but not so fun if they make you feel bad about what you have and wish you had $30,000 to sink into a new kitchen with marble countertops.

Prepare for the commercials in children's TV programming. If your kids watch TV, take time to discuss advertising and marketing with them in an age-appropriate manner. Make sure they understand that commercials have one goal: to sell a product. My kids know that advertisers aren't always truthful and that toys and games don't always live up to the hype their marketing buzz would have you believe. Now, when they see a commercial for the next hot toy, they're more likely to say "I bet that isn't as great as it looks" than "I want that!"

mom wisdom

"At one point, when a lot of the kids were developing entitlement issues, my husband declared a 'basic living' week. We ate oatmeal for breakfast, bologna sandwiches for lunch, and beans and rice for supper all of that week. The kids were not allowed any electronic devices that week, either. They seemed to learn some valuable lessons, and one daughter in particular is quite interested in not repeating the experience."

—Ramona, mom of eleven in Arizona

So what *do* kids really need? Judging by the current mainstream way of thinking, too many people think kids need and deserve the newest toys, designer quilts on their beds, and brand-name, stylish clothing. And of course, those things can be nice. But in our house, needs are as follows: food, clothing, and shelter. Those are the things we would die without, and they all cost money. Following closely after those needs are our non-negotiable wants: love, a feeling of security, education, reading material, music, physical activity, laughter, and entertainment. None of those things have to cost a lot—or anything at all, if done right! And after that come the true wants, like stylish clothes, new toys, books, and music; restaurant meals, knickknacks, and other non-necessities. Even the negotiable wants have a hierarchy; for example, in our home we tend to value experiences over things. So we'd be more likely to spend discretionary funds on a vacation than a new wardrobe.

We are very fortunate that we have all our needs and non-negotiable wants taken care of and enough of our negotiable wants as well. But it's helpful for me to keep that hierarchy in mind as I'm looking at our budget and making everyday purchases. If I buy my toddler that new, non-sale-priced sweater—even if it feels like I have plenty enough cash for it right this minute—what am I sacrificing? Thinking about that gives me a realistic idea of the true cost of a purchase. Sometimes I put it back, and sometimes I decide it's worth it and buy the sweater anyway. But at least I'm going in with my eyes open.

Cultivating Contentment

Okay, so we grownups—sometimes, after a little prodding—can understand the difference between wants and needs. But getting our kids, who aren't always privy to the ins and outs (and outs and outs) of our checking accounts may need some convincing. Here are some ways other Table for Eight parents help cultivate a sense of contentment with what material things they have—and keep their kids from having a permanent case of the "gimmes."

Changes of attitude. "I think that discontent is an attitude that really has nothing to do with budgets and income brackets. When something cool happens or comes our way, I will make sure to point it out. We, in turn, pass on what we can—whether it's outgrown clothes or a surplus of soup fixings. We don't need a huge pot of soup for ourselves, but for some uncanny reason, when I have the stuff to make a ton of soup, there coincidentally seems to be someone very ill that we know or several new mamas or stressed-out families who can use some."—Bonny, mom of five in Minnesota.

Seeing the cup half full. "It's easy to be grateful if you just keep your eyes open. We lived in the inner city for 19 years and every day, we saw people who had much less than we did. I try not to keep my thoughts on those who 'have,' but on those who 'have not.'"—Marie, mom of eight in Illinois.

Remember how the "other half" lives. "We were blessed with a built-in system for helping the kids realize they were 'rich' even though they were poorer than their friends. We adopted two older children from a third-world country, and those two were able to remember what it was like to be hungry, to have no indoor plumbing, and to not attend school. Their recollections and their appreciation of everyday things the others took for granted—like underwear—helped the other kids realize that not having the latest designer tennis shoes really was a minor issue. I think other families could accomplish some of the same realization by making sure their kids are aware of how large parts of the world live. Participate in a child-sponsor program and make sure your kids see the letters and literature; have them participate in church-sponsored trips to poor regions. Work with Habitat for Humanity to build housing in your own town, and your kids will see that they don't have it so bad. We didn't let them complain about sharing bedrooms or having less than others without reminding them that on a global scale we were among the richest of families, and that love matters more than big screen TVs and Game Boys."—Sharon, mom of five, Indiana.

Teaching Kids About Money Management

One of the best ways to live a money-conscious lifestyle is to get your kids on board. Teaching kids about managing finances accomplishes several key goals. First, it will help them be happier, more responsible, and allow them to enter adulthood with the tools to be financially secure. Too many kids never learn how to value, care for, and use money, and have to learn the hard way by going deeply into debt and making other costly financial mistakes as adults.

Second, opening your kids' eyes to smart money management will help you manage your own money better. They may be less likely to beg for things they don't need, or more willing to work or save some of their own money for purchases because they understand the value of a dollar. And they may even become your second conscience—if you know your kids are carefully watching the way you spend money, you might be more careful to spend wisely.

How much you tell your kids about your family's finances is up to you. Some families have a need-to-know policy, where the kids are only aware of financial decisions that directly impact them. Others have an open-door, open-book policy: parents discuss money and the family's finances candidly in front of the kids and may even invite their input and ideas. My husband and I adopted a semi-open-book policy. I don't tell my kids exactly how much money we make; frankly, they tend to be blabby and I don't know if they understand that it's not polite to talk about their family's income in public yet! But I will tell them when a purchase is outside our budget or explain to them how much a certain bill is and what that means in real-world money. For example, I might tell them that it takes three hours of work for Mommy to pay the electric bill. My kids also get an allowance that's theirs for being part of the family. They're required to save some of it, donate some of it to charity, and then they can blow the rest as they see fit.

 **mom wisdom**

"We check all the coins we get from change, and if it was minted in one of our children's birth years, that coin goes into that child's bank. It's a very small way to help them save some money and actually can add up over time."

—Cindy, mom of eight, Colorado

"This may sound corny, but my husband and I save all of our spare change. One month, many a year back, when we just didn't have enough to make the monthly mortgage payment, we cashed in our change and had $300! It is a big help and adds up."

—Lisa, mom of four, Pennsylvania

Here are some things other Table for Eight parents do to help their kids learn to manage money:

Use prepaid debit cards. "My daughter, who is nine, gets $20 a month. Half of it goes directly into savings, and half goes onto a prepaid debit card through our bank that she is free to use how she sees fit. She knows that if she wants to give gifts at Christmas and birthdays, her debit card must have the money on it to buy them. She is also free to choose to donate and has donated to different groups at different times."—Katie, mom of five, North Carolina.

Illustrate the mechanics. "When my kids are teens, they help balance the checkbook so they learn how to do it and see the money-in, money-out process. We are very open about our finances with the kids so they understand why we can't buy that $100 item. Our teens do odd jobs to earn money. We pay a very limited allowance—$1 per week from the time they are seven to 13 years old, and then $5 per week from 13 through 18 years old."—Cindy, mom of eight, Colorado.

Show kids what things cost. "My kids help me with the grocery list so they can see how it costs money to buy things. Sometimes we give them money to purchase things so that they grasp that money goes into everything we get and eat."—Amanda, mom of six, Michigan.

What's allowed on that allowance. "Our kids start earning an allowance when they are six. They have to save 25 percent in a savings account for college; we tell them that if they get plenty of scholarships, they can use the money to buy their first car instead. They have to donate at least 10 percent to charity, and they can choose what to do with the other 65 percent. We put no limitations on what they spend the money on, unless it's something inappropriate or not allowed in our family. We try to help them make good choices, such as saving up for big things or checking ads to see if the item is on sale somewhere. They also use their money if they want to do something that costs money that we don't have money allocated for, such as going to a theater to see a movie."—Mary Ann, mom of five, Michigan.

Get a job at home. "There is a lot of work around the house that my kids can get paid for. For example, we pay $3/hr for yard work. We work from the home, so the 16- and 14-year-olds can work in the office for $5 an hour. I will generally pay a child to clean my bathroom on a weekly basis. I work a lot with the kids to find a balance between responsibility and rewards. If they get to do an outside activity, what responsibility do they have to balance it out? Privileges without responsibilities results in spoiled kids, kids that feel entitled."—Carmen, mom of five, Washington.

As They Grow

It's a good idea to start thinking about what kind of expectations you'll have of your kids as they grow older. When your kids start driving, will they have use of the family car or be allowed to purchase a car of their own? Will they be responsible for gas, insurance, and maintenance costs?

Will your older kids—especially young adults—be expected to have a job, help with family finances, or pay rent? There's no right or wrong way to handle this, but having very clear guidelines in place can help prevent frustration and hurt feelings later. Here's how some parents feel about the older child's responsibility to the family:

Room and Board. "If my older kids are not in school and have a full-time job, they pay $150 per month room and board to live at home. If they complain, I remind them that they can't live anywhere else that inexpensively. When they become unwilling to do that, they need to find a place of their own. Even eagles 'stir up the nest' to get the young ones out on their own."—Marie, mom of eight, Illinois.

Driving is a privilege. "We had all the kids pay for their own auto insurance when they wanted to start driving. Amazingly, none of them felt like a driver's license was something they cared about at 16 when they realized how hard they would have to work to get one. Most of them started driving at 18."—Sharon, mom of five, Indiana.

You *can* go home again—sort of. "We have told our kids that they are welcome to live with us until they graduate from high school. If they choose to go to a local college, they may live with us while going to school full-time, rent-free. We also tell them that if they ever find themselves in a situation where they *need* a place to go, they will always be welcome at our house temporarily while they get back on their feet, but they will be paying rent if they aren't a full-time student or if they've already received their bachelor's degree. I think that if kids have clear expectations from early on, you can avoid a lot of the discomfort of sorting out the financial aspects once you are in the situation. Our kids know that we will always take them in if they need a place to go, but they know it will not be a free ride."—Mary Ann, mom of five, Illinois.

The cost of a college education shared. "We told each of our kids that for college we could pay their tuition to an in-state school (or an equal amount to any school they wanted to attend). We told them that during college they could live in our home without contributing toward rent, food, or utilities if they wanted to attend college locally. Those who went away to school had to cover their living expenses. After college, my attitude is no free rides—the exception being if one of them had an injury or illness that required them to be off work for a long time. Of course we would pay their expenses then. Our kids like having their own apartments, though, because in our family moving back home also means following our rules (to a certain degree). If they want total freedom, they have to finance it!" —Sharon, mom of five grown kids, Indiana.

But What About College?

Financial guru Suze Orman tells parents to make sure their retirement is covered before they worry about saving for their child's college education. I agree; while our kids will have plenty of opportunities for scholarships, grants, loans, and other means they can use to finance schooling, we adults have limited time and resources to plan for our own futures. And if we run out of money in our old age, guess who's going to end up with the responsibility of caring for us—probably our grown kids!

Trust funds are great things if you can afford them, but don't worry that your kids are doomed to an uneducated future if you aren't wealthy. There are different ways you can get money for your kids' college education.

Scholarships

There are a lot of scholarships available for college students, and it's not just the 4.0 GPA scholars that qualify; there are scholarships that take extra-curricular activities, financial need, leadership, good citizenship, race and ethnicity, parents' workplace, and many other factors into account when making awards.

However, it's important to keep in mind that searching for college scholarships can be time-consuming, especially if you're looking off the beaten path. You can search for scholarships through a service like www. scholarships.com, but looking for and applying for aid through your child's chosen college is a more direct route: once your child has chosen a school, contact the financial-aid office. They should have a list of scholarships and grants, requirements, and application forms.

Government Grants and Loans

The year before your child heads off to college, you'll need to fill out a FAFSA: Free Application for Federal Student Aid (www.fafsa.ed.gov) One form will apply you for grants—money that doesn't have to get paid back—subsidized loans, which aren't charged interest until your child graduates, and unsubsidized parent loans, which are charged interest while your child is still in school. The interest rates are generally low, so federal student aid loans are a good option.

Keep in mind that government grants and loans, and some private need-based scholarships take into account how many people in your family are attending college at once when making awards. So if you will have two or three kids in college at one time, you will probably qualify for more money for each child.

College Savings Plans

If you can afford it, it's a good idea to put money away for your kids' education—even a little bit here and there adds up. But keep the money out of your kids' names: when it comes time to apply for financial aid, your child's assets will count against them at a significantly higher rate than the same money would if it was in the parent's name. For example, if a child has $5,000 in savings, the government assumes that the child has 20 percent of that amount—or $1,000—available to help pay for school. If it's in an account in the parent's name, they only expect 5 percent of it—$250—to be put toward education. What does that mean for you? If over time you manage to carefully sock away thousands of dollars in your kids' names, they could each end up with a significantly smaller financial aid award than they would if you kept the money in a college-savings plan in your own name. Two plans to look out for are the 529 College Savings Plan or the Coverdale Savings Plan.

Start Locally, Transfer Later

There's also the community college route. Plenty of young adults have worked through their first couple of years at a community college, getting basic general education requirements under their belts as they save money and acquire a high enough GPA to qualify for scholarships at a four-year university.

Financial Planning for Big Families?

Whatever it is you plan to do about your child's education, it might be a good idea to sit down with a financial planner to help you map out a long-term plan. You might think of hiring a financial planner as something that's only for people with a lot of wealth to manage. But nothing could be further from the truth, says Melvin Carrington Smith, Sr., CFP®, ChFC, a financial planner, father of five, and grandfather of five. According to Smith, proper planning is essential when you're raising lots of kids—and you don't have to be wealthy to benefit from the services of a financial planner.

"Because the cost of raising children has gone up significantly in recent years, it's essential that parents identify priorities and make a plan to accomplish those priorities," says the Birmingham, AL-based Smith, who is also the founder of the Financial Discovery Forum, a not-for-profit organization that aims to help people better understand how to plan their finances. Financial planning, says Smith, can help parents think about tough questions like how much and what type of life insurance to buy, why they might need disability insurance, why they need a will and how to create one, and why and how to start saving early for retirement and college. "When you consider that over 90% of workers are not able to retire comfortably, you can see the importance of financial planning for just about everyone," says Smith. "The old saying is really true, 'If you fail to plan, then you have planned to fail.'"

The biggest obstacle to financial planning in a big family is trying to keep everybody happy with their slice of the pie, says Smith. "It's really important that parents talk to their children and let them know the overall financial situation." You don't have to go into details, he says, but kids need to understand that money is finite and needs to be managed properly. "Together, the family members need to address what really comes first, second, third, and so forth. Everyone needs to get a piece of the action, but at the level they need, not necessarily the level they *want*."

Smith emphasizes that parents should make sure their own retirement plans are fully funded before they start college savings. "When a parent retires, there isn't anyone to give them financial assistance to live on for the rest of their lives if they haven't saved enough. At least with college, there are scholarships, grants, and financial aid to provide assistance." Also, if your retirement funds are very healthy, you may be able to provide your children with assistance—maybe helping them pay off student loans or put a down payment on their first house—later, when they're adults and you're able to pull from your investments.

For many of us, part of the American dream is that our kids get into a good college—and certainly, a college degree can make life easier down the road. But there are plenty of families, large and small alike, that simply can't afford to put their child through college. If that's your reality, find ways to work around it—probably through a combination of grants, and loans, contributions from you, and contributions from your child in the form of work-study, merit-based scholarships, or perhaps working a part-time job while in high school and college to contribute. Make it clear to your kids that while you value higher education, you're going to need their help making it happen. If they value it, too, they'll rise to the occasion—though for some kids, it takes a few years after they graduate before they feel ready to make that commitment, and others may choose military service, working a trade, or some other route instead.

Everyday Savings

It's great to have a healthy attitude when it comes to money, but it also helps to be able to hold on to some of it! In the last chapter we talked about saving money on groceries, but there are still a lot of things kids need—and yes, want—that *can* cost you an arm and a leg, but don't have to. These tips and ideas might help you save money when you're buying for your big family.

Repair, Reuse, Recycle

We live in a disposable society. When something, such as a toaster or blender or even a TV, stops working in your house, what's your initial response? Far too often the typical American shopper just tosses out the broken item and buys a replacement. With stores full of mass-produced items that aren't always the highest quality—and a dearth of handy people who really understand how to repair appliances, fix ripped seams, and remove stains—it may seem cheaper and easier to just buy things new than take the time to fix, repair, or clean.

But besides the hidden cost—more trash in landfills and junkyards, more waste produced during the manufacture of new things—it's just not dollar-smart to keep buying cheaply made items, using them for a while, and then throwing them away and buying more. Unfortunately, many of us weren't raised with an understanding of where—or why—to get high-quality new and used stuff or how to repair items that still have lots of life left, so these resources can help you:

Look at your local Freecycle listings: www.freecycle.org. Users of the e-mail list and online message boards post the items they have but no longer need, and you can claim them, for free. Or you can put up requests for items you want in hopes that another member has one they're looking to unload. The service is free, and each "chapter" consists of people local to your community, so there's no shipping involved. Freecycle users give away anything from clothes and toys to appliances, furniture, and a variety of strange odds and ends (I've seen dryer lint, Styrofoam packing peanuts, and shredded paper offered). Sometimes you have to weed through a lot of stuff you don't need to find that treasure, but it can pay off bigtime; after my toddler broke the antenna on my cell phone recently, I got a perfectly good "new-to-me" model from a Freecycle posting. It saved me a couple hundred dollars.

Check out Craigslist. These online classifieds have spread from their Californian roots and are now available in 450 cities across the United States. You can find everything from jobs and cars to used electronics and furniture to free stuff at www.craigslist.org.

Look around your community for thrift and surplus stores. Goodwill and The Salvation Army are great places to start, but there may be other opportunities you don't know about. For instance, the non-profit organization Habitat for Humanity sells surplus and used building supplies at a big discount through their ReStores: www.habitat.org/env/restores.aspx. If you are not sure where to find surplus or used goods in your community, visit the website for the Reuse Development Organization at www.redo.org for a list of local reuse centers.

mom wisdom

"In our house, garbage night is also known as Sunday Night Shopping. It's one way to acquire kid-quality furniture, such as desks and dressers. Usually you have to sink a few screws into them, but that's not all that difficult."

—Brenda, mom of four

New Baby, Used Stuff

Don't fall into the trap of thinking you need every contraption under the sun for your baby. As you know, they grow fast, puke, and poop a lot—often on their precious little outfits—in those first few months, so spending a lot of money on clothes really doesn't make sense. Items like bouncy seats, swings, and monitors can make your life easier, but aren't necessities—and hardly ever need to be bought new. Look around your church, thrift stores, and yard sales—chances are good you'll find plenty of barely-used baby "gear" you can pick up for a song and a dance.

Here are a few tips for saving money on those must-have baby items:

A basic layette. This usually consists of however many onesies and t-shirts, gowns, creepers, receiving blankets, and socks you'll need to make it from one laundry day to the next (keep in mind that you probably will get behind on laundry with a new baby!), plus one or two warm blankets. Assume your baby will have a diaper blowout or leak at least once a day while you're planning how many of these to buy. But absolutely don't buy the majority of these items new! At thrift stores and yard sales, you can find basic layette items for as little as nothing because people are just trying to unload them. Around here, 25 to 50 cents is pretty standard pricing for yard-sale newborn basics.

Diapers. Now that generic disposables are cheaper, better quality, and more readily available than ever before, the cost difference between cloth and disposable diapers for one baby is negligible. But consider that you can hand down cloth diapers from baby to baby to baby, and it's easy to see that cloth diapering can save a big family plenty of cash over the long haul. But keep it simple: a dozen or so prefold diapers and a handful of high-quality Velcro or snap wraps, and you're good to go. Now that cloth diapering is becoming trendy, deluxe and downright beautiful cloth diapers are on the market. Just remember what your baby will be putting *in* that diaper before you plunk down your hard-earned cash, and try to keep cloth-diaper shopping from becoming a pastime.

Sling or baby carrier. Baby Bjorns are a very comfy way to carry newborns, but your baby will outgrow it fairly soon. I recommend a good adjustable sling for older babies and toddlers, particularly if you plan to add another baby to your family when your current baby is still young enough to be to carried a lot. You can double up slings, carrying a baby and a toddler or twins at the same time. A good carrier will make your life a lot easier, enabling you to hold your baby and get things done at the same time, so shop wisely. Again, check with other moms, consignment stores, and eBay for bargains.

As Your Children Grow

When your older children need clothes, buy with handing down in mind. Most kids don't need a huge wardrobe. A few pairs of jeans, shorts, and pants, and a few t-shirts, sweatshirts, and/or sweaters, plus a nice outfit or two for church and other special occasions is plenty. In fact, I find that when I have too many clothes for my kids, some nice stuff invariably gets shoved to the bottom of a drawer and doesn't get as much wear as I would like. Also try to stick to separate items that can be worn with almost anything else your child owns, rather than two-piece outfits that only go with each other. That way, when your child outgrows a top, you can pass it down to the next child before the pants.

When you shop with mixing, matching, and handing down in mind, your initial clothing investment should last through several children, only requiring you to fill in a few holes here and there. Some things to look for when you're buying:

High quality. If you're buying for your oldest, spending a little extra for clothes that will stand the test of time and many different children makes sense. Check thrift stores, yard sales, eBay, second-hand and consignment stores, Craigslist, and Freecycle for bargains. If you shop second-hand stores, you can easily find well-made clothes for cheaper than you would have spent on new, lesser-quality items at a discount or department store.

Durability. Rugged fabric and features like double-layered knees in pants and jeans can give your kids' clothing more life and pass-down-ability.

Gender-neutral. Resist the temptation to buy an entirely pink and lavender wardrobe for your little girl. It's fun to splurge on a few frilly items, but if you get girls basic jeans, pants, and tops for the majority of her wardrobe, she'll be able to pass a lot of it down to younger brothers. Plus, pink shows a lot more dirt and stains than jeans! This works in reverse, too: boys' styles that consist of plain colors or stripes and simple patterns instead of trucks and cars will probably be easier to pass down to future girls.

Classic styles. Invest in classic items like solid-colored sweaters, basic and long-sleeve t-shirts in solid colors, and jeans with a neutral leg (neither tapered nor very flared). For older kids who want more trendy clothes, these basic items can still form the "bones" of their wardrobe. Then they can add a few more fashionable pieces or accessorize with jewelry, belts, hats, etc.

Many of us—myself included—weren't brought up knowing how to sew and mend as our mothers and grandmothers were, but it's a useful skill to have—even if it just makes the difference between throwing away that shirt with a ripped seam or missing button and fixing it. Check your local college's home economics extension program or your community center for a basic sewing class.

Consider this note on seasonal clothes: just because something isn't technically in the right season doesn't mean you can't get some use out of it. All my sons were born in the fall and early winter, so we've lucked out in that they usually can wear the same clothes at around the same time as older siblings did. But because they haven't all grown at exactly the same rate, plenty of times one child has wound up with, say, a pile of short-sleeve t-shirts in January. We still use them, though. Short-sleeve t-shirts can be worn as pajamas or undershirts. Or you can layer them under a button-up shirt or over a long-sleeve shirt (my boys especially like this look). Heavy wool sweaters may be out come July, but a long-sleeve t-shirt paired with shorts makes a perfect outfit for evening or morning play on cooler days. When you're packing away nonseasonal clothes, make sure you aren't too rigid about what constitutes "summer" or "winter" clothing. I try to keep several items from each season easily available for each boy—we never know when we'll need it, whether we experience some freaky off-season weather or go on a vacation to another climate.

Dolls, Cars, and Balls

When my oldest two sons were little, I wasted so much money on toys that I am actually embarrassed to think about it. Now, I'm much pickier. Plastic junk does not enter my house unless the kids get it as a gift or in the occasional Happy Meal. The funny thing is, I made a mental no-buying-junky-toys resolution a year ago and have stuck to it all year; and nobody seems to notice at all. The fact is, the kids barely even played with the stuff they used to get. It would be the hot item in the house for a few hours, and then get completely forgotten about. Strangely, even though I've bought so few toys this year, we still seem to have many more than we did last year. I think they've learned to reproduce.

Of course I'm not advocating a toy-free house! Once in a while—as long as your house isn't already overrun with them—a silly plastic action figure can be a fun splurge. And certain toys and playthings stand the test of time:

The classics. Blocks, stackable cups and rings, play food, trains, dolls and dollhouses, and other classic toys can take a lot of use and will be enjoyed for years to come.

Outdoor toys, sports equipment, bicycles, and ride-on toys. Anything I can do to encourage my kids to play outside is worthwhile in my book. Again, look at Craigslist and consignment shops before you buy new.

Legos. A basic Lego set has given my kids many hours of fun. If one of your kids is really, *really* into Legos, it might be worth buying the specialty sets. Otherwise, don't bother. Just divide up some of the special pieces, remove them from the basic set, and rotate them every few months so your kids will always feel like they're playing with "new" parts.

Around the House

Keep in mind that in a big family, a bed may be slept on by many children, and dresser drawers will be opened many, many times by many little hands. You'll want good quality furniture that's built to last, so that "bargain" dresser at the big box store that's made mostly of particle board may not be such a bargain after all.

I find that the best place to find quality furniture at a discount is second-hand shops. Because the pieces are older and still standing, you know they are strong enough to handle some abuse. Generally, junky stuff would have fallen apart before it ever had a chance to be donated. It's a lot cheaper than buying new at the furniture store, and unlike the stuff from the discount stores, it's already assembled. A table or dresser that looks awful but feels sturdy you can always repaint, and you can add new hardware.

No matter what your family's size, it pays to give close attention to energy costs. But when you've got a big family, you have more kids to remind about not wasting electricity—and more needs that you can fill with those extra pennies you'll save through conservation. So keep in mind these things.

Be consistent. Keep heating and cooling costs to a minimum by setting your thermostat at a consistent and reasonable level. If your thermostat is on a timer, you can set your home temperature to go down at night and then heat back up right before it's time to get up in the morning. If you don't have a timer on your thermostat, the long-run savings may make the investment worthwhile.

Start reminding kids early and often about conserving energy and water. If your kids learn the value of not being wasteful, little things—like watering a plant with that last inch of water they don't want to finish or turning off the TV before they leave the room—will become second nature to them. And over time, those little things will add up and save you a lot of money, as well as leaving a smaller footprint on the earth.

Good insulation is a must. Make sure your house is well insulated and that your windows and doors are snug and free of drafts. If you're purchasing a new home or making renovations to your current house, high-quality windows and doors are a worthwhile investment. Curtains with insulated or blackout linings help keep heat out in summer and cold out in the winter. You can buy insulated curtains, or add blackout lining to the curtains you have with a sewing machine.

Saving Money on Activities

Because I value experiences over things, it's hard for me to skimp on activities like lessons, sports, trips to museums, and vacations. But you can give your kids rich experiences without spending much at all. Check out these ideas:

The barter system. Do you have a talent or skill? Maybe your local music teacher would be willing to barter in exchange for lessons.

Look for freebies. Museums generally have free or discounted days for the public. And it might be worth purchasing a family membership at your local science, history, or children's museum; many museums participate in programs that allow you to use your membership for free admission to museums in neighboring towns. For example, for $55 a year, my family membership to a local museum allows us to get into the Museum of Science and Industry in Chicago—free (generally it would cost our family well over $55 just to visit once). Do make sure that your membership, whether it's a reciprocal membership or at that specific museum, actually covers *your* family's size, though. For instance, a "family/household" membership at the Shedd Aquarium in Chicago only covers two adults and four kids per visit—if you have five kids, you have to purchase a "family plus" membership.

Check out your library. Libraries have more than books—you can get DVDs, music, computer programs, magazines, and more. Using the library's website, you can search the catalog and reserve books to pick up later—a lifesaver for we parents of many who don't relish the idea of trying to browse while our toddlers pull books off the shelves and our big kids whine about being bored.

Look for free entertainment. During the summer, check your local parks and recreation department or newspaper for free outdoor concerts and festivals. High schools and colleges often have inexpensive—or even free—theatrical productions.

Search out small towns with movie theatres. Unless you've got tons of disposable income, you might not find yourself hitting the movie theatre with all your kids very often. $7 or $8 per movie ticket times 6 or 7 or 8 people … ouch! But movie theatres in small towns are often still family-owned and operated and may boast a very inexpensive ticket price. Some big movie theatre chains also offer discounted family nights, which can be a big budget saver. Or check out a drive-in movie, where you generally pay a lower admission price, or where the cost is per car, not per person—a budgetary boon for big families.

Beat the high cost of sports. Sports can be expensive. In our house, the rule is that each child picks two sports per year that he'd like to participate in. As the kids get older, we hope that they will settle into a sport they really love—hopefully not hockey, which has a reputation for being horribly expensive! I think the way you handle sports really depends on your family culture. If athletics are really important to you, you'll naturally make them a high priority and budget for that. If you're like me and sports-neutral, you'll just hope your kids pick something cheap!

Volunteer with your interests in mind. If there's someplace you'd love to go all the time but can't afford regular trips, consider volunteering or working there part-time. For instance, museums hire volunteer staff, and often free admission is a perk. And your local health club or YMCA may offer free membership to employees or volunteers. Considering that YMCAs also offer low-priced and free activities for members, a free membership is a valuable thing for a big family to have!

For ideas on vacationing and taking fun outings without going into debt, check Chapter 11.

mom wisdom

"Living a healthy lifestyle is saving us money. Avoiding the drive-thru and other convenience food, getting regular exercise, and eating very healthy and drinking a lot of water means better mental health, more energy, and less feeling lousy for all of us."

—Bonny, mom of five, Minnesota

Like anything worthwhile, raising kids takes resources: time, energy, love, and yes, money. But you don't have to put yourself in the poorhouse to raise a bigger-than-average family. If you raise kids with a healthy sense of what they need versus what they want and try a sensible attitude when it comes to consumerism, the thrifty-living tips above will begin to come naturally. Here's a list of resources, books, and websites that will help you pinch pennies and hold on to more of your dollars:

- **www.stretcher.com** The Dollar Stretcher, a webzine with cash-saving tips on nearly every conceivable topic.
- *The Tightwad Gazette* **series by Amy Dacyzyn** These guides to penny-pinching, now classics, go way beyond the obvious for people who are seriously committed to frugality.
- **www.makingallowances.com** A website dedicated to teaching children about money management.
- **http://financialplan.about.com/** Information, tips and resources that will help you learn more about making short-term and long-term financial plans.

School Days

Let's face it: educating all the kids in a bigger-than-average family is a bigger-than-average job. More kids in school means more homework, more field trips to chaperone, more paperwork coming home, more permission slips to sign, and more fundraisers to annoy you. You must have lots of clean socks and underwear on hand at all times, as well as plenty of school clothes or uniforms. There are a bunch of immunization records to file and health forms to fill out, and more and more forms: vision and hearing screening forms, proof of residency forms, forms to apply for free and reduced-price hot lunches, forms to request a phone call when the grounds are sprayed with pesticides. There are discipline codes of conduct to initial, attendance policies to review, and a plethora of important dates to post on the fridge.

As if that wasn't overwhelming enough, half the time one kid's conference or after-school sport or activity conflicts with another kid's.

Choosing Schools

Deciding on what school or schools to send your kids to can be a big problem for parents of many: what if one of your kids wants to attend the arts school across town while the other will do best in the small classroom environment of your neighborhood school? Is it fair to send only one of your kids to an exclusive private school if that's all you can afford—even if the other kids are doing fine in the local public school?

As with any other decisions you make in a big family, you need to make schooling choices based on the good of the whole, while taking into account the needs of the individuals as well. Will the family time lost in shuffling your kids to a bunch of different schools be worth the benefits to the kids from being in those specific programs? Are your individual kids more likely to benefit from going to school alongside their siblings, or could they benefit from establishing a little independence and their own identities?

"We had to decide whether to put all our kids in public school, or some in public and some in private—we couldn't afford to send all of them there," says Mary, who has five kids. Because one of their sons was having a hard time in his class at the local public school, they decided to enroll him in a local Catholic school, which had smaller classroom sizes and more personalized attention. Because the other kids were doing fine in public school, Mary and her husband Dan kept them there. Now, two of her children attend a magnet program for performing and visual arts; two attend a neighborhood public school; and her son is still in the Catholic school—and, Mary says, all of them are thriving. "It seemed unfair at first to have one in private school while the rest were in public school, but the reality was that we had to make a decision based on what was best for everyone. It didn't make sense to deny our son the school that he really needed just because we couldn't afford it for everyone, especially since everybody else was happy where they were."

Laura, a mom of four kids, weighed the same kind of decision, but ultimately decided to keep her kids together in the neighborhood school. "My son was interested in a math and science magnet across town, but it would have meant spending about an hour in the car each day picking him up and dropping him off—which would have made it nearly impossible for the rest of the kids to participate in any lessons or sports. We compromised by letting him take part in math- and science-oriented after-school activities at his neighborhood school and taking him on regular trips to science museums in any city we could drive to in a day."

Volunteering

I hardly ever volunteer in my kids' classrooms or offer to chaperone trips. I'm pretty useless because my hands are always full with my one- and three-year-olds, and my van is full of booster seats. But I can contribute in a lot of ways that don't necessarily include coming into the classroom. Because I'm a writer, I try to find volunteer activities that play to my strengths. I've written the descriptions for items at the live auction and recently wrote a kid-friendly adaptation of Shakespeare's *Twelfth Night* for the kids to perform. Talk to your child's teacher or principal and tell them about your skills and schedule; chances are good they've got tasks they could really use your help with that you could do from home or during a time that works for you. If it's important to you to spend time in your child's classroom, maybe you can swap child care with another parent whose kids go to your school.

And when it comes to fundraising, I have a personal no-guilt policy for nonparticipation. I do participate in the book fair and the school auction, because everybody can use more books and the people who attend the auctions walk away with some nice, reasonably priced stuff. But I don't allow my kids to badger friends and relatives to buy stuff they don't need— period. Sure, once in a while one of the kids comes home with something that looks like it might actually be worthwhile, like chocolate bars or huge tubs of cookie dough, but in order to be fair I just say "no" to all fundraisers that involve catalogs, points, and prizes. I'd rather just write a check to the school for $10 or $20 than allow my kids to take part in competitive sales. Who wants to be hit up not once, not twice, not three times, but *four* times by the kids in my family selling junky jewelry, knick-knacks, and wrapping paper?

The Homework Headache

Ah, homework. Some kids have an hour of it per night … and if you've got four or five or more kids in the house, one hour times all those kids can mean an entire night of homework.

Even if your kids have a far more reasonable amount of homework than that, you'll need to be organized to make sure they get it all done without you wanting to tear out your hair. I choose a time early in the day to attack homework; if they wait too long, everybody's tired and it's far more likely that the homework session will end in tears (probably mine). For us, the best time to do homework is directly following the after-school snack. Then, nobody's hungry or tired, and once homework is done, we can all relax and enjoy the rest of the evening.

Find a Place

Where's the best space to do homework in your house? For older kids or those who can easily work independently, a logical place might be a desk or flat surface in their own bedrooms. If your kids share bedrooms and have a hard time concentrating if they're working together, you might have to give each child a time slot for when he or she can use the room to do homework. Kids who have difficulty concentrating or who need a lot of help with their work will probably do better working near you. I put my oldest son at the dining room table with his homework while I load the dishwasher. That way, I'm not so close that he comes to rely on me for help with every single problem, but I'm close enough that he can ask questions when he really needs to; plus, just having me nearby and available lends him moral support.

If all of your kids need supervision while working on their homework, you might need to think creatively: you can't be everywhere at once, and it could take all evening to sit with them one by one, but having them all sitting around the table might prove to be too big a distraction. Another option is creating a "cubicle" for each child to work in. Remove the top, bottom, and one side of an empty large cardboard box, and you've got a miniature folding cubicle that your child can put on the table if he needs a quiet place to work. Kids in big families might especially like the idea of having their own portable, private haven to work in. Let the kids decorate the boxes or hang "Do Not Disturb" signs on the outside, but if your child is very distractible, it's probably best to make sure the inside of the box is plain cardboard. You can also use tri-fold presentation screens for this purpose.

If you've got all of your kids working at once, be sure to leave a place for yourself to be available for moral support and assistance. It might be best to sit somewhat out of the way to encourage independence while still being available. A chair in the corner with a book or magazine is a good place to sit and keep an eye on things. "I work on my knitting while the kids are doing their homework," says Mary, who has five kids. "It's a good way to be nearby and ready to help when I'm needed, without getting impatient when things are moving slowly."

Not all kids can work in the quiet, but how can you accommodate different kids who need different levels of background noise to concentrate?

A washing machine or dishwasher running can provide a low hum for a kid who does best with a bit of "white noise," but shouldn't be too distracting to other kids in your family. "My oldest son is the only one in the family who can't stand any noise while he's working. Since he usually works at the table alongside his younger brother, they take turns; one day my oldest son wears earplugs while the younger son listens to music on the stereo. The next day my younger son listens to music on his headphones."

Here are a few additional tips:

Keeping track of elusive supplies. In a big family, pencils seem to go dull daily, babies and pets chew up erasers, and pen caps mysteriously go missing. In short, supplies can't always be counted on to be in good supply, unless they're kept up and out of the reach of smaller hands. To avoid that last-minute search for the only remaining pencil in the house—which can really put a damper on high homework spirits—create a mobile office: fill a shoebox or plastic storage container with all the supplies your kids need for doing homework and place it on a high shelf or in a closet that the little kids can't get into.

Post-It reminders. In our house, the kids used to fight for my attention when doing homework—they all wanted answers to their questions at the same time. I started leaving pads of Post-It Notes next to each child as they worked. Now if they have a question while I'm busy helping a sibling, they can jot it down on the Post-It, stick it next to the question or passage they're having trouble with, and move on to the next problem or continue reading. When I'm done helping the sibling, the Post-It Note is there to remind them what they wanted to ask.

Roger, will help. If one of your kids works pretty well independently but still wants to be able to reach you in case he gets stumped, try walkie-talkies, suggests Dr. Sally Hoyle, a psychologist and the author of *Same Homework/New Plan: How To Help Your Disorganized Kid Sit Down And Get It Done*. That way you can be anywhere in the house, whether it's helping another child with homework, folding laundry, or just sitting with your feet up, and still be available for a quick question.

Tuning out. Make sure the phone ringer is turned off, as well as any other electronic media that could cause distractions, like the TV or instant messaging programs.

Extra-Curriculars

Sports and after-school lessons can be great enrichment activities for kids, but with a bunch of them wanting to do a bunch of different things, extra-curriculars can easily become too much of a good thing, disrupt routines and bedtimes, take away from family time and schoolwork, and leave kids generally overwhelmed and over-tired. And often extra-curriculars conflict with each other, making it nearly impossible to "do it all." So how can a big family allow their kids the experience of extra-curriculars without letting them take over their whole lives?

Consider Placing Limits

Bonny, who has five kids aged four to thirteen, limits her kids to one activity at a time, plus church activities. "More than one activity at a time would max our family out," says Bonny. "If it's something that doesn't work for the family, it's not something I could consider having my kids do."

"We've cut back a lot here," agrees Lisa, who has four kids. "I think it's too overwhelming; we used to do swimming and martial arts at the Y, in addition to Cub Scouts and some sports. It's just too much for them and for us! We only do Cub Scouts now, and most times, we can't attend the meetings if they're on a weeknight. Homework and studying must come first, and we really try to adhere to a decent bedtime. Having a meeting at 7 or 7:30, when we are ordinarily getting into pajamas, is just too much. It makes getting up the next morning and functioning too difficult."

Put Older Kids in Charge of Their Own Schedules and Transportation.

If you have good and safe public transportation in your town, taking the bus to practices or lessons might be a great way for your teen to participate in activities that are important to him without stressing out the younger members of your family, who may have earlier bedtimes or stricter schedules. Teens can also get themselves to their own activities by walking, biking, arranging for their own rides, or—if they're old enough and it's okay with you—driving. Putting the responsibility of transportation in your teen's hands is a great way to weed out the activities they really care about from those they might not be all that committed to in the first place.

Consider Family-Oriented and Self-Directed Activities.

Taking the kids on outings to zoos, museums, parks, and sporting events on your own schedule is a nice way to expose your kids to everything from arts to athletics while working around your own family's schedule.

It might seem like paying for supplies and activities would make enrichment activities financially impossible for a big family. But if you keep your eyes open, you can find free educational activities in nearly any metropolitan area.

Public libraries are for more than just books. You can usually check out educational DVDs and videos; books on tape and music; computer programs; magazines; and much more. Plus, many libraries offer free or low-cost activities and other programming you can use to beef up your curriculum.

Look for local scholarships. Parks and recreation departments, non-profit arts organizations, nature centers, community centers, and YMCAs very often offer need-based scholarships for admissions and special programs. If you don't qualify for scholarships or grants, see if you can volunteer in exchange for a free membership. These special offers aren't always advertised, so be sure to ask.

Look for special discounts. If you're a homeschooler, ask your local bookstore or educational store if they offer an educator's discount on books or other materials. Many extend this offer to homeschooling families as well as teachers. And keep your eye out in local stores, restaurants, newspapers, online, and the phone book for coupons. Also look into discounted "educator" admission to local zoos, museums, and other cultural institutions.

More for homeschoolers. If you're a homeschooler, you might find the cost of private lessons and club sports for all your kids to be prohibitive. Check with local public and private schools. Some make their extracurricular activities and sports teams available to homeschooled kids.

Affording Private School

If public schools aren't an option for your family, you may be considering private schools, but then recoiling in horror when you consider multiplying the tuition cost times the number of your kids for thirteen years each. Consider this: to pay full price for a private school with very reasonable tuition ($5,000 a year—a steal in most communities) for all four of my children from kindergarten to graduation would cost $260,000!

This might seem impossible, but a lot of options can make private school less expensive:

Check about sibling discounts. Many private schools offer discounts for two or more siblings, but in some schools, this amount is so negligible that it's not really helpful for somebody with a lot of kids. On the other hand, some religious schools, like Catholic schools, may anticipate a lot of big families and offer steep discounts for second, third, and subsequent children. My kids go to a small Catholic school, and the third (and there-after) child's tuition is so cheap it's practically free. Also, religious school is often substantially cheaper for contributing members of the congregation.

Seek out financial aid. Many private schools seek economically diverse populations and offer a lot of financial aid in the form of scholarships and need-based grants to attain it. "It really pays to take the time to apply for scholarships. Don't be intimidated by paperwork," says Jennifer, who has five kids.

Do your homework. Some organizations give grants and scholar-ships for tuition, and your school might not know about it. If the school doesn't advertise that it offers scholarship money, ask anyway. Sometimes, the principal has a certain amount of money he or she can use at his or her discretion—you may just have to be the squeaky wheel. It never hurts to indicate that you're ready and willing to help out by volunteering your time and talents to the school, either.

Take advantage of fundraising opportunities. Many private schools participate in fundraising programs that allow you to save money on your school tuition while shopping. SCRIP is one such program: you can pur-chase gift certificates that are good at hundreds of merchants, and a per-centage of the purchase price is donated back to your school—and applied to your tuition account. Also, some private schools participate in programs with local stores that distribute cards you—or your parents, in-laws, and other family members—can swipe when making purchases, and a small percentage of your purchase is credited to your tuition account.

Other Private-School Issues

One thing that many parents love about smaller private schools—the close-knit sense of community—can feel like a drawback to some kids from big families. Sometimes kids with lots of siblings can feel a strong need to break away and make their own identity—and it can feel stifling when they attend the same small school with all their siblings. And if a young student is weary of being compared to a high-achieving older sibling, a private school may make it more difficult for that child to make his or her own way.

And private schools that are exclusive, offer highly-specialized curriculum, or are very achievement-oriented may have been the perfect choice for your first child, but aren't right for younger kids. Struggling in a school where a sibling is excelling can be difficult for any child to deal with, and a big part of helping each of your children meet her potential is by finding an academic environment that helps her shine. A private school may also not have as many options to choose from when it comes to sports, arts or other "specials," and if that's important to your family or some of the kids in it, it's definitely something to keep in mind. "Our oldest son, who's in third grade, goes to a tiny Lutheran school where there aren't many opportunities for sports, which he doesn't mind at all," explains Eric, who has four kids. "My daughter, who's in fifth grade, started there, too, but then she started showing signs of serious athletic ability, and it's important to us that she is able to pursue that. So in the morning I drop our son off to the Lutheran school on the way to work, while the bus picks our daughter up to go to the public school." Eric says it's working fine for now, but he worries a little that his two youngest children, who aren't school-age yet, will have needs that require choosing yet another school. "I just hope our future doesn't include four different sets of school paperwork to keep track of!"

Bottom line: even if you love a particular school, that doesn't mean it has to be a fit for all of your children. When your kids go to a private school, it's easy for it to start feeling like a second home—and you may feel obligated or it may seem easiest to send the entire family there. But what if one of your kids has a learning style that doesn't fit in at the school, or would simply prefer to attend a different school? Just because your kids all share your genes, that doesn't mean they'll all thrive in the same educational setting. Don't feel that just because some of your kids attend a specific school all of them must—even if you love the teachers, administrators, and other parents.

Your Child's Peers

One of the most challenging things about having a lot of kids in school can be managing their peer relationships. A parent of four or five kids probably doesn't have time to be running all of them to a variety of different friend's houses and after-school activities every evening. And besides, isn't after-school time supposed to be family time? I asked several moms of Table for Eight families how they handle playgroups, peer groups, and other "friend" issues with their children. These are some of their answers:

Do help kids find their own friends. "Friends are very important. Kids need to interact with kids their own age and they need a chance to develop relationships outside of the family. I think the need for outside friendships is as important for kids in a large family as it is for singletons."—Carlena, mom of four, Ohio.

Do remember that three is sometimes a crowd. So your nine-year-old has a friend coming over from school, and you're hoping your seven-year old will get an automatic playdate out of the deal. It's tempting to try to form threesomes when you've got closely-aged kids. And of course, kids that close in age can and will play nicely together ... sometimes. But when closely-spaced siblings spend a lot of time together, an outside friend may be considered a hot commodity, and one of the kids may monopolize the new friend and leave the other sibling out. Of course, there's no excuse for a kid being mean to a sibling, but it's important to recognize that your children will probably, at some point, want friends of their very own. Try making arrangements that allow your child some privacy with her school buddies: maybe you could arrange for your child to meet her friend somewhere besides your house after school or set up an outside activity for the child who's likely to be the third wheel. Best yet, find other families with closely-aged sibs, and make after-school playdates a group affair.

Do make your house the place to be. You can save yourself a lot of driving around and also keep a close eye on who your kids are hanging out with and what they're doing by making your home an attractive place for neighborhood kids. This is especially helpful for big families, because it's hard to keep track of where a bunch of kids are if they all scatter after school's out. Keep them interested in hanging out at your house, and it's much easier to keep tabs.

Do befriend other parents. When you've got several school-age kids, each with his own after-school agenda, you need all the watchful eyes you can get. Make friends with other parents in your community. The parent grapevine can be an extremely effective way of keeping tabs on what your kids are up to without them even knowing about it—though telling them you've got eyes everywhere can be a powerful deterrent. My kids know that when I want to find out something about their behavior at school, I just go down to the bookstore. The bookstore's owners are all loyal lunchroom volunteers, and they know *everything*.

Don't over-do it. In a big family, your kids already have a lot of built-in playmates and may actually need less outside social interaction than you'd think after a busy day of school. Plus, experts increasingly agree that kids today are over-scheduled and don't have enough time to just play. "I haven't been to a playdate in ages," says Jill, mom of four. "We just don't have the time and my children don't seem to need it. I'd prefer to see my children grow deep roots with a few friends than shallow roots with dozens."

mom wisdom

"I like to try to get my oldest child, who's eight, over to a friend's house or to have a friend over occasionally so he can be around someone his own age, but for the most part, my kids really get along really well together and complement each other well. In fact, as I type this, they all went up to the oldest child's room to snuggle in his bed together and watch a movie. It is adorable. That is definitely a benefit of having a large family."

—Lisa, mom of four

Homeschooling Lots of Kids

Of the big families I know, about half of them educate their kids at home. People with lots of kids might choose to educate their children at home for many reasons: they may have religious beliefs that line up well with homeschooling, or they may be less than thrilled with the public school options in their area but unable to afford private school tuition for many kids. Whatever your reason for considering homeschooling, you may encounter resistance and criticism from well-meaning people who doubt your ability to teach "all those kids" as well as a classroom teacher could.

But is homeschooling hard when you've got lots of kids? Actually, "It's easier!" says Jill, a mother of four who started homeschooling her oldest daughter, sent her to private school for two years, and then took her back out again. "When she was in school, all we did was drive, drive, drive, and do homework all night. Then my son began preschool, so add in even more driving … plus parties and meetings." Jill says that rather than feeling busier now that she's homeschooling, she just feels like they traded the evening hustle for a busier morning and early afternoon. "Evenings are so much more peaceful!" she says. "I love that I'm not constantly rushing my children in the morning, too."

Ramona, who has eleven kids—nine of whom she's currently homeschooling—agrees that on the whole, it's easier to homeschool a large family than it is to send them to school. "We are able to streamline the process. I think it is much easier than trying to get nine kids up and out of the house early in the morning and then dealing with peer issues when they come home," she says. Because Ramona has several kids with special needs, she knows that homeschooling also makes it possible to meet the needs of kids with widely differing abilities, without having to enroll them all in different schools.

Of course, homeschooling a big family does present a few challenges. For instance, what do you do with the little kids in the family who want to be underfoot while you're trying to teach your older kids?

"My five-year-old loves to 'do school,' so she is happy sitting by us working in her workbooks, coloring, and looking at books," says Jill. "I also try to involve everyone when I can." Jill admits that her 20-month-old can be a challenge to work around. "She is constantly grabbing scissors, taking crayons, dumping the flash cards. I try to schedule time with one of the children doing a specific activity with her, like blocks or puzzles, when possible. That really helps. Other times she just wants to sit in my lap or nurse while I'm teaching."

Activities That Work for Everyone

If you plan to enroll your kids in activities, you may have a hard time finding places that will accommodate all of them at once. Try your local YMCA: many will have classes for homeschooled kids, or you can enroll your children in evening sports or lessons. The plus is that there is usually child care available, and sometimes a lounge or open-play area for siblings. And you can exercise, swim, or take part in another class while you wait. "My three youngest do age-appropriate classes like sports and arts at the YMCA," says Bonny, who homeschools her five children ages four to thirteen. "I utilize their free child care when necessary, and my oldest kids are big enough to either stay home or shoot baskets, play pool, or do their schoolwork if they come with us."

So how does Bonny keep from living her life in the car, driving kids from this activity to the next? She gives her older children's activities priority and makes activities for the younger kids work around their schedules. "For instance, the three younger kids are each taking a sports class, but we chose the ones that are back-to-back on a night when the thirteen-year-old has to be at the pool anyway, so it all fits together," she says. And they limit their activities to a few places close to home—the local high school, where her thirteen-year-old practices with his swim team, the YMCA, and their church.

Finding Friends

Another challenge a big homeschooling family might face is finding other home-learning families with a wide enough age range of kids to provide friendships for all your children. When I homeschooled my boys, almost every other family in our group had one or two elementary-age kids. That meant that most lessons and activities were geared toward kids in that age range, and it wasn't always possible to bring my toddler along. It could even be a challenge just to "hang out" with our homeschool friends, because their houses weren't usually set up for little kids and often the baby was the odd man out. If finding large homeschooling families is a challenge for you, looking to religious homeschool communities may help, as there are sometimes more big families in those groups.

Another solution may be simply rethinking the way you view home education. Instead of involving all the kids in tons of activities, it's okay—

sometimes even preferable—to put the "home" back in "homeschooling" and stay family-centered in the activities you choose. Your kids can make friends with other children in the neighborhood, from religious organizations, and in club sports, lessons, and other activities during after-school hours and on the weekend.

And you may find that a more home-oriented focus strengthens your children's relationships with each other: "We're not huge on playdates, especially for the younger kids because they do have each other," says Bonny. "And I found that, once my oldest began homeschooling, she was much more eager to spend time with her little sister. When she was in school, I always thought that after she'd been gone for seven hours, she should have a little time to spend with her little sister, but the opposite was true back then: after spending all day with her friends at school, she only wanted to spend her after-school time with those same friends. The sibling relationships in our family have really been strengthened by homeschooling."

Can You Teach a Big Family?

Keep in mind that in a typical classroom, a single teacher is managing between twenty and thirty children. Even if you have ten kids, you still have fewer individual personalities and needs to take into account—and much less "crowd control" is necessary. A lot of the six or seven hours a child spends in a school environment are spent lining up, waiting their turn, or transitioning from one subject to the next—which takes considerably more time when you've got 30 kids than when you've got 5 or 6. Plus, because you know your children so well, you can focus the work directly to their abilities and learning style—much less wasted time. Many homeschooling families find that they can get through all their school work for the day in an hour or two—or even less. "If I can get thirty or so minutes each day with my older kids, we are set," says Bonny. "Most of their work is done independently, so they can do that in their bedrooms or in the living area if the little kids are playing in the bedrooms."

Ramona has a similar experience with her kids, nine of whom are currently homeschooled (the other two have graduated). "Since our kids are older, most of them basically make their own schedules. They know what work needs to be done in a day and they do it on their own, letting me know when they are finished with each subject."

Is It Expensive?

Homeschooling a big family can be surprisingly economical, because a lot of materials, books, and curriculum items can be passed from child to child. "We pass the books down as we are able," says Ramona. "It helps to purchase hard-cover books which can be reused and are not consumable." Ramona says that purchasing a table-top copier can be a huge money-saver, because you can copy from texts and workbooks instead of buying multiple copies.

There are also a lot of websites where you can print out free work-sheets for all different subjects, from penmanship to arithmetic. Try online homeschool swaps or eBay for inexpensive, gently used curriculums and other materials. This is also a great place to unload stuff you no longer need or that was a good fit for some of your children but not others.

Enrolling in a "virtual" public school is another great way to keep costs of homeschooling at a minimum. Some school districts offer a virtual charter or public school through the K12 program, a curriculum that can be administered at home using a computer. In the areas where K12 partners with a public school, you get to use a computer and materials and have access to a teacher, for free. Though using a program like this removes a lot of the autonomy that some homeschooling parents enjoy, other parents may find the organization and contact with a teacher reassuring.

What if Both Parents Work?

Even though the idea of homeschooling lots of kids with two busy work schedules might sound nearly impossible, many families make it work. Carmen, a mom of five, works from home during the early morning hours (her husband works a different shift) and homeschools her kids later in the day. Bonny's husband works full time, while Bonny works part-time at the YMCA, which earns her and her kids a free membership. She homeschools her kids around her work schedule: "I've never considered that 'doing school' needs to happen at certain times of the day or certain months of the year. We don't really follow the school calendar or the school day schedule."

Even in single-parent households or when both parents work out of the home full-time, homeschooling may be possible if you can find homeschool-friendly child care. Ask a local homeschool group for recommendations—another family may have a homeschooling teen or nearby college student who's available to baby-sit during your work hours. Or they may have recommendations for a homeschool-friendly home daycare provider. For more information on finding child care for big families, visit Chapter 5.

Off to College

A number of studies have shown that children from larger families are less likely to attend and finish college. No big surprise there: a college education is expensive enough to tax most parents' budgets, even if they have just one child. Very few people I know can pay for college entirely out of pocket, no matter how small their family.

But that doesn't mean that college is out of reach for kids in big families. In Chapter 7, we discussed ways that college can be attainable even for financially-strapped families. Most of the parents of big families that I surveyed said that college is definitely on the horizon for at least some, if not all, of their kids. "College has never seemed optional," says Jill, who has four kids. "We are currently investigating how to start paying for it. In my husband's words … 'Scholarships!'"

Like anything else, where there's a will and some creative thinking, there's a way. But keep these things in mind when you're helping your child plan for college:

Stress well-roundedness in high school. Scholarships are based on more than just a GPA; they may look for qualities like leadership or artistic potential as well as many other areas.

Start your search for scholarships and grant money early. "I always just assumed my oldest would qualify for federal financial aid," says Tracy, mom of six. "It was very upsetting when it didn't come through. With her not qualifying for federal aid, it also eliminated a lot of aid that either the state or the university would have put up." And when you look, go beyond the standard financial aid form: get online and look for scholarships that aren't well-known. Many thousands of dollars in aid go unused each year because nobody applies for it.

Plan on making your home available past high school. With today's tuition and housing rates, it's very difficult to get through college without taking out loans, which your kids will be paying off for many years. Allowing older kids to stay in your house during college can ease that burden considerably. It's also a less distracting environment for a young college student than a busy dormitory might be. Yes, the "college experience" is important to many young adults, but it can happen later, once they've gotten a handle on college life and have a little more maturity under their belts. Plus, having older kids in the house can benefit the entire family: your youngest children will benefit from their relationship with the oldest kids for a longer time, and your college-age kids can continue to help with chores and can chip in with baby-sitting to help cover their room and board—a great way to get them used to juggling several responsibilities at once.

Be a smart consumer. Consider all the costs of sending your child away to school, including the area's cost of living and travel to and from home.

Chances are you've got a lot of different personalities and learning styles to work around when it comes to choosing the schooling option—or options—that's right for your family. And when you're trying to coordinate dropping off, picking up, and extra-curricular activities, other factors like starting and ending times, availability and cost of after-school programs, and location will factor in big-time. Balancing the needs of each individual child against the needs of the whole family can be a challenge, but luckily, today there are so many options that it's easier than ever to find a fit for all your kids' different personalities and abilities. Just keep in mind that there are a lot of ways to get a good education, and as long as you're involved in their education, chances are good your kids will do just fine.

Discipline and Child-Rearing

When people hear that I've got four kids—especially four boys—they often say, "Better you than me." Or "How do you stay sane?"

When I ask what they mean, the truth comes out: people who have been overwhelmed by an experience involving one or two children—their own or maybe a bad baby-sitting memory from long ago—tend to assume that having three or four or five or more children in the house would take the situation up a notch, from "overwhelming" to "chaotic" or "just plain crazy."

True, our house does sometimes resemble a four-ring circus, with each kid loudly going through his own personal meltdown while I stand by helplessly and consider pouring myself a stiff drink. Chaos and a breakdown of discipline happen to the best of us! But with reasonable and firm boundaries and a proactive outlook, your kids can be well-behaved and respectful, and grow into balanced, responsible adults—even if you've got a bunch of them.

I actually think bigger families have a few clear advantages when it comes to discipline issues. For one thing, brothers and sisters can act as the sibling police. Constant tattling can be annoying, but it also means you're much more likely to find out if a kid is doing something really, really stupid or danger-ous. Second, by the time you get to your third or fourth kid, you get better at figuring out what works, what doesn't, and which fights are worth picking.

But there are some challenges, too. Nobody can be in two places at once, let alone four or five. If your kids are close in age or in spirit, they may become very adept at working together to carry out—or cover up—mischief. And, because kids are all unique and may respond differently to certain techniques and approaches, having lots of kids means you might need to have a very well-stocked parenting toolbox.

Advantages of discipline in Table for Eight families	Challenges of discipline in Table for Eight families
The kids police each other.	The kids police each other.
More hands to help.	More fingers to point.
When the kids cooperate with each other, they can make your life easier.	When the kids cooperate with each other, they can get away with a lot more.
Siblings learn from each other's mistakes.	Siblings pick up on each other's bad habits.
More conflicts mean more learning opportunities.	More kids means more opportunities for conflict.

So let's look at these tips and methods other parents of many recommend for raising happy, well-behaved, and responsible kids—and keeping your house reasonably calm and under control!

Sibling Squabbles

Even brothers and sisters who love each other's company fight sometimes. In fact, in our house the kids who are the closest fight the most! It's natural for kids to clash once in a while, but that doesn't mean you have to allow disharmony to take over the household. Here are some tried-and-true methods for settling sibling skirmishes:

When possible, let them work it out themselves. Refusing to get involved in minor tiffs forces your kids to work through them together, which can be a great way for them to learn to navigate difficult social situations later on in life. Besides, when you have more than two kids, there are just too many possible storylines going on at any one time for you to really understand the background behind the current drama. If you jump in and take sides without really knowing what's going on, you run the risk of making one of your kids feel unheard or escalating the situation even more. Think of your role as a relationship referee or facilitator—not a micromanager.

Don't be afraid to step in when it's warranted. This includes when one child is being physically or emotionally bullied. "We try to let the older two work out their squabbles themselves, but if voices rise too high or we think things might get physical, we step in immediately," says Michelle, mom of four kids ages one, two, six, and seven. "We insist that they talk to each other and explain why they got angry, and ask for each other's forgiveness when they calm down. We stress family unity and also stress that to get on each other's nerves is normal, but that you have to repair the heart that you hurt with your words."

Don't typecast your kids. Depending on how the majority of fights seem to play out in your house, it's easy to start viewing your kids as a set of roles: the bully, the victim, the peacemaker, the instigator. But some kids—even the quietest and littlest—can have a sneaky way of instigating fights while flying well under Mom and Dad's radar. And once a kid knows that being the victim gets him a certain amount of attention or sympathy, he may well try to use that position to his advantage in the future. "One of my big issues right now is my ten-year-old son; he is trying to manipulate emotions by being the 'poor little picked on one,'" says Carmen, mom of five.

Split 'em up. When nothing else is working, try keeping the squabblers apart for a while. In my experience, sometimes kids fighting a lot means they're just spending too much time together, are fighting to establish their own identities, or to get special attention from you. Taking them out separately for a special errand with Mom or Dad or enrolling them in different activities may give them the space they need.

Don't indirectly reward bullying or instigating. Sometimes kids pick on their brothers and sisters because they're trying to get attention. If one child punches his brother in the arm and you deal with it by punishing the puncher, he's succeeded in getting your attention in a negative way, and the hurt child may feel ignored. On the other hand, if you immediately give your attention and sympathy to the sibling who's been wronged, you're both supporting him and refusing to "reward" the wrongdoer with attention. When you have lots of kids, it's important that they learn quickly that negative behavior isn't a way to get attention. On the other hand, this kind of behavior might be a cry for attention from a child who doesn't know any other way to get it. So after the dust clears from the fight, have a talk with the instigator to find out where he's coming from—and what you might be able to do to help him feel more heard.

mom wisdom

"One of our biggest squabbles when we had four teenage girls at home was over 'borrowing' clothes from each other and whether that required permission or not. Each of the girls wanted her sisters to be punished for borrowing without asking but thought her own borrowing was okay because it was 'only for emergencies.' We sat the four of them down together and told them to decide on a consistent policy—either they always got punished for borrowing without permission, regardless of reason, or they didn't get punished—in the end they decided they would stop complaining about unauthorized 'borrowing.'"

—Sharon, mom of five grown kids, Indiana

Different Strokes for Different Big-Family Folks

By the time most parents have their second child, they often start to realize that no one child-rearing method is right for every kid. And by the time you're on number three or number four, you're sure of it. Whether you're trying to calm a fussy baby, establish a naptime routine for a toddler, or get a preschooler to eat her peas, what works for one child is almost guaranteed not to work for the rest. Of course, it's the same story with discipline techniques. And it can feel like there's so much at stake—your child's development and your sanity!—as you're trying to figure out what works the best for each child in your house.

There are a lot of excellent child-discipline books on the shelves (I've listed a few at the end of this chapter). Just remember that if something doesn't work, it might not be because you're doing it wrong! Nobody has all the answers for every child, and that includes your mother, the woman down the street with two seemingly perfect children, the teller at the bank, the cashier at the grocery store, your pediatrician—and yes, even child-development experts!

mom wisdom

"We treat our children differently because several of them have special needs. Those children are far harder to discipline due to their individual issues. For example, was she lying or did she honestly not know that it was wrong to do something because she can't mentally grasp it? Our other children understand the issues related to their special-needs siblings, and there have never been any complaints over the different discipline techniques."

—Cindy, mom of eight, Colorado

Also keep in mind that you are going to change as a parent over the years you're raising children. You may have started off with some very specific ideas about how you were going to handle your kids, but your style is likely to change. "With my first couple of children I was *very* strict," says Shirley, who has five kids. "As I got to number five, I found that I didn't have the energy to keep them all in line, so the younger kids enjoyed less strictness." If there is a wide spread in your kids' ages, you may find that age, maturity, different circumstances, or a changing world-view also makes you a very different parent from when you began.

One of the hardest things for me to realize and accept when my family started to grow is that I couldn't be the same mom to three kids as I was to one. And I couldn't be the same mom to four kids as I was to two. But you know what? That's not all bad. I'm definitely spread thinner, and there are days that I look at my kids and wonder how I'm going to get them all to adulthood alive, much less as functional, responsible and decent human beings. But on the positive side, I have developed a lot more patience. And just as important, my expectations of both my kids and myself have changed.

Sometime between having my second and third child, as I watched my two older children grow from toddlers to preschoolers to big boys, I began to understand that I don't make my parenting choices just to get from one day to the next, but for the long haul. And I could see that despite all the little—and yes, even the big—mistakes that I made when they were babies, my two oldest kids were still growing into kind, decent, and fun people. Knowing this gave me tons more confidence with my third and fourth babies—and I know they've benefited from it. One of the things many of the parents I spoke with said was that having lots of kids made them realize that at any given time they might have several different ways of dealing with discipline issues among their kids. While one child might respond well to time-outs, others might only need a raised eyebrow cocked in their direction to whip themselves into quick shape. While some kids respond well to incentives and rewards, others are more intrinsically motivated or seem to respond to the natural consequences of their actions. As long as you're paying careful attention not to typecast your kids (the "bad" one, the "rowdy" one, the "good" one), it's okay to choose different discipline tools based on what works for that particular child at that particular time.

mom wisdom

"In our house we practice something called 'tomato staking.' When one of the children is going through a challenging stage, I keep him or her physically close to me—sometimes, as close as a few feet away, but definitely no further than a room away— all day so that I can keep an eye on the child, offer encouragement as necessary, and thwart misbehavior before it even starts. I don't play with the child, but involve him or her in whatever I'm doing—cleaning, cooking, or what have you. I find that this gets to the root of many behavior issues. Sometimes, kids act up because they are looking for attention, and tomato staking allows me to give them lots of one-on-one attention. Sometimes they just can't control their impulses and need close supervision for a while, and tomato staking offers that, too. And sometimes, the child I thought was starting trouble was actually being picked on by a brother or sister, and tomato staking gives him or her distance from the situation and gives me a better idea of what's going on."

—Emily, mother of seven, Utah

But It's Not *Fair!*

Of course, any time you appear to treat one child differently from another, you open yourself up to that tired old complaint: "It's not fair!"

Which begs the question: *can* life really be fair for the kids in a big family? While your kids might say "no way," don't worry—because most kids go through a period of being hyper-focused on fairness (and how unfair their own lives seem) they'd probably feel the same way if they were only children, too.

mom wisdom

"The kids do notice when we take different approaches, and that is something we take the time to explain to them. We also explain to them that Mommy and Daddy are learning every day also, and that we reserve the right to change techniques based on what we think works the best that day."

—Michelle, mom of four

When you're considering the needs of so many different people, you have to take a close look at how the wants of one person affect the needs of the whole group. In my opinion, it's not important or possible to make every situation 100 percent equal for everyone involved. And the more kids in the house, the less time you have to explain and justify your choices to your kids—so don't do it. Be sure the decisions you make are as just as possible, and work toward an overall balance, but if you have to, don't be afraid to let your child know, in no uncertain terms, that you have made a decision in the best interests of everybody involved and it's no longer up for discussion.

An approach like this may very well raise gasps from friends of fewer kids, who may have gotten caught up in feeling a need to carefully explain each parental decision to their kids. There's nothing wrong with offering an explanation if you've got the time or energy for it, but it's hardly child abuse to say "Because it's what I've decided—end of story." In my house, opening the floor to discussion about every decision I make can set off a never-ending chain reaction of questions and protests. Sometimes I'm

147

flexible enough in my decision to entertain counter-arguments. But often the decision is non-negotiable, and I don't feel guilty saying so.

Taking an approach of overall balance, rather than trying to hyper-manage each individual situation until it's completely fair, might mean that sometimes one child gets a bigger slice of the pie—figuratively or literally. But down the road, more likely than not some other decision will weigh in the other child's favor. That's what "fairness" really is—the big picture.

This is a far more realistic introduction to the way things work in the real world, where individual transactions and interactions are rarely 100 percent equal for both parties. Life requires a lot of compromise, and sometimes, submission. Growing up in a big family gives kids many opportunities to become flexible people who roll with the punches instead of fixating on injustices they can't control.

When kids are at what I jokingly call the "avenger for justice" stage, though, they aren't always able to look at the whole picture to remember that, although this situation didn't go in their favor, others have and will. Unfortunately, it's easy for a child to blame anything he sees as inequity in his life on having lots of siblings. It's understandable, but usually inaccurate!

"Kids have to learn to understand that 'fair' doesn't always mean they get what their friends are getting," says Sharon, whose five kids are now grown. "If you have lots of kids, you have less money or time per kid—but we tried hard to divide our time and money evenly between the kids. We used hand-me-downs, but we made sure the youngest didn't always wear castoffs. Our definition of 'fair' is that everyone got their needs met, and we divided the extra time and money evenly among wants." Jeff, who has five kids, agrees. "I hate to do the whole 'back when I was a kid' thing with my own sons, but sometimes I just can't resist because it's really true—parents were just different then, and it really wasn't expected that you'd try to make everything fair for your kids. I don't recommend sounding like a broken record, but sometimes when I remind my kids that they are lucky that their biggest problem is that their brother might have gotten a bigger pancake than they did—not that they didn't get any pancakes at all—they get the picture."

So in addition to trying to keep the scales balanced, it's important to drive home the idea that life isn't fair for anyone, whether he is an only child or part of a big family. This also helps to redirect your child's focus away from a self-centered "what's in it for *me*?" attitude to a more global perspective that includes the thoughts and feelings of those around him.

For Michelle, mom of four, this outlook on life fits in perfectly with the religious worldview she is trying to impress on her kids: "We try hard to be fair, but we also remind kids that the world isn't usually fair, and that suffering is part of life. Since we're Catholic, service and sacrifice for others is part of the faith tradition we are teaching our children."

The complaint "It's not fair!" is a great way to spark a dialogue about what fairness really means. "Life isn't always fair, and that's a great learning experience for the real world," says Cindy, mom of eight. "We've had some great discussions due to a child not thinking something was fair." Cindy says that if there is a genuine imbalance among her kids, she will try to make it up to the other child—but that protests over petty "injustices" won't get a child much sympathy in her house: "If they are upset because their sibling got the last piece of cake so that gave them one more than someone else, they need to get over it!"

Of course, you don't have to be Catholic or religious at all to teach your kids the value of service to others and selflessness. And "It's not fair!" can give you an opportunity for discussion.

On the other hand, when you've got a lot of kids, with a lot of different agendas and desires, it's sometimes all-too-easy to let the whiniest—er, *squeakiest* wheel get all the grease. Don't make the mistake of always responding to the child who hollers the loudest. The quiet, laid-back kid who always seems so well-adjusted could be crying out inside for you to take notice of her needs, too.

Controlling Chaos

Do big families have chaotic houses? According to my panel of big-family parents, that seems to depend on your definition of "chaos." If you can be perfectly calm in the midst of a gaggle of children (and perhaps a pet or two) running in circles, talking, bickering, or singing—and sometimes all at once—then you might not find living with a big family particularly chaotic. And then there are the rest of us, who are occasionally driven to distraction by too much noise and motion. And if you're tired or over-stimulated to begin with, a little confusion goes a long way in creating grumpy, overwhelmed parents. So how can Table for Eight parents stop the household insanity—or at least cope with it?

Set a quiet tone for the house. Play calming music, burn candles or aromatherapy in soothing scents, or keep the TV off or turned to a reason-ably quiet volume. Don't allow competing noise—no radio and TV on in the same area of the house, for instance. Try to speak quietly. These things won't always keep kids from being their often exuberant and loud selves, but it may encourage a calmer attitude—and at the very least, it may put you in a more peaceful frame of mind and more likely to be able to cope with the noise. "I used to like to watch NASCAR on the weekends with the volume up loud—I loved listening to the sound of the cars driving by," admits Jeff, a father of five boys. "I'd do the same thing with the news, or when I watched movies—I'd have the surround sound on and the volume cranked up. It took me a while to realize that whenever I was watching TV turned up loud with the surround sound on, my youngest kids would start acting crazy, wrestling, yelling, jumping all over the place. I finally realized that the noise level was really getting them riled up, so now I only use the surround sound when they're outside playing or in bed for the night."

Block it out. When nothing else works, a pair of earmuffs or earplugs can be a great bedlam-buster. "What a great way to block out competing stereos, TV, and loud phone conversations!" says Sharon, mom of five.

Make sure the house is at your neatness comfort level. It might take a little extra time to stay on top of it, but many of us require a certain level of order to feel functional—and for us, disorder and mess can make the house feel downright frenzied. How messy the house is can affect our per-ception of how chaotic it is; for instance, if my kids are screaming and run-ning in circles on a clean floor, I feel a lot less stressed out than if they're walking quietly on a dirty floor. Figure out what your triggers are—piles of laundry? dirty dishes in the sink?—and make sure that eliminating them is part of your household's daily routine. Decide whether it's better to do those tasks yourself or delegate them to your kids.

Personally, I usually choose to do the things that are most important to my sanity myself. The last thing I want is to encounter unswept kitchen floors and a paper-covered table at 8:30 P.M.—and *then* have to confront the kids to take care of it. By that point, I'm already grumpy, and the interaction isn't likely to go well! I take care of my "trigger tasks" myself and choose chores that can be done imperfectly, or on a slower schedule, to delegate to my kids. I'd much rather butt heads with my kids over something like dusting shelves, which don't really bother me, than dirty floors, which definitely do! If you do put your kids in charge of one of your trigger tasks, invest the time to make sure they learn to do it right, and make sure they have an incentive to get it done on time and are accountable enough to follow through without constant reminders.

Get regular time to yourself to recharge your batteries and replenish your well of patience and calm. "When we have dinner, sometimes with everyone talking and being loud and having a great time, I realize that it's driving me bonkers! I generally leave the dinner table, go to the other end of the house to my room—my sanctuary—and lay down with the lights off. In about twenty minutes, I feel civilized again, and I'm ready to be pleasant," says Carmen, a homeschooling mom of five who also works at home.

Every mom needs a place she can go to and be alone for a few minutes when she's on the brink of losing it, and it's even more important for a Table for Eight mom. Whether yours is the bathtub or a corner of your bedroom, try to make it a restful, comfortable, and attractive place to grab a few minutes rest. Stash your nook with light reading material, a comfy blanket, a soft eye mask, or whatever you need to create an atmosphere of peace and calm—even if you can only grab time alone for five minutes at a time.

Enforce a nightly "noise curfew." When you've got babies and toddlers in the house, this can be more difficult, especially if they have unpredictable sleeping patterns. But older kids—even those without strict bedtimes—can follow quiet-hour rules. "When our kids were older, we had a rule of 'quiet after 9:00 P.M.,'" says Sharon. "After that time there was no TV allowed, no music that could be heard outside the bedroom, no showering, no doing laundry. The kids could go to bed, do homework, read, or do whatever quiet activity they wanted, but no noisy stuff."

Try to keep a sense of humor. "Sometimes my husband and I just look at each other and laugh at the chaos," says Michelle, mom of four. If you can't laugh, try faking it. Studies have shown that faking laughter gives you some of the same stress-relieving benefits of real laughter, and who knows—it may put you in a laughing frame of mind.

 **mom wisdom**

When everybody is talking at once, it's sometimes impossible for a parent's voice to rise above the din. Here's some ways other parents of lots of kids get attention when they've just got to be heard:

"Sometimes you can go over to the children making the most noise and gently hug them—the touch seems to get their attention more than yelling would."

—Michelle, mom of four

"I rarely have to scream. I get the offender alone and speak in a calm but firm tone. They understand I'm the boss."

—Shirley, mom of five

"I holler 'Hey!' and then speak. If you make a ridiculous idle threat like 'If you don't quit, I will never feed you again!' it gets their attention, and they will usually stop—with a laugh—and let you speak."

—Carmen, mom of five

"I'm not one for loud voices, but if the kids ever heard me raise my voice they shaped up immediately. My spouse isn't like that and at times shouted to be heard and to try to get some order. I think my method worked better—as my son once said, 'Mom said "damn,"' and we knew we were in big trouble."

—Sharon, mom of five grown kids, Indiana

"My mother used to hiss at us—that caught our attention!"

—Angie, mom of six, Michigan

"I call out once and then make my voice get softer; they have to get quieter or they can't hear me. Or I just stand there and stare, and that gets their attention."

—Cindy, mom of eight, Colorado

"I walk softly and carry a big stick, so to speak. I find the quieter I am, the more I am heard."

—Carly, mom of four, Ohio

"If nobody's listening to me, I will sing loudly or whistle. That usually gets them to stop what they're doing and look at me!"

—Christi, mom of six, Virginia

Keep them close. When you're around your kids a lot, it's much easier to nip the beginnings of confusion in the bud before it gets out of hand. "I am usually most effective with the children if I am right in the middle of activity with them," says Angie, mom of five. "I am able to lead them better and appreciate them more if I am playing or working in the midst of them."

Level with the kids. Tell your kids that the commotion is making you grumpy, and ask the older kids especially to help set a good, quiet example for the younger ones. During a calm time when the kids are receptive, you can come up with a code word that you'll use if things are getting too out of control.

If you can't beat 'em, join 'em. Like anything else, chaos is more fun when you're a part of it. I've been known to belt out "Help me, I'm losing my mind!" in my best opera-singer imitation. Sometimes all you can do is add to the noise and try to relieve a little of your own stress by being silly and loud right along with them.

Allow yourself to lose it sometimes. Face it, life with a lot of kids is stressful, and not always fun. In fact, sometimes parents of many can feel like we're barely hanging on to a thread of control ... over our kids or our own emotions. Parental meltdowns happen sometimes to the best of us, and to the rest of us, they happen a *lot*. Don't bottle up frustration, anxiety or anger. It's not a good idea to let loose all your pent-up emotions on your family, but in an age-appropriate way, you can tell the kids that their behavior is upsetting you. If you're having a bad day and are upset for no one reason in particular, confide in your spouse or a good friend. If you feel angry, anxious, or sad all the time, consider seeing a therapist, counselor, or other professional.

It's often hard for parents, particularly moms, of many to admit when they're having a rough time with discipline or child-care. We worry that people will judge us for having more kids than we can handle, or that they'll think we brought it upon ourselves. Worse, we may have allowed them to put us up on a pedestal of perfectly pulled-together parenting, and it can be very difficult to admit that we don't know it all, and aren't really an all-natural earth mother with perfectly-behaved kids. But you know the saying about being your own worst enemy? It definitely applies here. Let go of the idea that you need to hold up your own family as an example of why big families can work. You don't have to prove anything to anyone except yourself and your own kids.

No Bedtime Battles

I have to be honest; we don't exactly have the bedtime situation under control in our house yet. With a toddler who sleeps in our bed and a preschooler who's currently trying to drop a nap and wreaking havoc on his sleep routine in the process, only our two older kids are on a reliable bedtime schedule. And that's fine with us for now. Some big families put a higher priority on order and routine, establishing very regular sleep habits right from infancy, and that works for them. But no matter what your approach to nighttime parenting is, getting a big family down for the night can require some work and forethought. Here's how some larger families handle the logistics of bedtime:

Divide and conquer. Assuming you're married and your spouse is home every evening, splitting the kids into two groups, with each parent tackling one, can be an easier way to handle bedtime. For instance, in our house, I start the bedtime routine with the bigger kids—toothbrushing, reading out loud—but my husband finishes by getting the kids tucked into bed. Then I get the three-year-old settled into bed while my husband gets the baby to sleep. By 9:00 at night, I've been nursing and holding the baby for most of the day, and I'm ready for a break from him. At the same time, tucking my three-year-old in and taking a few minutes to snuggle is a nice way to ensure that we stay connected, because his wants sometimes take a back seat to the baby's needs during the day. Another approach is to handle the entire bedtime routine yourself one night and trade off with your spouse the next day. The divide-and-conquer approach can work with morning routines, too "I really like doing bedtime with the kids, and actually make a point of doing it as often as I can," says Paul, a father of five kids including a six-month-old baby. "My wife is a teacher, so by the time I get home after 6:00, she's already been home for two hours. And of course with feeding the baby at night, she's not getting as much sleep, and she has to pump milk during the day while she's at work. Basically, she's on mom duty all day and night, even when she's working. So I let her have twenty minutes at night to herself while I read books to the kids, tuck them in and rock the baby to sleep. I figure that's the least I can do, and it's a nice way to spend time with all of them, too."

Make bedtime family time. Sometimes parents—myself included—rush bedtime, eager for a quiet household and some time alone, which can be rare when you have lots of kids. And of course, there are those crazy days when everyone is so tired and cranky that all I can do is hope that they make their way to their beds and don't come out again until morning, when we can make a fresh start. But overall, I find that when I don't spend enough time with my kids in the evening before bed, they suddenly erupt with questions, requests, or long complaints they just have to get off of their chests *after* I've already tucked them in.

dad wisdom

"Sometimes when I come home from work tired after a long day and am met with a bunch of kids jumping all over me, I mentally fast-forward to when they're in bed and I can have some time alone with my wife. But then I tend to fixate on bedtime all evening, which makes me not really enjoy the time I do have with the kids. Sometimes it's a shock to the system to go from being at my office, which is quiet and orderly, to home, which, well, *isn't*, but when I force myself to slow down and enjoy a nice family dinner, help with homework, or go kick a ball around the yard instead of trying to rush everybody off to bed, I enjoy my family a lot more ... and my wife is a lot happier with me when they finally do get off to bed and we have our time alone."

—Mark, father of five, Vermont

Gathering the family together a little while before lights-out for toothbrushing, story time, talking, and cuddling offers a guarantee of togetherness at the end of a busy day. Older kids can read to the entire family, or all the children can take turns reading from a book. You can pile into a bed or onto a big sofa together and enjoy a half-hour or so of quiet reading and cuddling, listening to a story on tape or some music, and quietly talking. If your kids are very busy during the day or if you or your spouse work long hours, everyone may really appreciate a calming and reconnecting ritual like this before heading to bed ... which could eliminate some of those last-minute ploys for attention. And it will give you something to look forward to at bedtime, rather than just wishing you could get it over with.

Accept reality. Before I had kids I imagined that I'd put them to bed every night at 7:00 and they'd go instantly to sleep, leaving my husband and me with hours ahead of us for adult time. And when I had just one child—and later, when I had two—I was sometimes able to pull something like that off. But with four kids in the house, the reality is that bedtime is no longer completely smooth. It often takes an hour or longer to get everyone down and out for the night, by which point I'm pretty wiped out, too—sure, I might have enough energy for a couple of episodes of *Good Eats* on Food Network, but that's about it.

My husband and I decided not to set strict sleep schedules for our kids when they are babies, which is part of the reason it takes so long for us right now. Because we've chosen to take a relaxed approach to bedtime for our babies, we've had to accept that, while we have small children in the house, bedtime will be somewhat disorganized.

And eventually, when we decide it's time for their bedtimes to become more reliable, there's likely to be some resistance from the kids. The way I figure it, you and your kids are going to have a struggle over sleep at some point—whether it's while they're babies or when they're older. We chose to wait and have it when they were older rather than do the sleep-training thing with our babies. But that doesn't mean we're doomed to a bed full of teenaged kids! We haven't had much trouble getting our kids to develop healthy, independent sleep habits as they got older, even though they started off with pretty relaxed sleep "schedules." My point is that there's no one "right" way to do bedtime with your kids. Parents of lots of kids have to be able to find something that works for their unique family. It might not look the same as the family down the street, whose one child religiously hits the sheets at 6:45 P.M. and sleeps twelve hours at a stretch. After all, even if you are lucky enough to get one kid who sleeps like that, what are the chances you'll get four or five?

Sometimes, though, sleep deprivation can become a critical situation, especially when you've got several small children who aren't sleeping well at night yet. If you are having a difficult time functioning during the day due to lack of sleep, you need real help. You can't parent well when you're chronically tired, and it can make ordinary activities like driving or cooking dangerous, too. Ask your spouse to take over bedtime for you a few evenings in a row so you can try to catch up on sleep, hire a baby-sitter to watch the kids so you can take a nap … whatever it takes. Babies are biologically wired to be unpredictable sleepers, but if things don't start to improve as your child gets bigger and you just aren't getting enough sleep, you may need to employ some gentle sleep-training methods. Take a look at some of the books I've included at the end of this chapter for help.

Dealing with Stalling

One child's last-minute request after lights-out can be contagious, leading to an avalanche of stalling tactics from the tried-and-true "I need a glass of water" to sneakier bedtime-deferring techniques like reading with a flashlight under the covers or sneaking into the kitchen for an unauthorized snack. And when kids share bedrooms, they often keep talking and laughing long past bedtime. These tips help keep bedtime stalling to a minimum.

Set a timer fifteen or twenty minutes before bed. Tell the kids they have until the timer dings to take care of all their last-minute business: drinks, trips to the bathroom, etc. After the timer dings, it's time for bed—no excuses.

Set the stage for nighttime independence. Have your kids gather all their "bedtime supplies"—water and anything else they think they may need to have access to at night—and find a place for them near their beds.

Get them to work together. If your kids share bedrooms and you have a hard time getting them to stop whispering and laughing, offer them a reward if they can fall asleep—or pretend very convincingly—within five minutes. Or use the same kind of reward approach you might remember from summer camp: tell the kids that the first bedroom that becomes—and stays—completely quiet will get a reward at breakfast. It can be something simple—like an extra pancake or being served first—but it'll prompt the kids to work together to "win."

Routines, Rituals, and Rewards

In my household, routines and rituals are the key to keeping everything peaceful and functioning. My kids are more cooperative and their behavior is better when they know what to expect next, whether it's how I will deal with a certain behavior or about when they'll get up, eat lunch, take a nap, or go to bed.

Notice I said *about* when. Rigid schedules work for some families, but relaxed routines can be a better bet. Life can be unpredictable with a big family, and you'll need to be somewhat flexible in order to keep things from falling apart if there's a change to the usual timeline.

Outside activities like sports and lessons can make sticking to routines more challenging. As I've noted before, it's important to weigh the benefits of any activity for that one child against the ways it might affect the entire family. As Sara, a mom of five, who tries to limit outside activities for her kids because too much rushing around can throw off the home routine, leading to over-tired kids, says, "There is no substitute for good rest when it comes to expecting good behavior from your kids!" This limiting decision can be a tough one because parents today are expected to be pretty child-centered in the way they arrange their time. But I prefer to think of myself as "family-centered" rather than child- or adult-centered.

Family routines aren't just about when things happen, but also *how*. In a big family, to have a system for keeping track of your expectations of each child, as well as behavior infractions and rewards can be very helpful. This system can be a plus for both you and your kids: at any time, they can see exactly what's expected of them and how they're doing so far, and you don't have to clutter up your brain by trying to keep track of it all mentally!

Ramona, a mom of eleven, has a point system for keeping track of duties, chores, and consequences. "When my kids finish something, they either come and tell Mom, who checks them off on her handy dandy clipboard, or they write it on the white board so that Mom can come along later and make all of the necessary notations. At the end of the day each child gets two points if they got everything done on time, but points get taken away if they did not. When they lose a certain number of points there are specific consequences, such as doing schoolwork on Saturday or not watching videos."

Karen, mom of five, has a point system as well—but hers focuses on rewards instead of consequences. "My kids get points for doing what's expected of them—chores, homework done on time, etc. I don't reward them every single time they do something right, but when they get to twenty points—which usually takes them about a week—they get a small treat, like an ice cream cone. I also allow them to pool their points for bigger rewards, which encourages them to work together to get them. I find that it breeds a kind of positive 'peer pressure' in the house, where the kids are working toward goals together." Carmen, mom of five, has a system called ARCS—Attitude, Room, Chores, and School. If a child's ARCS are in check, he or she can have privileges like visiting with friends. "I love cause and effect," says Carmen. The built-in consequences for not following through on ARCS make it very easy for kids to tell if they are meeting expectations and makes "punishment" unnecessary a lot of the time. And best yet? "Mommy's emotions are completely taken out of the equation," says Carmen. Instead of trying to make decisions about consequences in the heat of an angry moment or allowing your kids to talk you out of a consequence because you're distracted or stressed, a logic-based cause-and-effect system like Carmen's ARCS spells out very clearly what the expectations are and what will happen if they aren't met. It makes it much easier to be consistent and fair.

It's also important to know what your goals are for your kids. What do you want them to learn about life? What kind of people do you want them to become? With limited time to spend individually with each child, you really have to know what you want to accomplish with them to make sure they absorb the lessons you want them to learn. "The best tip I can give is to look at your values—what is really important to you, and what isn't," says Carmen. Carmen, who educates her kids at home, said that when she and her husband started homeschooling, they made a list of the four most important values they wanted to pass on to their children. Number 1 was a strong faith, number 2 was reading, writing, and arithmetic, number 3 was character, and number 4 was life skills. "Can they change the baby, change the oil in the car, fill the gas tank, open a bank account, make dinner, sew on a button, change a flat tire, use a computer, buy groceries, pick out good produce?" asks Carmen, who feels that many parents don't do a good enough job of making sure their kids have the abilities and skills they'll need to be responsible, competent adults.

When people ask me whether it's possible to raise good kids if you've got a lot of them, I say "definitely yes!" In fact, having a lot of kids has actually forced me to take a closer look at the way I discipline and teach my kids and what kind of effect my actions will have on the kind of character they develop. At the end of the day, it's more important to me that my kids grow up to be responsible, well-adjusted, unselfish people with a healthy sense of perspective than it is for them to be happy all the time right now. Because of that realization—and in order to keep the house from sinking into total bedlam—I've tightened up on some things, but I still make sure the kids feel loved and feel like they have a voice.

It's possible that you'll run into criticism from people for being "too strict" with your larger family. You may take some flak from people with smaller families—or, amusingly, people with no kids at all—who mistake a no-nonsense attitude for overly harsh parenting. But as long as you set those firm limits in a loving way—after all, the word discipline means "to teach" rather than "to punish"—your whole family may be better off for it.

Of course, my household is still far from perfect. There are definitely days when it seems like I'm grooming juvenile delinquents, and days I'd be embarrassed if a neighbor looked in the window and saw how my family— including myself!—is behaving. I figure I'll be learning for the rest of my parenting life, until my last child leaves the house. Maybe I'll get parenting completely figured out by the time I have grandkids—too bad I'll have to keep it to myself!

These resources can help you with the some of the trickiest discipline issues:

How To Talk So Your Kids Will Listen and Listen So Your Kids Will Talk, by Adele Faber and Elaine Mazlish (Piccadilly Press, 2001). This time-tested book has sold nearly 2 million copies. It gives some great techniques for communicating with your kids without nagging, threatening or yelling.

Siblings Without Rivalry: How To Help Your Children Live Together So You Can Live Too, by Adele Faber and Elaine Mazlish (Piccadilly Press, 1999) A #1 New York Times Bestseller, this favorite deals with the causes of sibling rivalry and offers useful solutions for helping kids get along. Faber and Mazlish each have three children.

Positive Discipline: the classic guide to helping children develop self-discipline, responsibility, cooperation and problem-solving skills (Ballantine Books, 2006), Jane Nelson, Ed.D. Written by a marriage, child and family therapist—who also happens to be a mother of seven—this classic manual helps parents create a relationship with their kids that doesn't include punishments or pleading.

NO: Why Kids—of All Ages—Need to Hear It, and Ways Parents Can Say It, David Walsh, Ph.D. (Free Press, 2007). In this book, a psychologist and father of three makes the argument that raising kids in a culture that says "yes" to everything isn't doing them any favors. The book advocates a reasonable parenting style that emphasizes that kids need to experience logical consequences, delayed gratification, and disappointment in order to build a strong character.

The No-Cry Sleep Solution: Gentle Ways to Help Your Baby Sleep Through the Night, by Elizabeth Pantley (McGraw-Hill, 2002) This book, written by a professional author, parenting expert, and mother of four isn't a sleep-training manual. Instead, it offers gentle methods for moms who are wary of sleep training to help their babies sleep for longer and longer stretches at a time.

Sleep Solutions for Your Baby, Toddler and Preschooler: The Ultimate No-Worry Approach for Each Age and Stage by Ann Douglas (Wiley, 2006) Written by an experienced author and mother of four, this book operates under the mindset that there is no one right way for children to sleep, and presents the research and a variety of solutions so that parents can decide.

Piece of the Pie: Helping Everyone in the Family Get Enough of You—and Become Their Own People

The other week, I took my four sons to the park. It took a few minutes to get the two big kids out of the back end of the van, unbuckle my three-year-old and set him in the grass, then go to the other side of the van, unbuckle my toddler from his car seat and set him down on the ground. The outing hadn't even started yet, and already I was tired!

The five of us headed for the playground and I started scouting for the perfect place to put my keys, extra jackets, water bottle, and assorted other stuff. It had to meet these criteria: I'd have to be able to stay very close to Owen, because he's at that wants up-wants down-wants up again phase, and isn't too sure on his feet. I'd have to be within eyesight of William, who at three, wants to play independently but still needs supervision. And I'd have to be at least within shouting range of Jacob and Isaac, who are nine and seven. Oh, and I'd need to be able to sit down from time to time, too, because all that chasing Owen around was going to be exhausting.

I finally found a good location by the baby swings and started pushing Owen. But soon, William shouted for me to catch him at the bottom of the slide, and Jacob and Isaac begged me to push them on the tire swing. "Please please please please!" all three pleaded in unison.

"I'm only one person, you guys!" I protested. "I can't be everywhere at once!"

Looking around at the other parents, pushing their one or two children on the swings, I felt a momentary twinge of guilt. Is it fair to ask my kids to wait for my attention? I wondered. After all, they didn't ask to be born into a family where they'd have to constantly compete for a slice of my limited time.

Then I thought back on my own childhood. When I was growing up, my mom didn't even take me to the park—I biked there myself. I played outside from sun-up to sundown most days, only coming home for meals or to take care of my chores. Most of my friends had the same kind of freedom. But it never would have occurred to me to ask my mom to play with me or push me on the swings—that's what other kids were for. Did I feel neglected? Absolutely not.

Raising the Bar

As families have gotten smaller, we've raised the bar on what constitutes good parenting. It's hard to say which came first, the chicken or the egg—in other words, have parenting standards been elevated because people are having fewer children, or are people having fewer children because the standards are so high?

According to Andrea O'Reilly, founder of the Association for Research on Mothering at Toronto's York University, the answer may be both. "Having fewer children allows us to do this intensive, child-centered mothering, and the higher the parenting standards, the more difficult it is to meet them with more than one or two children." O'Reilly, herself a mother of three, recalls that when she was two years old she was in the playpen, her sister was in the stroller, and her brother was tied to a tree as her mother did the laundry—and that was a common practice among mothers on her street. While children tied to trees would probably be grounds for a visit from Child Protective Services these days and would make even the most laid-back modern mom cringe, maybe we've swung too far in the other direction. "Today's parents have become their child's entertainer, confidant, and social manager," says O'Reilly.

In fact, some experts say that modern parents have actually become *too* child-focused. In an article for the website www.babble.com, parenting author Katie Allison Granju wrote of today's mother: "We may no longer be 'professional homemakers,' but whether we stay home with our kids, or work outside the home, we've turned parenting into its own, highly stressful, endlessly demanding, often joyless undertaking." Granju, who is the author of the forthcoming *Let Them Run With Scissors: How Over-parenting Hurts Kids, Families, and Society* (Soft Skull Press), cites a study by the research group Public Agenda, which found that 76 percent of American parents describe raising kids today as "much harder" than it was when they were kids. Despite modern conveniences and fewer children on average, how can parenting be getting *more* difficult? Because, argues Granju, we've all become harder on ourselves—and each other. Maybe that's one of the reasons many people feel ill-equipped to have more than one, or at the most, two children: they've set their own parenting standards far too high.

Time and Tradeoffs

I'm with my kids a lot. I love to talk to them and enjoy being with them, whether I'm helping them with their school work, reading aloud to them, or going for a walk. I like to listen to them tell me about their friends or hear about their schemes while they help me load the dishwasher or mix the batter for banana bread. But the fact of the matter is, I don't have as much undivided time to spend with each child as I did when I had three, or two, or one. And I'm okay with that.

As it turns out, all four of my kids got what they wanted at the park that day. After I pushed Owen on the swing for a few minutes, I caught William coming down the slide—and then William "helped" me catch Owen coming down the slide. Then we moseyed over to the other side of the playground, where I gave the big kids fifteen or twenty spins on the dizzying tire swing while their little brothers laughed on the sidelines. Yes, everybody had to wait, and yes, everybody got less of my time than they would have if there had just been one of them. But what they lost in attention from me, they gained in the joy of spinning and sliding with their brothers.

Giving Them the Time They Need

Of course, all kids need one-on-one time and attention sometimes, and living in a big family can make that a challenge. Here are some ideas for making sure each child in your family gets enough of "you":

Take a different child along each time you run errands. When you have a baby in the house, it's often tempting to take her everywhere you go, but try leaving the youngest home with your spouse and take your middle or older children to the store or bank. Small babies often seem to need Mom the most, but a solo trip with you will help your bigger kid more than your short absence will hurt the baby. "In our family, each child other than the baby gets special time every weekend. We manage this three weekends out of four. Even if it's going to the grocery store 'just with Dad,' it's special time," says Cindy, mom of eight.

Express love—lots of it. "That's something my husband and I put as our first priority. We act very loving with each other, to show them that Mommy and Daddy love each other, and we are very open with each child about how much we love them," says Michelle, who has four kids.

Even when they're all together, single your kids out often with a compliment or comment meant only for them. I make sure to say each child's name and ask a specific question, meant only for him, during family mealtimes or when they come in the house after school. I ask everyone else in the family to be quiet while that child answers my question; if I didn't ask for quiet, the more talkative kids in our house would jump all over themselves to interrupt, and one of the kids might not feel heard. I even do this with my youngest son, though he can't talk at all yet. I want to make sure he doesn't grow up feeling like he can't get a word in edgewise.

Eat dinner as a family as often as you can. There's a wealth of evidence linking the family meal to lower incidences of drug use, pregnancy, and other risky behaviors in teens. When you eat dinner together, you have a chance to sit face-to-face with the people in your family, making eye contact and connecting with everyone individually and as a group.

Multitask. Most of us have at least one or two times each day where our bodies are occupied, but not our mouths or brains. Long walks or bike rides and chore time are perfect opportunities to connect with your kids, maybe one or two at a time.

Make yourself available. "Every now and then I go to bed really early and then lay in bed," says Cindy, a mom of eight kids. "Each child has ten to fifteen minutes of time to come in and talk about anything they want to. They love those times—they have my undivided attention, and anything is fair game to talk about." Cindy admits that she has to set aside at least an hour to give each child his or her time!

Focus. If a child comes to you with a problem or question, remove yourself from visual or mental distractions. Put down your book, set your laptop aside, turn off the TV, or move your chair away from the computer, and listen until he's done. "When any child comes to me for any reason, I work hard to give them my total attention until they are done with their question or need," says Cindy.

Take advantage of snippets of time. When you've got a baby in the house, finding time for older siblings can be really hard, so you may have to get creative and make it very clear to your other children that, though you'll be busy with the baby and that may make it difficult for you to go to them, they can always come to you. Minutes just before bed and early in the morning are sometimes more convenient for setting aside time to spend one-on-one with children. "My four-year-old and I share some sweet early-morning moments when she comes in my room before anyone else wakes up," says Angie, a mom of six.

Get creative. "Each year for Valentine's Day, we would give the kids a card filled with coupons we made," says Sharon, mom of five grown kids. "The coupons were for things like 'Go out to dinner alone with Dad,' 'Go to the movies with Mom,' or 'Spend an afternoon with Mom and Dad at the park.' The kids could 'spend' their coupons over the next year. They had to give us a bit of notice, but the coupons were specifically for one-on-one time and the other kids stayed home. All of the kids really loved getting their yearly coupons and always used them."

Tell them you love them unequally. "I love all of you the same" isn't what your kids want to hear, says Elisa Medhus, M.D., mother of five and author. "Kids want to feel they have a unique relationship with you." Medhus makes sure her kids know what she thinks is special about each of them. Medhus also employs a "Buddy Day" every week with each of her five children—on that child's day, a brief one-on-one outing with Mom is the highest priority.

Realize that time doesn't have to be scheduled or focused on play to be "quality." Chatting with your child as you ride in the car together counts and so does cuddling up on the couch and reading, even if you're reading two different books. Often just being together is enough. Closeness and touch can speak louder than words.

Know what matters to your child. "I try to keep up with what's going on personally with them in their little social lives," says Shelley, mom of five. "Just being able to talk with them about what really matters to them seems to do the trick. Let's face it, we don't have a lot of time with each one. But they know I'm paying attention when I ask them about specific things going on with them. Then, they speak up about the other things going on that I don't already know."

Above all, don't listen to critics who say that kids in big families are shortchanged by not having enough time with their parents. Most people I know with lots of kids spend just as much time with them collectively—and sometimes a lot more time—than the parents I know with fewer kids. It's all relative, and a larger number of kids doesn't necessarily mean less time available for each kid as long as we are mindful to make ourselves available—as any parent should be!

Helping Your Kids Be Themselves

How many of you remember being referred to as "Becky's sister" or "Bill's brother" instead of, well, yourself? It's an unfortunate fact that, especially in a bigger family, some people will probably try to lump your kids together or typecast them—the "pretty" one, the "smart" one, the "athletic" one—based on their own assumptions. Of course, kids in big families have their own distinct personalities, but you might wonder how to help your child's identity really shine, especially if she's shy, quiet, or following in the shadow of a particularly well-liked older sibling.

"We encouraged the kids to be involved in their own activities and pursue their own interests," says Cindy, a mom of eight children. To do that, she had to think creatively about ways to foster independence and individuality in some of her kids. "One of our daughters was very dependent on her sister, so we asked the school to separate them so that the dependent child would develop her own friends and interests," says Cindy. And, because her adopted children originated from two different birth families, Cindy noticed that people would often try to categorize "Someone would say 'X and Y really love ballet' and I'd say, 'No, X loves ballet, but Y actually has no interest in it. She loves reading.' Gradually, people quit seeing them as two groups of kids and saw them as individuals instead."

Sometimes, making a real effort to support and nurture each child's unique personality can give him the courage and confidence to carry that identity out into the world—no matter what assumptions other people might make about him. "I get to know who each child is, and have everyone in the family relate to them as a real person, not a type," says Angie, mom of six kids. "I try to encourage their interests. For example, my oldest is really interested in cooking, and I buy her ingredients to experiment with to hone her skills. My eleven-year-old started a club that meets twice a month, and I take him on numerous trips to the store to prepare for his meetings. My six-year-old is interested in accomplishing things—she's determined to learn to play the piano, to speak Spanish, to do handstands and bridges. I teach her what I know and cheer her on in what I don't. My four-year-old is very interested in nature, and I gave her a box to collect items from our walks together. My two-year-old is athletic, so I like to teach him to play kickball, soccer, basketball, and bowling. The baby is just getting into the swing of things. I try to pick up on her cues to be snuggled—or left alone."

Does Birth Order Matter?

How much stock you put in birth order stereotypes might depend on whether you identify strongly with wherever you wound up in your family's lineup. I was the baby of my family and had a lot of the personality traits we babies are supposed to have: creative, easily bored, and extroverted. And taking a close glance at my family, it seems my kids fall into pretty typical birth-order patterns, too: my oldest son is serious, a perfectionist, a worrier, and a nurturer. My second son (first middle) tends to be reserved and unexpressive; it's easy to overlook his feelings, and he has tried hard to set himself apart from his older brother. My third youngest son is the family clown, making everybody laugh. And the baby of the family is definitely outgoing.

But then, they have a fair number of the "wrong" personality traits for their birth order, too. Jacob, the oldest, isn't particularly driven—at least not yet. My second-born isn't a people-pleaser. My third born isn't at all a "lost" middle child. And it's too soon to tell for sure with the baby of the family, but so far he's not all that laid back. Researchers disagree on how much importance birth order really has in a child's developing personality. Critics of birth-order research say that other factors, like child spacing, familial relationships, and economic circumstances when each child gets added to the family, make a bigger difference. And your own birth order may affect how you'll relate to your children, too: a firstborn may feel more sympathetic toward her firstborn child, while a middle child may feel a connection to his middle children.

But while the jury is still out on whether birth order really predicts personality, some of the personality traits just make common sense. For instance, firstborns are often said to be controlling, but it only makes sense that an older child would try to use his size and age to his advantage when establishing a pecking order among his brothers and sisters. And if middle children get "lost," it's probably because they never get the one-on-one time with their parents that comes with the experience of being either the only baby in the house or the last baby in the house. As for the baby of the family, well, I can say from experience that we often do get picked on, and our parents may be so tired by the time we come around that we get away with a lot more!

Birth-order stereotypes aren't a hard science, but they do provide an interesting context in which you can consider your children's behavior and personality traits. For instance, knowing that my oldest son is likely to feel put-upon or take on a lot of responsibility for his younger siblings makes me more conscientious about dividing the load fairly between him and his brothers. And understanding that my middle kids might feel left out has given me extra incentive to get one-on-one time with both of them, asking about their feelings and connecting with them. And as for my youngest, I'm aware that my "baby of the family" status might prompt me to empathize with him more than the other kids in the family, so I'll be careful not to let that affect the way I parent him—or the rest of them.

I'll also take care to make sure he learns to do things for himself before he leaves the house; having a lot of big siblings around, I've noticed, means that the baby of the house often never has to lift a finger! My sister's baby, the youngest of four, didn't learn to crawl until long after his first birthday.

While some babies just don't crawl until after a year, Quin didn't even try—all he had to do was look at a toy and half-heartedly reach for it, and one of his big sibs would grab it for him.

If your household includes adopted or stepchildren, these additions can really throw a wrench in your birth-order assumptions because a middle child in your house may have been a firstborn in her birth family. "We have adopted children who were firstborn but are the fifth or eighth child in our household," says Cindy, mom of eight kids. Some of her adopted children fit the stereotype that goes along with their placement in their family, while others fit the stereotype of their birth order. Others don't fit any stereotype at all. "They are who they are, and we find ways to encourage them in their strengths," says Cindy.

Carmen, who has five kids, says that her kids do fit into the birth-order stereotypes pretty well but that hasn't been a problem in her household. "My oldest is the book-smart, straight-As, honor role kid-typical firstborn overachiever. My next child is a typical middle child—wants attention and gets it through questionable behavior. The next one is a typical middle child but is a mama's girl and very opinionated. And the youngest is trying to constantly get one over on the other ones and me. But my kids have no major problems with identity; they are very much their own people."

Sibling Relationships: Beyond Rivalry

One of the best things about having a big family is the tremendous gift a child with lots of siblings has—a large, built-in support system that can last his whole life through. Of course, turning out kids who enjoy and get along with their brothers and sisters enough to stay close their whole lives can seem like an impossibly lofty goal when they regularly bicker. But siblings can, and very often do, get past rivalry to become the best of friends. Here are some tips from experienced parents of big families—some with adult children who have remained close—on how to keep kids from fighting like cats and dogs and how to help them form close bonds that will last a lifetime.

Do things as a family. "Expect your kids to help each other even if they complain. Make sure you create opportunities for all of them to get together during the year—Christmas, birthdays, and other holidays—when they get older."—Shirley, mom of five grown kids.

"Too often these days families spend so much time apart, especially with all the activities to choose from for kids. We participate in some activities—swim lessons, scouts—but we also make time with the family a priority."—Michelle, mom of four.

Do things everyone loves. "I always get everyone together for board games, hot dog and marshmallow roasts, stories, dancing—something that we all love to do and do well as a family. I include everyone in most everything we do, like kids' ballgames and school performances." —Sheryl, mom of six.

Don't take no for an answer. "My husband got down on the floor and taught the little girls to play together and to be best friends when they were very young: two and four. He played with them and taught them to take turns and share by modeling it and directing it. Now, two years later, they are inseparable. He also insisted that the 15-year-old stick up for the 11-year-old when they were very young, seven and four. All of the children are strongly encouraged to be kind and loving and helpful for their younger siblings. Even the two-year-old is gentle and loving to his baby sister."—Angie, mom of six.

Establish a buddy system. "We have a buddy system in our house. Since we have four older children and four younger children, every Monday the older children have a new, younger buddy. So for that week, they do a great deal of taking care of that younger child—getting them what they need, changing diapers, helping them get dressed. That one on one time has been invaluable in creating close bonds between them all. The little ones look up to and always want the attention of their older siblings and the older kids adore their little siblings; because of the special needs of several of our children, our other children are learning very valuable lessons about people that are 'different' and how to relate to them. I think their compassion and understanding is wonderful and will help them throughout their lives. Our children are very close and readily available to help each other whenever needed. They all play together daily and help each other 'grow up'—that's one of the wonderful strengths of home-schooling."—Cindy, mom of eight.

Baby-Sitting Little Sibs: How Much Care is Fair?

The American public—particularly those of us who have, or want to have, really big families—was fascinated by the Discovery Channel show about the Duggars, a family in Arkansas with 16 kids. But when I discussed the Duggar family with other parents, many of them protested passionately over the fact that in the Duggar household, the children have work to do—real work, the kind that actually helps to keep the home functioning, not playing at sweeping with a toy broom.

And that work includes helping out with younger brothers and sisters. The older kids help out, in part, by bathing and dressing their little siblings and helping care for them, using a system that pairs older kids with little ones. The very idea seemed foreign and antiquated—cruel, even—to some of my friends. "When do those kids get to be kids?" they asked. "Why should they have to do the parents' job?"

But I see it a little differently. With today's brand of competitive hyper-parenting, many parents spend an inordinate amount of time worrying about how to make their kids smarter, more musical, more athletic—more likely to be successful. Our kids are no longer expected to help run the household; now they are household projects in and of themselves. It may look like we're giving them more, but are we really giving them what they need to be successful adults?

It's not enough that kids get into an Ivy League school or become accomplished pianists or athletes. Part of becoming a happy, competent, and just plain good person is learning to care for others, share the work-load, or put somebody else's needs before one's own. What about the satisfaction of knowing they're valuable, needed members of a household?

Most of us don't have huge families like the Duggars anymore, and many of us enjoy spending our disposable income on our kids and having more one-on-one time to lavish on each child. And that's fine. But in removing all responsibility from childhood, something has been lost: a sense of purpose, some perspective that will help them be more compassionate, responsible, and selfless.

When I ask my older sons to help out with their younger siblings now and then, I'm hardly wrecking the mostly care-free childhood they most certainly enjoy. But I hope I'm teaching them an important lesson about putting someone else's needs above their own.

So is it not fair—there's that f-word again!—to expect my kids to help care for their siblings? I don't think so. The way I look at it, we're all a family, and we all have to pitch in to keep the family functioning. Part of the "work" involved with being a family is caring for the youngest members. As those youngest members grow up, we will find other work for them that helps to support the family.

Eventually, my older kids will be out of the house, and the younger ones won't have little brothers to care for. With fewer people in the house, their workload will no doubt be less than it was for their big brothers. But I really think that they are the ones who will be missing out, not the other way around! I guess we'll have to regularly borrow younger cousins to look after—otherwise, how will my youngest learn how to change diapers or burp a baby?

That said, it's very possible to take the concept of older siblings helping out with younger siblings too far. You can't blame kids who feel bitter or resentful if they're expected to be second parents to the younger ones—after all, they didn't ask for a bunch of siblings, and every kid deserves a chance to be just a kid.

But a lot of teens don't mind watching their younger siblings from time to time—some may even want to do it—and having a baby-sitter living right in your house can be really convenient. Here are some ways you can keep from expecting too much from your teen as a built-in baby-sitter:

Be age-appropriate. A preteen may not be mature enough to be left home alone with the kids, which is unfortunate, because they often make the most eager and fun baby-sitters. But preteens can be very good mother's helpers, keeping the little ones out of your hair while you check your e-mail or get dinner on the table. Just make sure you aren't expecting too much: though your preteen may seem mature in comparison to younger kids, he is still forming critical judgment skills and may be easily frustrated, distracted, or worn out by watching a busy youngster. If your smallest children are still at the "running out in the street" or "sticking chokable objects in mouth" age, you may want to keep a very watchful eye while your preteen gets used to baby-sitting.

Make sure they're ready for it. Will your younger children recognize their big brother or sister as an authority figure? If your younger kids see the sibling in charge as just 'one of the kids,' there is likely to be a serious breakdown in the chain of command the minute you leave the house. Trouble establishing authority is more likely to be a problem between a teen and the older kids in the house than it is to be between a teen and the baby of the family, so it might be a good idea to ease your teen into sitting by having her watch a younger child first, and seeing how that goes. And make sure you think as critically about your own teen as you would any other sitter you were considering hiring: are you sure she'll know what to do in an emergency? Does she know how to call paramedics or what to do if there's an accident or fire?

Be mindful of their "off" time. "Jacob, will you keep an eye on Owen while I use the bathroom?" "Jacob, will you help Owen get out of his high chair?" "Jacob, will you play with Owen for me while I fold this laundry?"

There's nothing wrong with asking for a hand from the older kids every now and then, and in our house, nobody seems to mind playing with the baby. But my oldest son Jacob is so eager to please and agreeable when I ask him to do something that it's sometimes only too easy to lean on him more than I probably should. When I notice myself doing that, I always take a minute to tell him that I realize I have been asking a lot of him, that I appreciate his help, and that he's free to go have some time to himself … while I make very sure to keep the little ones from following him. It's not always easy to be the oldest of four, and though I know I'll screw up and expect too much from Jacob at times, at the very least I can let him know that I don't take him for granted.

Pay them. If you had another teen come into the house to baby-sit your kids, you'd pay them, right? Paying your own kids on the occasions that you do ask them to baby-sit can go a long way toward keeping the older child from feeling used—as well as giving them incentive to do a good job. Some parents consider sibling care to be part of what a teen is expected to do in exchange for his allowance, but I think it's smart to separate out regular allowance from baby-sitting pay. It's a psychology thing: even if you know in your head that part of the child's allowance is earned through baby-sitting, he's likely to see it as an extra service he provides for free on top of his other chores—especially if he's the only one in the house old enough to baby-sit.

Give notice … and/or allow your teen to opt out. Though there are times when emergencies come up and you don't have prior warning, it's not fair to repeatedly spring baby-sitting on your teen, who probably has plans of his own. If you can give him a few days' notice, he'll be able to arrange his evening to accommodate your plans. You can also encourage your teen to partner up with another friend you trust for tag-team sitting. That way, if your son isn't available on a night you need a sitter, his friend can pinch-hit; and when his friend needs a backup, your teen can step in. When they're both available, they can keep each other company on the job (though you may want to hide the snacks).

Don't use baby-sitting as punishment or consequences for misbehavior, bad grades, or as a way to "earn back" privileges. Mopping the floors, yes. Washing the car, okay. Caring for little siblings—never! This is a sure way to breed resentment between brothers and sisters, and besides, if a kid feels surly and indignant about having to baby-sit, he'll probably do a crummy job of it.

Redefine baby-sitting. Here's the situation: you want to run a few errands sans children. Your eleven-year-old is eager to baby-sit her five-year-old sister and eight-year-old brother, but is too young to be left home alone with them. Your sixteen-year-old would rather not be bothered with entertaining the tots, but will be home and available. Why not make your eleven-year-old the "baby-sitter" and your sixteen-year-old the "house-sitter," and let them split the fee? That way, each child gets what he wants: your preteen gets to earn some cash and feel like a responsible adult, your teen gets to earn money without actually having to play with the little kids, and you have two people in charge—one who will gladly play with the younger children, and one who will be responsible if there's an emergency.

What About Mom and Dad?

"How do you find time to keep making them?" a stranger asked me one day. She was, of course, referring to my children. I suppose she thought that having kids makes it impossible to find enough time for romance to create more of them. Obviously, she was wrong in addition to being rude.

But fundamentally, I suppose she had a good question: how *do* parents of many kids keep their own relationships strong?

I've never been big on "date night." For one thing, finding a sitter who's willing to take on four kids—and who doesn't charge a week's pay for it—isn't always easy. My eldest son isn't old enough to baby-sit yet. And when you take into account the hassle of finding the sitter, leaving instructions, making plans, and getting everyone settled down for the sitter; and then when you factor in the expense of paying for the sitter and whatever it is you're planning to do outside of the house ... well, "date night" loses its luster pretty fast.

That's not to say my husband and I never go out alone. Sometimes, when we've been lucky enough to find a local and willing baby-sitter or during periods of positive cash-flow, we've gone on quite a few dates. But honestly, having a date night hasn't made much of a difference in the state of our relationship, either way: when we're feeling connected, date night is the icing on the cake, but we can also be pretty happy hanging out at home watching HBO after the kids fall asleep.

We might both sigh aloud that we'd like to get some time away, but our motivation is that we both want to eat a nice dinner, share a drink, see a show, listen to some music, or just have some peace and quiet—not that we feel like our relationship is unraveling because we "only" get to see each other at home. And when we're out of sync—and yes, we've definitely been there—a date night doesn't solve whatever problems are lurking beneath the surface.

And though I understand the reasoning behind the advice that parents should 'put the marriage before the kids,' I don't like the idea of pitting my kids against my husband as if it's some kind of competition. I don't put my husband "first" or "last" any more than I rank my kids in order of importance.

Of course, it's important to put in the effort to keep your marital relationship strong. Not only is it the best thing for you and your spouse, but your kids also deserve an intact family if it's at all possible for you to give them one, and they'll learn a lot about healthy adult relationships by watching you relate to each other. But my point is that even if regular date nights aren't an option for you, you can do many different things to keep that connection alive.

Speak each other's "love languages." And let's face it, ladies, that means making sex a priority—or at least ranking it somewhere above clipping your toenails or bleaching the trash can. When you've got small children clamoring for your attention, it isn't always easy to get in the mood—believe me, I get it! But for your husband, sex isn't just a shallow pastime. If you just can't get on board for an hour-long romance-a-thon, try surprising him with a quickie in the bathroom. Taking away the pressure of always having to initiate will mean a lot to him. And the chances of parents of a lot of kids regularly finding an hour for sex is pretty unusual, anyway.

At the same time, gentlemen, figure out what it is your wife needs. Physical affection, and yes—communication—are probably important to her. And it wouldn't kill you to make an effort to keep up with stuff your wife needs you to do around the house without tying it directly to some kind of sexual trade-off. Nothing kills the mood like a man doing the dishes only because he expects to get some nookie as a reward. On the other hand, watching him mop the floor because he just wants to make her life easier can be a very powerful aphrodisiac.

Go high-tech. Use the power of technology to stay in touch while one or both of you are at work. E-mail, instant messaging, text messaging … chances are good you have access to at least one of these forms of communication. Use them to send practical, silly, and romantic messages to each other throughout the day. A big plus—the kids can't hear what you're saying.

Go to bed together. Even if you have little kids who aren't on a regular sleep schedule, even if one of you has work to do late at night, make an effort to at least go into the bedroom together for a little while before one of you goes to sleep. This is probably the quietest, calmest time of the day for both of you, and it's a perfect opportunity to talk about what's going on in your lives or just watch TV together without a constant flow of kids running in and out. "I think TiVo saved my marriage," jokes Ron, father of five kids ages 8 and under. He says that bedtime can be so crazy some nights that he and his wife rarely knew when they would be off-duty for the evening … and by the time they got in bed and started flipping through channels, there would be nothing but half-finished shows they had no interest in watching. "Before you knew it one of us would be snoring and the other one was checking e-mail or reading." But then Ron started recording reruns of their favorite sci-fi show, which comes on too early in the evening for them to catch. "Now we know no matter what time we get to bed, we've got an hour of good television ahead of us, and we never miss a night. It's incredible how fun it can be just to lay next to each other and watch a good show."

Stake a claim on some couple time. Unless all of your kids are very young, chances are good your oldest ones are responsible enough to take over for a few minutes so that you and your spouse can have some private time, whether it's for romance or just talking about practical matters. A good time for this is right after dinner. The kids won't be hungry, so they won't bug you for food. You'll both be fed, so you won't be irritable. And it's not too late in the evening, so neither of you will be too tired.

Make time for your friends. It might seem counter-intuitive, but one of the best ways to keep your marriage strong is to take time away from it. No person can be everything to another, and especially if one of you stays home with the kids, your need for adult conversation and companionship can become intense—too intense for just one person to fill. Keep your outside friendships strong so that you always have somebody to talk to about the things that matter to you and do the things you love with—especially the things your spouse isn't as interested in. And if you encourage your spouse to do the same, the two of you can save your time together for conversations and activities that you're both into.

Don't be afraid to draw boundaries. When you have a house full of kids, it's only too easy to let them run all over your personal space and time. If you can't get your kids to respect your couple time or requests to be alone, you may have to set some firm rules. Some parents don't ever allow kids in their bedroom. Others have a lock on the door, and they use it. Or a "do not disturb" doorknob sign like they have in hotels may work. Do whatever it takes to get the message across that Mom and Dad aren't to be disturbed.

Make sure you're both on the same page when it comes to birth control and the possibility of more pregnancies. Even if you aren't ready to say "all done" when it comes to having more kids, the fear of becoming pregnant again before you're ready can put a serious damper on your love life. This can be especially intense while you've got a baby or young toddler—you're still trying to get some semblance of a figure back, you may be nursing and not sleeping well, and it's hard to get away from the house for more than a few hours at a time. Or perhaps you have a very clear memory of some of the less-pleasant aspects of pregnancy, birth, or postpartum. The idea of starting all over again from scratch can be terrifying, and combined with the libido-lowering hormonal fluctuations that happen during the first year or so after having a baby, for a mom the idea of having sex can be so unappealing as to be practically repulsive. I've explained my intense aversion to sex during the first year or so after a baby is born as something like a biological urge *not* to get pregnant! And then you've got Dad, who, while maybe not relishing the idea of expanding the family at the moment, also doesn't really know what it's like to experience pregnancy, birth, postpartum, nursing, or hormone fluctuations. Oh, no—his hormones are pumping at the same rate as ever!

So what to do about this difference in objectives?

It won't fix the hormone issue, but when Dad takes on some responsibility for family planning, it can help ease Mom's mind ... and that's half the battle. Fathers can buy condoms or help mothers keep track of their birth control pills or devices. Or, if you've chosen to utilize Natural Family Planning, Dad can take over a large part of the charting and record-keeping. The point, dads, is to make sure your wife understands that you aren't under-estimating her desire not to get pregnant again right now, even if you can't quite put yourself in her shoes. I can't guarantee she'll become a tiger right away, but at the very least, she'll appreciate your efforts—and it'll be one less obstacle to your love life.

Have some compassion. When your kids are small, it's easy to get weighed down by the intensive parenting they require. And if your kids are closely-spaced, your relationship may really feel the strain as both of you battle sleep deprivation, exhaustion, and sometimes accompanying anger and resentment ... for months or years on end. And as they grow, the physical demands of caring for lots of children can be replaced by a variety of emotional stresses. Either way, while parenting lots of kids can be wonderful, it can also stretch your patience to its limits—and unfortunately, married couples often take out that stress and anxiety on one another. As tempting as it can be, don't make your interactions a contest of who's working hardest, doing the most, feeling worst, or sleeping least. Instead, assume that your spouse has good intentions—even if you're pretty certain the workload isn't divided fairly—and come to discussions from that perspective. Remember the ubiquitous "I" statement: it's a lot more effective to say something like "I feel frustrated when I come home from work and the house is a pigsty," than "You never do anything around here," which will probably just lead to hurt feelings and defensiveness.

Ladies, you should be especially careful to watch out for passive-aggressive displays like slamming doors; eye-rolling; and huffing, puffing, and loud sighs. Half the time, men don't even notice the high-drama performance you're putting on for their benefit, which just leads to more frustration and resentment on your part. If you've got something to say, say it—calmly and directly. Otherwise, your husband really might have no idea how you feel.

Remember why you made all those kids in the first place. Don't become so focused on caring for your children that you forget why you started having them! When you were first married, you probably dreamed about having children to enhance your marital relationship, not to replace it. Every member of your family is important—and that should definitely include your partner. Your family is more than a collection of people: together, you're a unit, and each part of the unit has to be healthy in order for the whole family to be happy. By being careful to make sure everyone's individual needs are met, you'll go a long way toward having a big, happy Table for Eight family.

Having Fun

After my fourth child was born, I started dreaming about taking the whole family on a cruise vacation within a few years. So I logged on to the website for a popular cruise line to get a ballpark figure to work around.

I selected two adults—no problem. But when I tried to select four children, the web interface would only allow for three. That was my first indication that traveling with four kids might have just put me in a whole new world of inconvenience and cost.

Since then, we've made a fair number of hotel reservations and keep running into the same trouble. The reservation interfaces all seem to think I should pay an extra fee for the additional two children beyond the two they allow for (though they won't use any more space than the rest of us), or sometimes they tell me there are *no* available rooms to accommodate us and try to get me to book two rooms. Sometimes I fudge when I'm booking, reserving it for two adults and two children, and then spend the time until the trip worrying that I'll get busted when we check in. Perhaps we're a fire hazard, six people squeezed into two beds, but four of the people are pretty small and I'd rather have them right alongside me in case of a fire than in an adjoining room. And I really didn't want to sleep in one room with two of the kids while my husband takes another.

From hotel rooms planned for no more than four people, to figuring out how to get there, to taking a vacation without going into debt … no doubt about it, traveling with a big family can present some big challenges. In this chapter we look at some ways big families can take vacations—whether they're roughing it or traveling in style—without busting their budgets or (usually) breaking occupancy rules.

Where to Go?

If you just can't afford a Disney vacation for your whole family—or simply live too far away to make the trip—you still have many affordable options. But be careful: some theme parks are a bummer for larger families—they're often focused on thrill rides for big folk, leaving smaller kids without much to do except stand around and wither in the heat.

One easy winner for our family vacations—which often includes not just me and my kids but also my sister and her teenagers—is the indoor water park. The temperature is always balmy; you don't have to worry about rain; and there is usually plenty to do for everyone in the family, including Mom and Dad. If you book a room in a hotel/water park combination, you can go easily from your room to the park without having to leave the building or even getting dressed! Plus, a lot of water park/hotel combinations seem specially-made for big families, offering suite accommodations including fun bunk-style rooms for the kids.

The Oak Haven Resort near the Great Smoky Mountains National Park in Sevierville, Tennessee offers deluxe cabins fit for a big family—up to seven bedrooms, each with a 4-6 person hot tub on a screened porch, good-size beds, a playground, gameroom, pool, and more. For a really big family, these jumbo-size cabins offer a great value. The website can be found at www.oakhavenresort.com.

The Lake Mancos Ranch in southwestern Mancos, Colorado offers an authentic, family-friendly dude ranch experience for your big clan. Cabins are spacious, with two to three bedrooms, a separate living area, and two private bathrooms. There's lots for kids to do, like river rafting, a nearby national park to explore, family horseback rides, swimming, hayrides, fishing, panning for gold and other kid-friendly activities. Considering that the prices include all meals, activities, and gratuities, the cost is very reasonable—and young kids get a discount. The website is www. lakemancosranch.com.

Great Wolf Lodge, a family-friendly hotel/water park, currently has locations in Kansas, Ohio, Pennsylvania, Michigan, Texas, Virginia, Wisconsin, Washington, and Niagara Falls, Canada. Large rooms are expensive compared to regular hotel rooms but include admission to the water park and can be a surprisingly economical big-family weekend getaway. Visit the webssite www. greatwolf.com.

As theme park admission prices go, Holiday World in Santa Claus, Indiana, is about middle-of-the-road. But where Holiday World pays off big for large families is its refusal to nickel and dime you: once you're inside the park, food is reasonably priced and you get unlimited soft drinks or water for free. The park is well-landscaped, including plenty of shady areas to get out of the sun. It features plenty of thrilling rides for big kids, several play areas, and lots of rides for little ones. Holiday World includes a huge water park where you can get free sunscreen. If you figure that a typical theme park charges a few bucks a pop for a cup of soda or a bottle of water, you can see that free drinks can offer significant savings for a big family. Kids' tickets are discounted; babies under two are free; and you can purchase a next-day ticket for about half the cost of standard admission. The website is www.holidayworld.com.

The Oakland House Seaside Resort in Brooksville, Maine is an old-fashioned seaside resort where families can kick back, relax, and enjoy activities like kayaking, badminton, hiking trails, and more. Cottages can accommodate up to nine people. Prices include breakfast, dinner, housekeeping, and use of recreational facilities. Children under two are very inexpensive, kids from 2-5 are half the adult rate, and 6-11 are ⅔ the adult rate. Visit the website at www.oaklandhouse.com.

Resorts and Cruises

Many all-inclusive cruise vacations and resorts include tips, meals, beverages, and transportation, so you won't have to worry about digging into your pocket again and again. You will probably have to pay for things like recreational vehicles or in-port tours, however. Check carefully to see what's included in your resort or cruise before you book—sometimes, travelers are surprised by charges they thought would be covered.

Crystal Cruises offers connecting staterooms for big families; classes and activities that appeal to kids of all ages as well as adults; all-inclusive dining options including Kosher, low-carb, vegetarian, sugar free, and gluten-free meals; and child care. Families up to 14 can reserve a private room for dinners, and a Junior Activities Director will meet with your family privately at the beginning of the cruise to plan your stay.

Getting There

Where you're going probably isn't as hard a question as just how you're going to get there. Maybe your destination is an easy afternoon's drive or maybe you're looking at a longer trip.

By Air

Flying can be incredibly expensive for a big family. It may make more sense to start by looking for inexpensive places or dates for a flight, and then working from there to schedule a vacation around it. If you're thinking of using an Internet discount travel planning service, you may have to think again: Expedia and Travelocity allow you to book flights for a maximum of six people. Priceline will reserve tickets for up to eight people, while Orbitz.com will book for up to nine.

Keep in mind that airports generally aren't family-friendly places. For example, during a recent flight to California and back, during which I spent serious time in five major airports, I was unable to find one reasonably quiet place to nurse a baby, and even family restrooms were few and far between. Considering long waits for security, the long layovers that often accompany discounted tickets, and even the wait for your luggage to show up on the other end, flying may not be that much of a quicker or easier way to get to your destination unless you're traveling cross-country.

You'll also have to keep in mind what you'll do when you get to your destination. Will you bring all your car and booster seats, or rent them at your destination along with a vehicle? You can purchase a padded, protective container for car seats and boosters for about $35. That will keep them from getting damaged while being checked or while they're in the cargo area, and they are usually on wheels, which makes carting them around the airport a breeze. Most car rental companies will rent you car seats and boosters for an additional cost, but you may be more comfortable using your own—particularly because you probably won't have time to check whether the rental agency's car seat has been recalled, and you can't be absolutely sure it's never been in an accident, which could render it unsafe for use.

If you're flying, you may also want to allow extra time for recovering from the trip before jumping head-first into your planned activities. Flying can be hard on everyone, and it's likely to take you a long while to get off the plane, gather up your entire family's luggage, rent your car or find your shuttle, and get to wherever you're staying. By that point, you're likely to be bushed. "We usually plan a very low-key first evening," says Laura, mom of four kids including two teenagers. "Basically, we sit around the hotel watching a movie, playing board games, and eating snacks. Our older kids like to get away from the family a little after all that travel, so we let them go down to the lobby with a deck of cards or down to the pool. That way they get a little space and the younger kids get enough rest to be back to their normal selves the next day."

If you do choose air travel, remember to bring things to keep your kids occupied—giving each of them their own backpack stashed with snacks, water, books, and quiet toys is your best bet. Ask to preboard so that you can be sure to sit together and get settled in before the rest of the passengers come in. Note: be sure to check security rules before you arrive at the airport to make sure you can bring bottled water and other liquids aboard.

mom wisdom

"Air fares are a tough nut to crack if you want to go a long distance—we've had great success in starting looking for fares early, like six months ahead of time. We've traveled to Denver and Seattle in the last five years and never paid over $200 per ticket. Try searching at 1:00 A.M., when unused seats come back into the airlines' computer systems."

—Jackie, mom of eight, Florida

By Train

Traveling by rail isn't cheap, but it does offer glimpses of beautiful scenery, and the trip can offer a great experience in itself! Amtrak offers discounts for children—though only two children per adult qualify for the discounted rate—and AAA members. If you travel by train, don't book any activities or other transportation too close to your arrival time; Amtrak is notorious for running behind schedule. Be sure you're seated as close to the snack car as possible to avoid having to schlep all your kids back and forth between several cars every time they want something to eat. Better yet, pack your own snacks—the snack car can get very crowded during train trips and often has long lines. Meals are served on a schedule in the dining car. The food is generally kid-friendly, but get there early to avoid long waits for hungry kids.

If you need extra space, consider booking a sleeping room. A family bedroom sleeps two adults and two children, but you can book coach seats for some of your family and trade off using the beds. Sleeper cars also include shower facilities. Plan to book these way in advance, though, because they tend to go quickly.

Again, because Amtrak trains are so likely to run behind schedule, it's probably best to look at a train trip—particularly a long one with multiple stops—as a vacation in and of itself rather than a way to get to a destination. That way, everybody can just enjoy the sights, sounds, and scenery instead of stressing out about how long it's taking to "get there." For more information on rates, routes, and special offers, check out www.amtrak.com.

By Car

Generally, the most economical way to get a big family where you're going is to drive. For a lot of families, "getting there is half the fun," and driving allows you the freedom to stop at that great-looking family restaurant when everybody's getting hungry or to pull over to take a gander at the world's largest ball of lint and other great scenic stops along the way.

Unfortunately, driving can also take a long time, and bickering kids in the back seat can test any parent's patience. Here are a few tips for making your road trip as painless as possible.

One great way to drive on a long vacation and save money on hotel costs at the same time is to rent an RV or recreational vehicle. It might cost a thousand dollars or more to rent a large-size RV for a week's vacation, but even considering RV rates at campgrounds, that could be significantly less than seven nights' worth of hotel rooms for your whole family. June through August is the most expensive time for RV rental, so if you have flexibility to travel during other times of the year, you may be able to score quite a deal. Visit www.cruiseamerica.com for rates and info.

Pay careful attention to seating. It's often best to put a big kid next to a little kid if possible. That way, the bigger kid can tend to any emergency needs the smaller sibling might have. (Ever tried to console a screaming toddler unable to reach his sippy cup while you're driving 70 MPH down a busy freeway?) Also, big kids are a lot less likely to bicker with a baby sibling, and the younger kids are unlikely to say "Mom, she's *touching* me" if they're beside a considerably older sibling.

Music soothes. Bigger kids and teens will be a lot happier if they can listen to their own music, so it's probably worth investing in headphones and an MP3 player or personal CD player for them, if they don't have one already.

Take along a movie. A lot of families swear by portable DVD players for showing movies on long trips. One family reported bringing along two DVD players on each trip—one for the bigger kids and one for the younger ones.

Bring along your own munchies. Pack snacks that are easy to open, and avoid messy snacks that might spill all over the car if you hit a bump. Instead of buying soft drinks, bring water bottles and refill them at rest areas. You can also bring powdered drink mix to add to your water.

If you must rent ... "Car rentals are tough—not a lot of places rent 12-passenger vans, or if they do, they're really expensive. It just takes a lot of searching; we got an unlimited van rental last summer from Seattle for $1,500 for three weeks. We knew we wanted to do a loop tour of the Northwest and Canada, so we settled on several cities that would make good endpoints and searched for van rentals there."—Jackie, mom of eight, Florida.

Consider a Travel Agent

Due to the popularity of Internet booking sites, the average consumer now has access to some of the discounts that were previously only offered to travel agents. And the difference is? Travel agents make it their job to know when and where to find the best deals, which properties are family-friendly, and how they can help you plan the best vacation for your family within your budget. If you go with a travel agency, you also have a connection with a person who can help with any issues that might come up during the vacation. For example, "If a hotel is oversold, they'll bump the people who booked through the Internet because they're just making one person mad. If they're working with an agency, the relationship is more important—you aren't as low on the food chain," says Joy Thrun of Classic Travel in Okemos, Michigan. Some travel agencies charge small fees for their services, but if they can help you save money, it may be well worth it.

Where to Stay?

As you've probably already figured out, standard hotels aren't always a great option for big families. But look for hotels that offer adjoining rooms or suite-style accommodations with fold-out sofas. If you're okay with sneaking half your family in through the back door, you can also rent a cot or crib or just bring sleeping bags and put some of the kids on the floor.

It's probably worthwhile to get a room with a microwave and mini-fridge, because milk and a box of cereal can feed your whole family breakfast for a few dollars—as opposed to thirty or forty dollars or more to take everyone out to eat. Hotels with free continental breakfast can be a huge money-saver for families with lots of kids. If you plan on staying in the hotel for more than a night, a fridge and microwave are a must. Some extended-stay hotels and suites offer full kitchens, which will allow you to cook whole meals while on vacation … if you really want to, that is!

Also, when you make hotel reservations ask about special deals. "Once, we went to Green Bay for four days and three nights. Our plans were very last-minute, and when we called the hotel, they had just had a cancellation on their king suite," says Marie, who has eight kids. "The room featured a king-size bed with a hot tub, a kitchen, and a large living room with pull-out sofas. Typically," says Marie, "the hotel would have insisted that the family of ten split up into two rooms, but since it was a last-minute cancellation and they were eager to fill the room, the hotel was willing to allow all of us to use it." Because the hotel included an indoor water park, which was free for hotel residents, and the kitchen allowed them to eat inexpensively, they were able to have a Table for Eight vacation on a small budget—just $800 for four days, including gas, food, recreation, and a hotel room for ten people.

mom wisdom

"We're a military family, so we have access to the Armed Forces Vacation Club: www.afvclub.com. Basically, it's timeshares/hotels all over the world that members of the military and their families can rent for $299 a week. They have them near tourist attractions in places like Orlando, Colorado, New York, etc. Most sleep six, some sleep more, and have kitchens. We can also buy gift certificates for other family members. Not many people know about this! Another option for military families are the MWR (Morale, Welfare & Recreation) rentals—you can rent pop-up campers, tents, and other camping gear at lower cost than normal rental places. And, there are military recreation areas like Ft. Fisher, NC, where they have little houses with 3 bedrooms, and garages, and public beach access right across the street. Full kitchens. They go for $600 a week in the summer months—which is a great deal in that area. We stayed with another family and all our kids—the adult couples each had a bedroom, the oldest kids shared a bedroom and the other kids crashed on the sofa beds so it was only $300 a family for a whole week at the beach. Not a bad deal!"

—Katie, mom of four, North Carolina

Bed and Breakfasts

Bed and breakfasts are usually privately owned and may be more flexible about occupancy than a large chain hotel or motel. They also may offer more creative uses of space and be a less expensive option than renting several hotel rooms.

Rent a House

Home or cottage rentals are often a far more economical and practical route for a big family. In most towns with any kind of tourism economy, you can find cabins, cottages, apartments, and entire houses for rent. Check Craigslist (www.craigslist.org) or www.vacationrentals.com for listings of vacation rentals. Just watch out for scammers if you go with a private company or individual.

Consider a Timeshare

Carla, who has four kids, has never spent a single vacation night in a hotel with them. "We have a worldwide timeshare that is large enough for our family and guests," she says. "We travel at least three times a year with the entire family, the children and I travel even more frequently to visit family members. We usually visit Florida, the beaches in South Carolina, Hilton Head Island, etc. Next year, we are planning a family trip to Europe."

Carla says that one big plus of her particular timeshare is that the accommodations are always suited to her family's size—it sleeps twelve. "We travel to resorts and always stay in large apartments with enough space for each person to have his or her own bed." Having a timeshare allows the family to stay in comfort and cook their own food. "We have a house with a full kitchen that's fully stocked. All we have to do is stop at the local grocery store after unpacking, and we don't spend any more money on food than we would at home."

Of course, not all timeshares sleep twelve people, so be sure to do your research to find out exactly what you're getting if you decide to go this route. Timeshares don't come cheap—a new timeshare can cost in the $10,000 range and up, though a resale timeshare is likely to be several thousand dollars less. Beware: timeshare companies are notorious for using high-pressure sales tactics, tacking on a lot of hidden fees, and even running outright scams. Do your research carefully before you even call a salesperson, and always read all the fine print before you sign anything.

Go Camping

Camping can be a fun family activity—but a campground can also serve as an inexpensive place for a Table for Eight family to sleep at night while scoping out local attractions by day. You can pitch tents, park an RV or travel trailer, or, in many campgrounds, stay in a cabin. Check www.gocampingamerica.com or www.koa.com.

Go on Vacation ... in Your Own Town

Okay, this idea might not sound very exciting. But be honest: how often do you really take advantage of everything your own area has to offer? "One time my husband took a week of vacation, but we stayed at home," says Marie, mom of eight. "Each day we planned activities that we normally would not have spent money on, like going to our local $7-per-person water park, riding the city trolley around the downtown area, going to the mini-golf park, going to see the latest Disney movie in a theatre instead of waiting for it to come out on DVD. Since we didn't have to spend money on accommodations, we spent our entire budget on enjoying activities, ordering pizza, and eating out at fun places like Chuck E. Cheese. It was a very inexpensive 'vacation' that the kids still talk about today ... one of the happiest family vacations the kids have ever had. Interestingly, the activity they reminisce most about? The twenty-five-cent trolley ride!"

Stay Focused

It's tempting to think of every vacation as an opportunity for cultural education, adventure, bonding time, relaxation, viewing beautiful scenery, eating fantastic food, visiting historical sites, and taking in kitschy monuments like enormous balls of twine ...

But in reality, a big family already has so much going on just getting from place to place that it's impossible to get all that out of one vacation—or heck, even five vacations! Even if you somehow managed to cram in good food, interesting culture, adventure sports, and hanging around in a hammock, by the time you got to the second day everybody would be so harried that nobody would be having a good time.

Instead, focus on one, or at most, two goals for each day of vacation. Maybe everyone just wants to relax and unwind. In that case, it's unrealistic to also schedule in meals in fancy restaurants or trips to museums, unless you plan to leave most of the kids at the hotel pool with your spouse while you go … (which is always an option!) Or maybe your goal is to show your kids the Grand Canyon or Niagara Falls. In that case, everything else comes second to that goal. The focus for your trip can be as specific as "let each child ride as many rides as he wants," or more vague, like "learn what it was like to live on a pioneer farm." Either way, if you have a goal in mind for each day of the trip, it'll keep you from getting distracted by attractions or options that don't matter to you as much.

Of course, I'm not advocating a highly-scheduled vacation. What fun is that? At the same time, I've noticed that vacations with four children can't have the same kind of meandering aimlessness that I often enjoyed while single or when my oldest son was a baby. It's just not as simple as carting the kids around to where I want them to go anymore, and being goal-oriented helps to keep the vacation from dissolving into a chaotic whine-fest. And make sure that you include your kids in your goal-setting … particularly the big ones. "I try to choose vacation destinations that have a lot of stuff for older and younger kids alike," says Sarah, who has four kids ages 16, 14, 8, and 6. "I find that my younger two are much easier to please, and will do pretty much whatever we ask of them, whereas my 16- and 14-year olds are much more likely to complain and do passive-aggressive things like get ready so slowly they make us all late getting a start on our day. If I include them in planning out the itinerary, even if they don't get to do everything they want to, they seem to feel a sense of control over the trip and are a lot happier and more cooperative."

Keep Your Sense Of Humor

Traveling with kids is always an adventure. Traveling with lots of kids can be an overwhelming cornucopia of noises, sensations, and smells as siblings touch one another without permission, crank up the music on their iPods so loud that everyone inside the car can hear it, cry, whine, snore, complain, eat pungent snack foods, fill their diapers, and remove their smelly shoes … sometimes, all at the same time. The only way to enjoy a big-family vacation is by keeping your sense of humor firmly intact. When your kids look back on a trip later, they'll remember that when things went wrong—sometimes, when every last thing went wrong!—you still laughed and had a good time. Sometimes, the biggest disasters make the best memories later (I can vouch for this, as I look back with very fond memories to the time my family of six drove from Michigan to Florida in 95 degree weather with the air conditioning broken … and then the car's reverse mechanism stopped working, so we had to push the car out of parking spots … and then, there was that incident with my dad and the time-share salesman …) If things go really wrong on your trip, think of it as your contribution to your kids' bank of funny memories. You'll all get decades' worth of fun rehashing the lost luggage, the puke that didn't quite make it out the window, or the hotel that turned out to be a total dive at family parties.

mom wisdom

"Look for deals. When my kids were little, the Marine Corp. Toys for Tots would let us get into Magic Mountain for free if we brought an unwrapped toy worth $5. That would save us lots of money. Disneyland had lockers that you can put food in so you don't have to spend lots of money on food in the park. The kids would each have a budget for souvenirs and could not go above that. Usually it was only a small trinket, but it made them happy."

—Shirley, mom of five grown kids

Advice from a Mega-Traveling Table for Eight Family

Tom and Jackie Lee are parents of eight and experienced travelers. The Lee family has vacationed in a variety of places, from a sheep ranch near San Antonio to a hostel in Banff in Canada. Here, Jackie shares her tips for making the most of a vacation with a big family—from choosing a destination to dealing with the inevitable vacation disillusionment.

Picking a Destination

"We sometimes search for farm or ranch rentals, but not something organized like a dude ranch. We look for family places that the owners are renting out to make a little money. We've stayed on a sheep ranch that had been in the owners' family for 100 years, a farm house on the bluffs of the Mississippi owned by a farmer whose Swiss ancestors had migrated there in the early 1900s, and an old farmhouse in the North Carolina mountains owned by a lawyer in Atlanta and used as a Boy Scout camp, so it had a shooting range, boating pond, and horses available to ride included in the rent. We've found that the best destinations usually lie at the end of a gravel road. Our kids all like the outdoors, and that's mostly where we focus. My husband and our oldest son like aviation/military things, so we've visited our share of plane museums and air force bases."

Finding Deals

"I use the Internet and AAA books to find hotels that allow children under 18 to stay free—not all hotels do. I've saved a lot of money by finding small, nonchain hotels. Also, AAA membership usually gets you a 10 percent discount at most hotels. You take a chance booking a place without seeing it, but I've only had one place I had to cancel when we got there because it was so bad. I usually pick unknown hotels by the website—if they have a good site with photos, I figure they've invested enough money to run the place well. By spending a lot of nights in small hotels on our last trip, we were able to splurge on the hostel in Banff, which, surprisingly, was the most expensive stay on the trip, even in Canadian exchange. However, it is one of the top five hostels in the world, and we did stay in brand-new private cabins."

Staying Sane on the Road

"We've found that about Day Three in a long driving vacation, the whole system will break down—I fall into total despair as to why we ever thought we could do this, the kids are fussy, my husband is out of sorts. But then we always regroup, figure out what we're doing wrong, and things get into a routine from then on. I tried to postpone Day Three this last vacation by spending the first three days on a little farm in Washington, but as soon as we got on the road, Day Three popped its head up, except it happened on Day Six this time! You can't get away from it, so you might as well prepare for it."

Economizing on Food

"We save on food by eating breakfast and lunch out of the ice chest. Our best purchase last trip was a Coleman electric cooler, which plugs either into your cigarette lighter or a standard outlet—eliminates having to fill a cooler with ice every day. At night, we'd buy milk and put it in the freezer in the hotel. In the morning, we'd eat cereal. Lunch is always sandwiches, fruit, and cookies. The kids get pretty sick of the limited lunch menu by the end of the trip, but it's not all that bad, and we can break it up with Subway or Wendy's once in a while. Another thing we do is bring a small microwave along, and bring it into the hotel at night. Then one of the parents goes shopping at the local grocery store for frozen dinners or deli dishes, along with a crudités tray and whatever food we might need for the next day or two, and we nuke dinner in the hotel. We save enough money this way to justify going out to dinner once in a while.

"A National Park Golden Eagle pass is a must on our vacations. We tend to stay away from destinations that cost more than a couple of dollars per person—it just gets too expensive. By using an AAA book and the Internet, we've found plenty of neat places to visit that don't cost a boatload."

Whether you're taking everyone across the country to visit Great Aunt Edna or just want to check out the destinations in your own backyard, traveling with lots of kids can be chaotic, messy, overwhelming, noisy—and fun. Don't let having lots of kids or a limited budget keep you from getting out and seeing the world. You'll run into bumps in the road, but at the end of the journey you and your kids will have great memories to think back on—even if some of those memories are less-than-perfect.

Making Time for Mom

When my youngest baby was a few weeks old, I decided to enjoy a much-needed bath. With my two oldest children home from school for winter break, my two-year-old in a Christmas-cookie induced sugar rush, and a new baby in the house, I really, *really* needed it. I do my best thinking in the tub, and I had several column ideas to mull over and a chapter of this book that I needed to map out mentally. Besides that, I just love the feel of relaxing in the warm water. Luckily, my husband was home to relieve me, so after feeding the baby, I headed for the tub.

The bathtub was full, at a perfect temperature, and scented with relaxing aromatherapy bath gel. I settled back into the warm, fragrant water, stretched out my limbs—sore and kinked from holding and nursing the baby—closed my eyes, and let out a sigh of relief, when ...

I heard the baby crying.

Had this scene unfolded eight years before and had the crying baby been my first son, Jacob, I would have been reaching for the towel. With my second child, Isaac, I might have given Daddy a minute to get it together, but I would have been on-edge and unable to enjoy the bath.

This time, I just turned the water back on so I couldn't hear the crying. When I turned it off—about a minute later—all I heard was luxurious silence (well, besides the inevitable household noise that creates a steady hum in my ears all day, every day. I've gotten good at ignoring that). One of the blessings of being a Table for Eight mom is that I've recognized my limits and realized that taking care of myself is important, too. I no longer worry that a few minutes of crying in Daddy's arms will scar a baby for life; I no longer delude (and disappoint) myself with dreams of a spotless house or gourmet meals on the table every night. I now allow myself space and time and some semblance of an inner life of my own. The challenge is that, while with each child I've added to the family, the more I've recognized and accepted that I have needs too, the more logistically difficult it has become to claim them. It's not always easy to find a sitter for four kids. The older ones have busy social lives and activities of their own. The youngest have basic needs that can seem to take up most of my day. So how is somebody who has kids—let alone a lot of kids—supposed to pay attention to her own needs? Is it really possible to make time for Mom?

Surrender to Motherhood ... but Don't Give Yourself up Entirely

Sometimes a mom gets knee-deep in parenting and is perfectly content to wade right in: I tend to get that way during the last few months of a pregnancy and right after I add a new baby. And that's great. Our kids won't be little forever, and some moms are very happy to shelve their nonmothering ambitions and interests indefinitely. If this is you, *great*. Don't worry, I'm not going to be one of those annoying people who try to tell you that what you really need is to get out of the house more often, that you should hire a babysitter or get a job or take up tennis. If you're happy with what you've got going on, who can argue with that?

But then there are the rest of us. Though, as I said, I tend to dive deeply and happily into pure motherhood for months at a time, something else is still always hiding right beneath the surface. It starts to gnaw at me, a little itch. And if I don't pay attention and scratch it, I end up feeling irritable, bored, and "blah." Though nothing's changed as far as I can tell, I start to feel like I'm not particularly good at anything. I'll remember those dreams I once had, as though I'm watching an old movie with a cheesy early 1980s soundtrack—but somehow I just can't tap into the energy to make them happen.

When I start feeling this paradoxical blend of boredom and fatigue— when I alternate wanting to go to bed for two days with wanting to run away from home—then I know the balance is off. Luckily, I've gotten pretty good at seeing it coming and averting it. But so many moms struggle with balance. How do we remain who we are while being good wives, mothers, workers, friends, and sisters? How can we be happy without feeling guilty? How can we raise good families without forgetting about ourselves?

Maybe you've already figured out how to balance your family with your own needs—getting out of the house now and then to spend time with friends, pursuing activities and causes that are important to you. If so, you might be tempted to skip this chapter entirely—you already know that taking care of yourself *is* taking care of your family. On the other hand, it never hurts to be reminded!

Or maybe you're just considering building a large family but are overwhelmed with the children you already have. You're wondering how anybody can be so thoroughly outnumbered by small, demanding people and still keep her sanity and some semblance of personality.

It can be done. Plenty of ordinary people—no full-time nanny, no addiction to amphetamines—with big families find or make time to care for themselves.

In fact, moms with bigger families may be better at figuring out how to strike this important balance. When my oldest children were two years old and an infant, I spent most of my time feeling blah, bored, and frustrated. My house was a mess; my hair was a mess; my diet was a mess. I'd lost myself and couldn't figure out how to find me again. Even simple tasks seemed so insurmountable that I really couldn't see any way to try to get more, not less, done. I already felt like a rotten mother most of the time. How could I justify taking time away from thinking about my kids and focus my energy on myself?

As I've added more children, I've become much better at caring for myself and for my kids. I won't lie and say things never get out of whack (see above) but I'm better at adjusting my expectations and figuring out how to reenergize, rather than beating myself up about it. For instance, through time and experience, I've learned that following a routine, getting out of the house regularly, and working toward a goal are good for me.

True, when you choose to have a lot of kids, you are definitely making a choice not to have as much time to pursue a career, hobbies, or other "selfish" pursuits. But simple self-care—which to me involves taking care of my health, getting enough sleep, and also feeling like a whole, interesting human being—isn't selfish as far as I'm concerned. When it comes to motherhood and ambition (note: when I say "ambition," I don't necessarily mean you've got specific career goals, either: it could be the desire to develop better cooking skills, to take better care of your body, to read more, or to take better photographs of your kids, etc.) there are two truths:

1. It is always possible to take some step, however small, toward caring for yourself, and

2. Taking care of yourself is taking care of your family.

Did you hear that? *Taking care of yourself is taking care of your family.* Repeat this idea a few times. You know that old saying, "If Mama ain't happy, ain't nobody happy?" Believe it: if you spend a lot of time with your kids, your disposition sets the tone for the household, and there's no way a home can be peaceful and joyful with a frustrated or resentful martyr for a mother.

"We all need time to ourselves," says Tracy, a homeschooling mother of five kids ages six to fifteen. "Giving to our children and spouses can be very fulfilling, but it's also very draining. We need time to ourselves to fill up again so we have more to give; it's not selfish to want and need something for ourselves." And here's the really great thing; you might think that if you spend whatever free time you can squeeze out of your day on pursuing goals that you won't have any time left for true leisure activities— you know, like enjoying some mindless television or taking a long bath. But you can make time for those activities and enjoy them more than you did before you had a big family.

And sometimes you'll find that the more energy you spend on yourself, the more energy you have to give to your family. Inertia breeds more inertia, but energy breeds energy. "I've found that by being active, doing yoga or hiking or even just getting out of the house for coffee with a friend, actually gives me more energy, so I am able to accomplish more in a day," agrees Tracy. "Often I'll feel like I'm not getting anything done, but if I just take half an hour to do some yoga or chat with a friend on the phone, then I'll feel good about getting back to folding that laundry or cleaning the bathtub."

But how do you find that time in the first place? How can you squeeze one more thing into your schedule between dueling dentist appointments and dozens of dirty dishes? It's not easy, but it can be simple.

Attitude Isn't Everything ... but It's a Lot

Sometimes, the real challenge is accepting the fact that there are only so many hours in a day and then figuring out how to make the most of the time you've got instead of feeling resentful about the time you don't have.

You may never be able to count on all your kids napping at the same time (hasn't happened to me since 2002). You may not even be able to go to the bathroom without small helpers tossing toilet paper in the tub and trying to sneak in a premature flush. I'm not going to pretend I never have those desperate, awful days where I want to run away from home and join a traveling carnival, but I find that a lot of the time, *happiness really is a choice.* Being frustrated and resentful takes up a lot of time and energy—time and energy that could better be used for reading a book, pursuing a hobby, or just kicking back with the kids—and being glad about it.

I know how hard it is to consistently have this attitude, especially if you're right in the middle of working through a particularly difficult stage with your child, dealing with a colicky baby, or just longing for some time and space of your own, and facing constant interruptions when you try to do something that means a lot to you. It can be frustrating—in fact, sometimes it can be infuriating. But "fake it till you make it" is an effective strategy when you need an attitude adjustment. If you feel stuck and discouraged, try "acting as if" you're content, confident, and energetic. You may not be able to will your child into effortless potty-training or your baby into sleeping longer than two hours at a stretch, but with some practice you can control your attitude—at least, most of the time.

Find Time or Make It

Most of us don't have long periods of free time stretching out in front of us, but that doesn't mean we have to bump self-care to the bottom of the to-do list. And you don't need a 25-hour day or heaps of disposable cash to take time for yourself, either by setting aside time for relaxation or by identifying your goals and starting to take steps toward fulfilling them. Instead of saying you "can't" relax or do something you want to because of time or money constraints, why not take a look at how you spend your time and money to see if there's anything less valuable to you that can go?

For example, even with how busy my life is, I still waste a lot of time: my vices are flipping TV channels (I don't have any programs I watch regularly—I just flip through the channels and mutter about how nothing's on! What a waste of time!), checking my e-mail obsessively, and lurking on a few parenting message boards online. When I am honest with myself, I know that to say I can't find 15-20 minutes a day to do something I really want to do (practice piano, work on some fiction) really means that I'm not disciplined enough to give up one of those time-wasters. And the truth is, those things don't add any value to my life, whereas accomplishing a long-held goal of learning to play the piano or finishing a novel does.

Some time-wasting is rejuvenating. For me, taking a long bath, sipping wine while flipping through a fluff magazine, or getting a pedicure are all examples of "good" time-wasting. And what is the litmus test? They leave me feeling refreshed instead of bored and blah (like the channel-surfing).

If your life circumstances make it impossible to add or find any time, consider asking for help. Maybe your partner can take over for a few hours a week while you take a class or just wander the library alone. If you're unpartnered, maybe there's a single-parent support group you can take advantage of. Your church may have a Mother's Day Out program, or you can start a baby-sitting co-op with some friends to give you a regular break.

There are lots of hours in a day," says Tracy, who besides homeschooling her kids also finds time for a daily yoga practice, musical pursuits, and much more. "Being very organized is part of what allows me more time for myself. If I don't keep my life scheduled and manage my time well, then there isn't enough time left over, and I'd be just zonked at the end of the day. I plan my time carefully."

Make Time for You Part of the Routine

Here's the thing about kids—it's very rare that they're going to come up to you and say "Gee, Mom, you look tired. Wouldn't you like to go soak in the tub for a while?"

As women and nurturers, we moms are used to looking out for everyone else's needs. When they don't reciprocate—and why would they, when we make it so easy for them to be cared for without giving it much thought?—we end up touched-out, tired-out, worn-out, and resentful. And then we feel guilty about being resentful. And then we feel resentful over the guilt we feel over our resentment.

But remember—your kids, and sometimes your husband, will take what you offer and still ask for more. If you offered them 24 hours a day of solid nurturing and care, they'd take it all and then say "Got any more of that?" It's not letting your family down to insist on time for yourself. Trust me, though they probably won't think to offer it, that doesn't mean they'll suffer if you just go ahead and take it. Oh, they may *act* like they're suffering, but think of the lessons they're learning: patience, delayed gratification, and selflessness. In other words, they'll get over it!

"I quite frequently hear what a busy mom I must be, and it's true that I am busy," says Tracy, who says her five kids are very accepting of her having a life outside the home. "My usual response is that my hands are very full, but I also have lots of helping hands. We work together as a team. All of the work doesn't fall on me. We all pitch in and make things happen. The children learned very early that mama can't do everything, and if we're all going to have time to have fun and enjoy ourselves, then the work has to be shared."

How can you seamlessly introduce "mom time" into the family's expectations? As with most other things in a big family, adding something new works best if you incorporate it into the daily routine. That's what Shirley, a mom of five, did to make sure she had time to follow her pursuits. "I'm a scrapbooker and I love photography," says Shirley. "I found that if I don't *make* the time, then I don't have it. I've learned to insist that I have some time every week to pursue my hobbies. Eventually the family became used to it—now it's a normal thing." Write it on the family calendar or whiteboard. Put one of your older kids in charge of getting dinner on the table on your book club evening, and make sure they know they have to be home. Make sure everyone knows that, on Wednesday nights, homework has to be done before 5 P.M. Whatever it takes to get the whole family on board, make it happen.

Of course, in a Table for Eight family, sometimes there just isn't enough time during the day to add in one more activity. So if you've got a lot of ambitions, eking opportunity out of an already-packed day may require some creativity and sacrifice. Carla, a mom of four and avid yogi who also loves to knit, write, and read, makes time for her own interests through a combination of getting up early, using available time to its fullest, and asking her husband and kids to pick up some of the slack. "I make my knitting and reading a part of my daily routine during my children's downtime," she says. "I have an evening each week that I set aside for my yoga class, and I stick to it. I also make certain that I jog a few times each week to get out of the house alone. I meditate and I get up before anyone else in the house so that I can mentally prepare for my day without distraction."

Help Them Help You Follow Through

Sometimes guilt over taking a little time for yourself can present itself in backhanded ways. Here's how it works for me: I'll think about going to yoga class all week. I'll toss that yoga class around in my brain until I can practically smell and taste yoga. And then an hour before my yoga class, I'll start coming up with reasons why I shouldn't go. Reasons like: dinner isn't ready yet, we already had delivery pizza once this week, and if I'm not here to help get dinner on the table, probably nobody will eat. Or the baby took a really long nap this afternoon, so he won't sleep while I'm gone, and it'll be as if I was away from him most of the day. And now that I'm thinking about it, gee, my back kind of hurts … maybe yoga would strain it?

It's all mental junk, and I know it! I want to go to the yoga class. My body's screaming for it, but my brain gets in the way. Coming up with "reasons" why I can't go to a one-hour yoga class is just a form of self-sabotage, so I try to be proactive. I'll let my husband know several times that day that I'm going to yoga class, so I don't get responses that consist of blank looks and "Oh, I didn't realize that was *tonight* …" (I used to get that a lot). I plan for an easy dinner way ahead of time and make sure that the after-school homework and chore machine gets started early. And most important, I have told my husband about my self-sabotaging ways and have asked him and my kids to help hold me to the commitments I've made to myself. When I put it that way, everybody is very willing to remind me that I've got (a class, a book group, whatever) lined up and that I should hurry up and go.

"My husband used to kick me out of the house when the kids were small because I felt guilty leaving them," says Tanya, mom of four. "I felt so much better after just browsing at a store or getting a cup of coffee and relaxing." Smart families will start to get the picture: a mom who has time to rest and rejuvenate is a happier mom, and in turn, the household is happier, too.

And remember that your kids and husband both will benefit from being left alone together. The more kids you have, the more crucial it is that their father is used to handling tasks like bedtime and baths, because your time will often be divided between the younger and older children.

Tracy says her husband Dave has gone out of his way to help her have a life outside of motherhood—partly because he loves spending time alone with his kids. "He's driven around with sleeping babies in the car and found ways to entertain them nearby where I was so that if they needed me he could just pop over and drop them off. He's extremely competent as a parent and a better housekeeper than I am. He loves being with the kids, and since I'm much more social than he is, he just enjoys the time he gets to spend with his children while I'm out getting a much-needed break and filling my social needs." Tracy says that her kids have always loved being left with Daddy. "I never leave them until they are comfortable being away from me. Until then I just arrange things so that they can come with me. The younger children are happy to stay home and have some special time with Daddy while I'm away. Aidan used to tell me that when I was gone they did 'secret boy stuff,' some sort of club that I wasn't allowed in. Dave has always made times when I was away into a special time for them to connect."

Simplify!

I'm a big fan of getting rid of time-sucking duties that don't feed your soul or feed your family. We can all identify the obvious time suckers—for instance, the volunteer tasks we don't really have time for but take on out of guilt. But what about the less-obvious thieves of precious time and energy?

Have you ever read one of those articles that advises women to learn to say "no" more often and thought "That doesn't apply to me! I'm not in any clubs, and nobody's asking me to volunteer to bake cookies"? But saying "no" isn't always as concrete as telling the PTA you can't serve as treasurer this year. People monopolize our time and energy in a lot of ways without coming right out and asking a favor. Do you ever:

- Lose valuable sleep worrying about volatile relationships?
- Spend time moderating disagreements between friends or family members?
- Get sucked into hours-long phone calls with drama-prone friends, listening to them gripe about their latest crisis?

Caller ID and voice mail were made for these kinds of situations! It may seem to go against every instinct in your body, but you don't have to answer your phone every time it rings. In fact, you don't *ever* have to answer your phone if you don't want to! I mean, once you've got bigger kids in the house, half the time it's going to be for one of them anyway. Train your kids on phone manners, and require that they take good messages as a condition for being allowed to use the phone. In other words, let them be *your* personal secretaries rather than the other way around. Or let calls go to voice mail, and respond after you've had time to think about whatever request or statement the caller is making. Everything, even answering your phone, is a choice. Exercise your power to choose!

Choose Your Friends Wisely

I know people who feel compelled to help mediate their friends' arguments. Frankly, if I had friendships that required that much arbitration, I'd rethink the relationship.

Part of the way I keep my life simple is by gravitating toward emotionally healthy, stable people who don't pick fights with me or each other. When it comes to friends, I've realized that often, less (or in this case, fewer) is more. The way I look at it is this: I spend a lot of time with emotionally immature people: my children. They're still growing and learning about social interaction, and it's my job to help them. I just don't have time to deal with emotionally immature grown-ups, too!

I also find that it's nice to have some other friends with bigger families. They tend not to be intimidated by us coming over (as my friend Hannah, who has six kids, says, "What's one more pound to an elephant?") and are likely to invite all my boys to birthday parties and the like, rather than just one or two of them. Their homes are set up for lots of kids, and they don't seem to get stressed out over noise, chaos, and even a bit of destruction here and there. They are also understanding about last-minute stuff that comes up when you've got lots of kids, and they "get" that sometimes it's easier, more relaxing, and more fun to just sit out on the back deck with a drink and chat while the kids run wild than it is to try to arrange for a sitter and go out. Those kinds of friends can be a lifeline when your life is too full and stressful to fit in one more obligation. The best kinds of friends to have are those who understand and accept you and your family wholeheartedly, and that's not always easy to come by with childless friends or those friends who don't understand why you'd ever want to have lots of kids. You might still have some room in your life for people who don't "get" your family, but if they take more energy from you than they give back, it's probably worth reconsidering spending time with them.

"I'm very fortunate to have a great homeschooling support group and lots of wonderful friends," says Tracy. "We trade off child care, help each other out, and share rides to things. If I have the two older boys out at a teen get-together in the evening and my daughter somewhere else, then we'll arrange with other parents in the group to drop off and pick up kids so that none of us have to do all the driving around. I trade off care, keeping a friend's children here in exchange for her keeping mine another day. The kids enjoy the time to play with friends, and it gives them opportunities to connect with other adults as well. Community is extremely important."

Homeschool and religious communities are a great place to look for other families with lots of kids. Or start your own Table for Eight support group; hang a flyer in your church, pediatrician's, obstetrician, or midwife's office, or a local grocery store; place an ad in the community newspaper; or go online to websites like http://moms.meetup.com.

Take Care of Your Body

Having lots of kids in comparison to having one or two is kind of like comparing a marathon to a 5K. They're both hard, but the marathon lasts longer, and you have to pace yourself a lot more. And while you might be able to make it through the 5K even if you haven't prepared yourself, you'd better be in prime physical condition before you start that marathon—or you could collapse way short of the finish line.

Taking care of yourself physically is imperative if you're going to be a happy, healthy, and effective mom. Add a poor diet and sleep deprivation to the everyday stress and exertion of raising lots of kids, and you're putting your physical and mental health—and possibly that of your kids if you're driving them around or using heavy machinery—at risk. So if you don't do it for yourself, do it for them. Get enough sleep, even if that means following the "nap when your baby naps" advice until your "baby" is ten years old. Take your multivitamins. Drink enough water. Try not to live on coffee. Sit down and eat real meals instead of picking at what's left after your kids are through.

A few months ago I was at a family party where the food was laid out buffet-style. Because the kids were out playing happily, I filled a plate for myself, sat down, and ate, and then called them to the table.

"What kind of a mother feeds herself before her children?" my grandmother asked.

I thought about what would have happened if I'd fed my kids—who definitely weren't starving—first. By the time I made four trips to fill their plates, answered all their questions about what was in each dish, and filled four cups with milk, some of them would have been ready for seconds. By the time I filled their plates with seconds, I would have been starving and irritable. And in the worst-case scenario, the food would be almost gone.

"A full one," I retorted. It's like the rule that, in case of an airplane emergency, you're supposed to put your own air mask on before your child's. Sometimes, Mom has to put herself first so she can keep taking care of everyone else … and nowhere is that more important than your physical and mental health.

Lower Your Standards

One way to eke more time out of your schedule is to prioritize. Decide what's important to you and what's not, and only put energy into the former. For instance, maybe you're saving $5 by clipping coupons every week, but you're spending an hour scouring coupon websites, pulling coupons out of the paper, and organizing them. How badly do you need the $5? Is it worth the time you're putting into the task?

Are you a perfectionist when it comes to housekeeping, cooking, or providing your toddler with sixty minutes of development-enriching "educational" play each day? If you enjoy these activities, by all means, continue. But if you're holding yourself to an unreasonable standard just because you feel like you "should," maybe it's time to cut yourself some slack.

Be Creative

So you can't get away every week, but you want to take drawing lessons. Or you're dying to go see a musician at a local venue but don't have the cash for tickets. Think outside the box to come up with workable solutions. Consider:

Barter. Do you have a skill or talent? Maybe you can work out some kind of a trade if you don't have enough money to pay for child care, lessons, or some other service.

Work your way in. Some performing arts venues employ unpaid ushers—in return, you get to watch the show for free.

Try books, DVDs, and the Internet to supplement traditional lessons. When I got my violin, I had an infant and knew I wouldn't be able to leave the house for lessons right away. So I bought a couple of books and a DVD primer to get me through the basics. In the meantime, I searched the Internet to get more familiar with terminology and theory. Even though I wasn't taking lessons the way I knew I'd eventually want to, I was still making progress and learning a lot in the meantime.

Make It Happen!

No matter how whittled-down you think your life is now and how little wiggle room there is for change, look honestly at the way you spend your time: *all* of it. And now imagine you are a pioneer woman 100+ years ago. You probably have a large family—a *really* large family by today's standards. You might have cooked every dinner over a fire (after killing and plucking a chicken from your yard and pulling vegetables out of your own garden). You most likely had to wash your clothes by hand. Even the simple act of getting a drink of water required a trip to the well. And without electricity, you had fewer hours in the day to get the bulk of the day's work done. But mothers then did it all and way more to boot. Are we so different? Is it really that we don't have enough time—or is it that we're filling our time with things that don't really matter?

We've got two basic choices when we're dissatisfied with our lives: figure out a way to accept how things are or make a change. What will you choose?

Look to the Future

Okay, so taking care of your own needs isn't easy. Maybe you're in a place in life right now where you're doing all you can and still can't squeeze out another drop of time for anyone—much less yourself. If nothing else, you can keep your spirits up if you keep a sense of humor and remember that it won't last forever. "I am totally sleep-deprived," says Sheryl, a mom of five who stays up too late and drinks too much coffee. "I'm just plain tired all the time. Emotionally, I am fine—no drama for me. Mentally, I am a little dull around the edges." Sheryl says she's always thinking about what she needs to be doing, where she needs to be going, and that there's just not room for much more in her life. But she knows it won't last forever: "As the kids get older, it becomes much easier," she says. "I have one more year until all my kids are in school for a full day, and then I might have a little square of time for myself."

Disclaimer:

While this chapter is intended to be a gentle kick in the pants for people feeling chronically victimized, all of the preceding is said with the assumption that you aren't ill, suffering from a chemical imbalance, or depressed. If you feel fatigued, lose your appetite, or have inexplicable aches and pains; or if you can't get a handle on feelings of sadness, hopelessness, anxiety, or guilt, please seek help from a doctor, counselor, or other professional. Remember—*taking care of your needs is taking care of your family.*

Suddenly Super-Size: When Your Family Grows in Groups

Not every Table of Eight family consists of a husband and wife adding one baby after another until they're "done." Families can grow in a variety of ways: maybe you've married somebody with children, and blending your two smaller families together adds up to one *big* family. Maybe you've adopted siblings or added older children to your family. Maybe you're a foster parent, so your household grows and then shrinks as children come in and out of your home. Perhaps you've given birth to multiples, doubling or even tripling your family size overnight. When big families don't fit the traditional family mold, special issues often come up.

Adoption

For many parents, adoption is a wonderful way to start or add on to their family. Some parents are so changed by the experience of adoption that they decide to adopt again (and sometimes, again and again!). And when parents adopt, children sometimes enter their families in twos or threes ... or even more.

Adopting Siblings

What happens when you adopt a group of siblings into a family that already has kids? Not only will your family grow quite a bit larger when you bring the kids home, but you'll also be adding children of various ages into the house which might cause your "original" kids to feel displaced. And while adopting older kids may mean you won't deal with some of the issues of bringing a group of newborns into the house—like sleep deprivation or diapering—you'll most certainly be dealing with things like discipline right away. In addition, you might have factors such as language barriers or attachment issues complicating matters.

"For us, the most difficult transition was going from three to five children," says Ramona, a mother of eleven, who had three biological children—ages three, six, and eight—when she and her husband brought home their first set of adopted siblings, ages eight and nine, from Russia. "Thankfully, we had about the same time frame of a pregnancy to prepare for bringing these two home, but it was still a shock. Suddenly, we could not allow the kids to get away with all of the little things we had before. It became apparent overnight that we were not as disciplined in our parenting as we had hoped we were! We scrambled to determine specific rules and how best to enforce them, while refereeing the new relationships and trying to teach our two new kids to speak English. Our older adopted child, a daughter, was also deaf, which presented its own unique challenges."

Ramona admits that the language barrier presented some unique issues during an unexpected move shortly after the adoption of one set of children. "My husband left to start his new job in a different state. I remained at home with eight kids, three of whom did not speak English. With the help of our church family and friends, we were able to pack up all of our belongings and eventually make the move ourselves. We only recently discovered that the middle child we adopted had no idea what was going on at the time, though. When asked at what point he finally realized we were moving, he answered, 'When we all got into the van and left the house.'"

Though she was at times nervous, Ramona brought yet another set of adopted siblings into their family a short time later … a group of siblings ages 12, 13, and 14. "The scariest part about bringing them home is that we had never parented teenagers before!" They adopted again and again. Ramona and her husband now have eleven children, ranging in age from 11 to 20, and credit the confidence to care for them all to their faith.

Though adding each new set of children presented challenges, Ramona says that she and her husband firmly believe that adding more children to the mix was one of the best things that ever could have happened to their three birth children. "We became better parents because we could no longer put up with the nonsense we had before!" she says.

Attachment Issues

Older adopted children may suffer from attachment disorders that make it difficult for them to bond with you and the other children in your family. You and the other kids in the house, who may have expected an instant close relationship with their new brother or sister, might find this difficult to deal with. "Three of our children came to us after disrupted international adoptions," says Ramona. "These girls went through much emotional turmoil in their first adoptive placements and have had varying degrees of trouble with this over the past few years. One daughter has only recently begun to call us Mom and Dad, after having been in our family for three years."

Melody, who has six kids—including two sisters who were adopted at ages six and nine—says that attachment disorders affected the way her new daughters related to her birth children. "They would play alongside their new brothers and sisters, but they didn't really participate at first. And they tended to stick to themselves, which was complicated even more by the fact that they didn't speak English ... they could speak to each other, but none of the rest of us could understand them. And they couldn't understand us, either!" Melody says that after she did a lot of reading about how to parent kids with attachment disorders, she was able to find ways to relate to her new daughters that helped them build trust. And, of course, it took time, too. "I'd say that parents who are looking at adopting older kids have to be honest with themselves about their expectations," she says. "Some of these kids have serious problems going back to how they were treated as babies." At the same time, Melody says she has no doubt her kids—all of them—have benefited from the experience of being part of a large adoptive family. "My biological kids learned so much about diversity and selflessness," she says.

Ramona agrees. "The way we see it, the kids will all be very well prepared to know how to get along with just about anyone they might meet in life, after having lived in our diverse family!"

If you're considering adopting older children, you should think carefully about how attachment disorders could affect your whole family—not just your adopted child. For more information on what you should know before you adopt—and how you can help kids with attachment disorders learn to trust again—visit http://attachment.adoption.com.

mom wisdom

"Each time we've adopted, our definition of 'normal' has had to change. With the first adoptions, I had set in my mind that things would be fine after six months. However, about that time the kids started becoming more used to us, and they began to relax and let their 'real selves' show more. This meant new challenges, which I did not feel at all prepared for. We all slowly adjusted, though. Honestly, it has been a matter of finding our new pattern of behaviors each time, rather than returning to what things were like before the adoption."

—Ramona, mom of eleven (eight adopted) kids

Birth Order Issues

When parents adopt older children into an existing set of kids, it's likely that some of those children will end up in a different place in the family lineup than the one they were born into ... i.e., a firstborn might become a middle child in your family. Some experts feel that adopting out of birth order has potential ramifications for all the children in a family and that all the possible issues should be considered carefully before making decisions about adoption.

Though you might not think birth order matters, for a child to give up the status of being "oldest" in the house can be hard. Also, adopting an older child can be difficult on the adoptive child—he or she may not be used to having younger siblings, may not be accustomed to carrying the kind of responsibility that comes with having a big family, may not be used to sharing possessions or space, or may actually be accustomed to "parenting" his or her younger siblings. There may be even more serious past issues, like abuse or neglect, that will make adjustment even harder for the entire family. If you are considering adopting an older child, please give all these issues careful consideration.

If you have already decided to adopt older kids, you can do a few things to make the transition easier on everyone:

Encourage individuality among your kids. You're probably already doing this with your birth children, but encouraging individuality can be even more important when you add older adopted children into the mix. If everyone is involved in the same activity, for instance, keeping kids from feeling like they're being compared to one another can be difficult.

Be prepared for gaps in academic and maturity levels. You may have to use very different approaches with your children and guard against comparisons to other kids in the family. Sharon, a mother of five grown children, adopted two of them—siblings—when they were nine and ten years old. "We tried to help them deal with rivalry by teaching them that each of them had different strengths and challenges. We didn't have set goals such as 'Get A's and B's in school.' Instead we had goals like 'Do your best in school.' Some of the kids were capable of straight A's, while others were seriously challenged to get C's. We tried to help them see those differences as normal and set our goals so that the kids could understand why we might have different expectations for each of them."

A variety of factors in your adoptive child's past may put them behind your birth children academically—or vice versa. It may be important to shield older, struggling children from the academic successes of younger kids in the family. Many families who adopt older children prefer home education for some or all of them because it allows for truly individualized learning without comparisons by grade level.

Find different ways to acknowledge the special status of each child in the house. If your oldest child by birth is no longer the oldest in the house, you will need to be sensitive to him possibly having hard feelings about that. Find ways to acknowledge the "oldest-ness" of both your oldest child by birth and the actual oldest child in the house. It may be that your adopted child is not ready for some of the responsibilities and privileges that your first-born biological child has. Try to distribute the responsibilities among the oldest kids in a way that matches their maturity level.

The oldest child by birth may not be the only child having difficulty adjusting to his or her new status. For example, if you've adopted a girl into a family that previously had only one girl, the "first" girl may feel that her position is threatened. If you've adopted siblings, you may find that your children tend to split into groups of siblings. "Despite our best efforts, the kids have kind of separated into two sets again now that they are older," says Sharon. "The ones who joined our family as older kids have serious bonding issues, and as adults don't relate well to their siblings." Though Sharon says she was able to help the children grow closer when they were living under her roof, as adults, they've grown apart into two groups again.

Getting Help

It's important to seek help for these and other issues that may come up during your adoption. Older adopted children can have attachment issues and other problems that may not be apparent until some time has passed. Look for social workers and adoption experts with expertise in this area, and seek out other families with older adopted children for advice.

For more information on adopting older kids, check out these resources:

Older Child Adoption is a website that offers advice and information on international and domestic adoption for children over two years old, including resources on attachment disorder and special needs: www.olderchildadoption.com.

Adoptive Families is a magazine and website with information and resources on nearly every possible kind of adoptive arrangement: www.adoptivefamilies.com.

The Foundation for Large Families is a support group for large, adoptive families, which also addresses adoption policies that are discriminatory to large families. If you've been told "no" to adoption because your family is already "too big," you'll definitely want to check them out: www.foundationforlargefamilies.com.

Foster Children

When it comes to blending foster children with existing kids, some of the same issues apply as in adoptive families. However, there are some pretty major differences: first of all, because there is no guarantee the foster children will be joining your family permanently even if that is your ultimate hope, bonding and relationship issues may be even more complex and challenging. But there's one issue that's unique to a foster family: how do you best set up your house to accommodate children who will move in and out?

Depending on the laws in your state, you may be required to follow rules for foster kids that don't match your own children's living quarters. Often, basement, attic, and tandem rooms—in which you have to walk through one bedroom to get to another, rather than the room having its own private entrance—are not allowable in foster care situations; foster kids can't share beds with other children, and you must separate their bedrooms by gender.

If your house is cramped, it may be difficult to create space that works for your family while still legally accommodating foster children, but with some creativity, you can do it. Here are a few ideas:

Convert a multipurpose room into a bedroom. Set up a multipurpose room that meets the criteria for a foster child's bedroom while also serving another purpose. For example, convert a guest bedroom or a storage room into a bedroom. If you will have just one foster-child bedroom, make sure any kids you foster are of the same gender. Pros: this arrangement allows you to bring foster kids in and out of your home without disrupting your other kids' sleeping space, and the foster child may enjoy having more privacy than he would if he were to share a bedroom with your kids. Cons: the foster child might not feel like "one of the group," and your children won't have as much opportunity to get to know him. Also, you'll have to make sure that whatever other purpose the room serves isn't disruptive to the foster child while he's in your home. For instance, a rarely-used guest room or place to neatly store your craft supplies is one thing—a cluttered catch-all room that you have to go into several times a day will probably make the foster child feel like an intruder.

Keep your kids' sleeping areas and living areas separate. In Chapter 2, we discussed a "dormitory" style bedroom arrangement, where same-gender kids are grouped several to a room for sleeping, with the majority of their toys and belongings in other areas of the house, where there's more space and storage. This can work well for bringing in foster kids, because all you'll need to do is add another twin bed—no worries about displacing "stuff." You'll be able to help your foster child feel at home by having a place for his things without it necessarily having to fit into the bedroom with him.

Special Considerations

When you integrate foster kids into your home, you'll also have to consider discipline, chores, and privileges and how you will deal with these issues in comparison to "your" children. It might be tempting to let things "slide" with a foster child, considering that he may be in your house temporarily. But the one thing many foster kids don't have, but want, is to feel like they "belong"—discipline, chores, and all. On the other hand, your foster children may be coming to you with a host of emotional and discipline issues that will require a different approach than you might take with your other children. The more kids you have, the more people there are whose needs you must consider before you take this step.

As desperately as foster children need good, loving foster homes, bringing foster kids into your house when you've already got plenty of kids of your own is a decision that requires serious research and thought. Your kids may be excited about the prospect of built-in playmates, but they probably won't consider whether, for instance, a foster child who's been sexually abused could be a danger to them. On the flip side, your children may be resentful about the idea of another child or children invading "their" space, without being able to truly appreciate how much they will gain from the experience of sharing their home, siblings, and parents with a foster child. These few resources can help you weed through all the "what-ifs" and make a decision that's right for your whole family:

National Foster Parent Association is a national organization that strives to support foster parents and be a strong voice on behalf of children: www.nfpainc.org.

The Pew Commission on Children in Foster Care was set up to develop recommendations to improve outcomes for the half-million children who are currently in foster care. It's got some eye-opening resources, such as a flowchart that traces a child's often-complicated journey through the welfare system: http://pewfostercare.org.

The Foster Care blog at adoptionblogs.com is written by an experienced foster parent of four (one biological child, two adopted from foster care, and one foster child). The blog covers a wide variety of issues that come up when integrating foster children into a household. Visit http://foster-care.adoptionblogs.com.

Multiple Births

If you're expecting twins, triplets, or more, you may be getting ready to double—or triple—or quadruple!—your family's size, literally overnight. While big families that grow one child at a time have months or years to adjust to the new size before adding a new child, parents facing multiple births will be caring for more than one tiny newborn while trying to parent older kids, too. Add on to that the fact that multiples can make pregnancy more difficult and the babies may be small and require extra care, and having multiples can seem overwhelming.

How will I care for them all? One day at a time. Parents of multiples have to learn to simplify, simplify, simplify! Laura, a mom of four—including a set of triplets—says she basically lived on the floor for months. "I didn't bother trying to move around the house during the day—how could I, when I didn't have enough arms to carry them all?" she says. "We camped out on the floor with my water bottle, books, snacks, and, of course, my nursing pillow."

Where will they go? While multiple babies do need a lot of care, they won't need miles of space … yet. Your house doesn't need to grow overnight to accommodate your babies, who will likely be happier sleeping in close proximity to one another than in separate cribs anyway. But you might find that you need more "gear" than you needed for your singletons. Even if you shunned gadgets like motorized bouncy seats for your single-birth babies, you may find that you just don't have enough arms to get everything done without relying on some tools to make your life easier.

What about my older kids? This is where having multiples can get especially tricky. Not only do you have several new babies competing for your attention, but you also have to make sure your older kids aren't lost in the shuffle. First of all, go easy on yourself. Kids are resilient, and while your older children may be resentful and jealous sometimes, they will adjust to having to wait a little longer for Mom and Dad's attention. In fact, a formerly-pampered child may benefit from the lessons learned in patience and sharing! On the other hand, you don't want your older kid or kids to feel forgotten. Try to involve them as much as you can in the babies' care. Even a toddler can run and fetch diapers and "help" you change a baby. Older kids can amuse one baby while you feed or change another. But make sure you spend some time with your older kids that doesn't revolve around the new babies. Even setting aside fifteen or twenty minutes of alone time—whether it's during those quiet moments before bed, during a walk, or while loading the dishwasher—with an older child each day can give you both an opportunity to reconnect.

Building your family through the birth of multiples can be wonderful, but it also comes with unique financial and practical issues. You'll need plenty of support from other parents who've been there. Here are a few resources that can help:

Mothers of Supertwins (MOST) is an organization supporting families with triplets, quadruplets, and more: www.mostonline.org.

TWINS Magazine is geared toward parents of twins and more: www. twinsmagazine.com.

Blended Families

Maybe you had one or two children with a previous partner, were divorced or widowed, and figured your small family was complete … until you got remarried to somebody with two or three or more children. Suddenly, that small family grew big—and threw two sets of siblings together, for better or for worse. Blended families may not always fit together as seamlessly as they did on *The Brady Bunch*, but it doesn't have to be an ugly fairy-tale, either.

Keeping It Fair

When it comes to assigning chores and responsibilities, handing out privileges, and distributing punishment, you may run into more snags than you would with full-blooded siblings. Stepsibs aren't accustomed to living together and may resent one another for a variety of reasons. They may not have wanted their parent to remarry; they may have thought their own parents would eventually get back together; or they may have had to move into another house and be unhappy about it. And then there's that birth-order displacement thing again. Not only that, but in a blended family, half of the time the chores, responsibilities, privileges, and punishments will be distributed by a stepparent, which may trigger resentment, protests, and hard feelings from stepkids. As impossible as it is to be 100 percent fair all the time, in a blended family you may have to focus more on fairness than you did when you were dealing with just your own kids, at least for a little while. Any perceived favoritism, whether it's toward your own children or your stepchildren, is likely to be felt keenly by the kids involved.

To keep things very fair, you may want to use a rotating chore schedule so that responsibility for those "least-favorite" chores is evenly distributed among all the kids.

Practical Considerations

If some of the children in your family live with you only part-time, you may face awkward transitions as your family grows and shrinks again as those kids come and go. If you don't have enough space in the house for each child to have his or her own bedroom, you may wonder whether to keep one room aside for the siblings who are coming and going, or if you should blend them in with the kids who live full-time in the house.

Where Will They Sleep?

Krista, who has two young sons and two teenage stepsons, has each "set" of boys share a room. Their three-bedroom house for a family of six was built that way by design, Krista explains: "We chose to do this because a five-bedroom house wasn't affordable, and a four-bedroom house would cause strife since some of the kids would get their own rooms while the others wouldn't. Somebody would feel duped out of a bedroom." While they considered splitting the rooms up differently—putting each younger boy with a teen—they ultimately decided that it made more sense to keep the boys separated into age groups. "If we split them differently, there would be the constant problem of the older kids feeling like the younger kids were invading their space," she says. "Plus, the older boys had shared a bedroom since they were born, so it's an easier transition for them and us."

David, the father of two kids—a son, 16, and daughter, 14—who spend weekends at his house and stepfather of 10- and 12-year old boys and a 14-year-old girl who live there full-time, says that he and his wife had a different approach when it came to blending their families. "We worried that with my kids only spending two days a week in the house, it would be too easy for all the children to form two camps instead of really living together—especially since my wife and I didn't get married until they were all older and kind of set in their ways." Their solution? Each of the younger three children has his or her own bedroom in the family's five-bedroom house, while one bedroom remains open for the older kids to use on the weekends as they see fit. "My kids have a choice—they can either take turns having their 'own room' when they come here on Friday and Saturday night, or they can bunk up with the same-gendered stepsibling." While his 16-year-old son usually chooses his privacy on "his" night to use the extra bedroom, David says his daughter almost always either invites her stepsister into her room for the night or sleeps in her room. "They see it as an every-weekend, all-weekend slumber party," says David. While his son doesn't necessarily choose to hang out with his much-younger stepbrothers all weekend long, David feels that spending every other weekend sharing one of their bedrooms has helped them grow closer. "It would be easy for him, as the oldest in the family and especially being so much older than the other boys, to retreat to his room, and we didn't want that to happen," says David. "With this arrangement, he can have one night of privacy each weekend, but on the night he kind of has to hang out with the rest of the family." Because his son is already 16, David doesn't anticipate there being many conflicts as his stepsons get older: "It helps that everyone has their own bedrooms all week, so the only time they have to share is on the weekend. And in two years, my son will probably be off at college, so the dynamics will change a lot. For now, though, the younger boys really look up to him and I think he likes that."

Table for Seven … or Three … or Five?

For Anna, who has two children from a previous marriage, two stepchildren—all of whom move in and out of the house during the week due to shared custody arrangements—and one child with her husband, Jack, the biggest adjustment, believe it or not, is cooking for the right number of people. "One day I'm cooking for seven people and have a huge pile of dishes to clean up," she explains. "The next day, my two oldest kids might be with their dad, while Jack's kids are with their mom, and I'm cooking for three. Then two of them come back and I'm cooking for five!" Anna deals by cooking ahead of time (see Chapter 6 for more information on once-a-month or once-a-week cooking) and freezing or refrigerating everything in two-serving batches. "Then I can heat up two, four, six or eight servings at a time. There's usually one serving left extra, but it almost always gets eaten. Hillshire Farms lunchmeat comes in reusable Glad containers that are the perfect size for two servings of casserole or lasagna!" Anna also makes sure there are always plenty of easy-to-grab foods around, like bagged salad kits, frozen burritos, and lunch meat and hoagie rolls. "I like us to all eat dinner together, but I have come to accept that we won't necessarily always all be eating the same thing," she admits.

Child Support

If you or your spouse—or both of you!—are paying child support for children from a previous relationship, blending two budgets into one can be complicated. In a big family, it's even more complicated because you have to figure out how to divide the pie into more pieces.

"I know a lot of women who want to have more children with their new husband, and see his child support obligations as an obstacle," says Maureen, who has two children from a previous marriage and two step-children from her husband's previous marriage—and is considering adding another child to the family. "To me, that's a completely backward way of looking at it. My husband's existing kids should be his first priority. I'd gladly have a few more children, but our financial reality is that we can only afford to add one more. But how could I live with myself if I griped about my husband supporting his kids just because I want to have more babies with him?"

Who's Working?

It's an unfortunate fact that many second marriages—statistically more than first marriages—will end in divorce. Why does this matter to you now? If you're putting aside your own career or education in order to stay at home with your stepchildren you should understand how it could affect you down the road—you may be out of the workforce for several years, therefore not acquiring job skills, experience, or Social Security, but be left without financial support if your marriage ends. The more children there are in your house—including stepchildren—the longer you could potentially be out of the workforce, and the bigger financial risk you'll undertake. Being an at-home parent—or stepparent!—can be a wonderful thing, but it's important that you make sure you and your children will be adequately supported not only now, but in the future. This is especially important if you're caring for children who are yours but not your husband's, or your husband's, but not yours: stepparents generally have no financial obligations to stepchildren if a marriage ends, and family courts are moving away from awarding extended spousal support and alimony.

Blending the Bucks

Money is a difficult topic to address, even in the most uncomplicated of marriages. Add child support obligations and differences in how families value and spend their income, and you've got a recipe for strain. It's a good idea to sit down with a financial planner to figure out your new family's long- and short-term financial goals—and how to meet them.

His Rules, Her Rules, Our Rules

Discipline and rules can be hot-button issues in a blended family. Each set of children may be used to very different rules, but with other kids in the house who will certainly notice any unfairness, it's not practical for one household to operate under two sets of rules. For example, Krista's house rules are very different from the house rules her teenage stepsons are used to at their mother's house, and that has caused some issues. "When my stepsons were very young, it was easy having two sets of rules, and the kids seemed to adjust well going back and forth. As they got older and the rules got a little stricter, there was some confusion and difficulties for them adjusting back and forth. The secret on our side was consistency … if there was conflict, it was very simple—we'd say, "That may be how it is at your mom's house, but this is how we do it here." Krista says that the fact that she is very much a co-parent in her home—for both her children and her husband's children—allows her to be both firm and loving while enforcing the house rules. "A large part of it for us, is that I have never behaved as if the older boys are someone else's children and therefore I have to treat them differently than my own. I show them the same amount of respect and attention as my children and I expect the same from them. I also don't leave it only to their father to deal with situations as they arise, as this is *our* family, not his family and my family."

In Krista's situation, taking a front-and-center role with her stepkids comes naturally, in part because she's been with their father since the boys were very small. But what about families that don't blend until later? In David's household, he says that taking such a direct approach could have backfired. "Like it or not, my kids are only in the house two days a week, and they've only known my wife for a couple of years. We had no interest in trying to force her into an active parenting role where they were concerned." Things were a bit different with his wife's children, because David lives with them full-time and their own father lives far away and rarely sees them. But even in spite of that, "We've sort of fallen into traditional roles, where my wife takes care of most of the child-rearing and discipline, and I am the fun-time guy," he explains. Because his own children are older and spend most of their time in a more permissive household, David admits that the "house rules" get pretty bent during their visits. "But we try not to present it as one set of kids enjoying different rules from the other," he explains. "We tell the younger kids that on the weekend, the rules change a bit—and for the most part, they benefit from that, too." For instance, on the weekends all of the kids get later bedtimes, can watch more TV, don't do as many chores, and are allowed to eat more junk food. "It's pretty easy to just pass most of the differences off as a weekend thing." David says he's comfortable with the way he and his wife handle their two separate-but-equal families: "I suppose some would disagree, but I think the notion that you can completely blend two families, especially when both families had years to develop on their own, is kind of unrealistic." Instead of acting like true siblings, David says, he'll be happy if the kids develop friendships and get along while they are kids. "I have no idea if they'll still be close in ten or twenty years—I hope they are, but I think I'm okay with however it turns out, especially since each child already has at least one 'real' brother or sister."

No matter how you decide to handle discipline in your blended household, to avoid resentment on either side it's smart to keep emotion out of the equation entirely. Come up with a system for assigning responsibilities and privileges, with built-in consequences for not following through on responsibilities. Then you won't have to worry that you're coming down too hard on your child because you want to make a good impression on your stepkids or that you may be inadvertently favoring your own kids. A chart or point system can help remove self-doubt and also make it less likely your kids or stepkids will feel they're being treated unfairly.

In some more extreme examples of nonblended blended families, the parenting, living arrangements, and even finances of each set of children may be kept completely separate. They may even have different sets of rules and privileges, and the "part-time" kids may feel more like guests than members of the family. Though arrangements like this can work well for some families, they can also lead to bitterness between the step-siblings, who don't understand why there are two sets of rules and expectations, and the kids may never have the opportunity to muddle through their differences and work out kinks.

Yours, Mine ... and Ours?

What really happens if you add a new child that's "his" and "hers," while all the rest of the children in the house are "yours" or "mine"? There may be a considerable amount of resentment and jealousy from older kids, and young ones will pick up on that tension. "I didn't really realize it was happening at first, but the amount of resentment my youngest stepson, who was five at the time, felt toward the new baby in our family went way beyond run-of-the-mill jealousy," says Mike, who has a teenaged son from a previous marriage, two step-children ages nine and seven, and a three-year-old child with his wife. "I think he felt really threatened by the baby, and who can blame him? Not only was he no longer the baby of the family, but the new baby belonged to both his mother and I. He probably thought we would love her more than him." And when Mike caught his stepson bullying the baby over and over, he admits that he probably didn't react in the best way. "I saw this big kid picking on my baby, and I'd explode," he says. "Looking back, it probably seemed like I was telling 'her' kid to keep his hands off 'my' kid. Finally, we just started keeping them away from each other. Now that both kids are older, the bullying has stopped, but they also aren't very close. I wish we had addressed it earlier, so that maybe my stepson would have felt less threatened and I could have put myself in his shoes a bit."

Though the kids born into a blended family never have to adjust to the new family the way the older kids did, there can be some pretty big drawbacks for the "ours," too. "I remember feeling really isolated from the rest of my half-brothers and sisters, like I was the outsider," says Erin, who was the only child who resulted from her parents' marriage—the youngest of five. "They were all older—like ten and up—by the time I came along, so in a lot of ways it was like being an only child." Erin later found out that, while the two sets of stepsiblings had been fighting before she came along, their mutual horror over their parents having a baby together was actually a bonding experience. "My sister admitted once that it was almost like I was the common enemy. She was joking, but I think there was a lot of truth to it. And they're all nice to me now, but I don't think I'll ever be as close with them as they all are with each other."

Erin, now thirty, admits she is bitter about her upbringing. "I feel like I got the worst of both worlds," she says. "My parents are getting old, and I don't know how much longer they'll be around. I have to share my parents with my brothers and sisters, and they all had kids way before me, so my kids have to share their grandparents, too. My other siblings all have two sets of parents, while I only have one. And the one thing I should have gotten out of having a big family, built-in friends, isn't really there because I'm not very close with my siblings."

Erin says there are two things she'd do differently if she were to remarry someone with children. "I probably wouldn't have another child, but if I did, I'd make sure not to wait until my youngest was ten years old," she says. "And I'd make sure the older kids in the house were really encouraged to accept the new baby." Erin also says she isn't sure she'd add just one new child to an existing blended family. "If there were two, at least they'd be in it together," she explains.

Not all "only ours" kids feel like Erin does. Sharon, who was also the youngest member of her family and the only one who was born to both parents, says her older brothers and sisters doted on her. "My parents made a point of bringing us all together, again and again, as a family. In fact, one of my earliest memories is of one of our weekly family meetings." Now in her late 20s, Sharon says she and her four brothers and sisters are very close. "I really don't think of them as half-brothers and half-sisters, though I guess that's what they are," she says. "I think my parents did a very good job of balancing their needs with mine so that nobody felt left out or resentful."

Each child in a blended family has experienced a significant loss, whether the parents divorced, one parent died, or a parent left, even if it happened very early in their lives. Multiply that loss by several children and add in divided loyalties, insecurities, and the upheaval of a parent remarrying, and you can see that coming together as a big, happy, blended family can be difficult. Get plenty of help and support for yourself and your kids as you go through this process. These resources may help: *One Family, Two Family, New Family* by Lisa Cohn and William Merkel, Ph.D. (Riverwood Books, 2004). This award-winning book acknowledges the complexity of blending families and offers unique guidance rather than one-size-fits-all advice.

The Smart Stepfamily: New Seven Steps to a Healthy Family by Ron L. Deal (Bethany House, 2006) This book, written from a Christian perspective, reexamines the myth of *The Brady Bunch* blended family and offers a step-by-step guide to help parents and stepparents move past the wounds of divorce and build a new life together.

The National Stepfamily Resource Center is a clearinghouse of information and resources for stepfamilies: www.stepfamilies.info.

StepTogether, a virtual chapter of the Stepfamily Association of America, offers message boards, resources, a chat room, and retreats for blended families to connect for advice and encouragement: www.steptogether.org.

Whether it's through remarriage, adoption, fostering, or the birth of multiples, adding lots of kids at a time can be both exciting and exhausting—so no matter what the circumstances of your family's personal population explosion, you'll want to make sure you have lots of support and information at your disposal before the "new kids" arrive.

Bunk Beds and Hand-Me-Downs: The Joys and Challenges of Table for Eight Family Life

We've covered a lot of the practical aspects of having big families—how to deal with the unique challenges that having more than the average number of kids can present. But what we haven't talked about yet is the feel-good side—the reasons people love having lots of kids, as well as the reasons people love growing up with lots of siblings—and the annoying side, too.

Stupid Comments, Snappy Comebacks

Every big-family parent has fielded them: the never-ending comments and questions people feel compelled to make about the number of kids you've got. Some of the comments are good-natured; some are outright hostile … and everything in between.

I group these dumb comments into a few categories:

Harmless

These comments are usually meant to be funny, sympathetic, or friendly. They don't bother me individually, though hearing them often can get old.

"Are you going to keep trying for a girl (or boy)?" Trust me, if it hasn't happened yet, I don't think "trying" is working …

"You must be a saint!" or *"How do you do it?"* Often, a frazzled-looking mom of one or two kids says this in a pleading tone. I look back to myself in her position and know that I would have had the same questions, so I try to take the time to answer her—and my answer is almost always "For me, it was a lot harder to go from one or two than it was to go from two to three, or three to four. Once you're outnumbered, you're outnumbered!"

"Are they all yours?" No, they just keep following me home like stray puppies …

"How many are there?" I can't remember. You'll just have to count them yourself.

"You've got your hands full!" Yes, I sure do … and I like it that way.

"Are you going to have more?" Are *you?*

Cluelessly Rude

"Do they all have the same father?" or *"Were they all planned?"* There's no good way to respond to comments like these because it's so unbelievably tacky that a complete stranger would comment on another person's sex life, fertility, birth control successes and failures, or the paternity of their children. In these cases, I think it's best to just give them an open-mouthed stare, or respond with something like "Did you just ask what I think you asked?" anything to make them think for a minute about what they've just said.

Just Plain Rude

"Better you than me!" Simple: "I agree." They may not get it right away, but it's fun to watch their expressions slowly change as they realize you've just insulted them.

"Don't you know what causes that?" "You mean it doesn't just happen on its own?" (Look angrily at husband.) "Honey, you've got some explaining to do!"

Or try one of these:

"Yes, and it appears I'm getting more of it than you are."

With dumb, innocent look: "I'm not sure. Why don't you explain it to me?"

"Don't you think that's a few too many?" Which ones would you like me to send back?

The Kids Have Their Say

Sure it's easy to make assumptions about how kids in big families might feel about having lots of siblings. But what's really going on in their heads? Here are what some kids have to say about growing up in a big brood.

The Good

"I love growing up in a big family. It has taught me how to relate to children of all ages and to become social with kids. I always have someone to play ball with, and I enjoy my little brothers and sister; they make me happy and even out the 'stress' of teenage-hood. When my life seems awkward, I always have my little ones to make me smile. My treasured moments are each of my younger siblings' births; didn't get to see them come into this world, but right away I got to hold them. Sometimes I wish I was an only child for selfish reasons; I could have more things and I wouldn't have anyone touching or ruining my belongings."—Kyle, sixteen, five siblings.

"I like to have a lot of brothers to play with. I always have something to do and someone to do it with."—Brian, ten, five siblings.

"I like all my brothers. I like playing with them, and I like that they teach me stuff like baseball, football, guitar, and piano."—Maddie, six, five siblings.

"In big families, you can have more people in games, you can talk to anyone, and do things together. It's fun with a whole bunch of people; you have a lot of advice if you have a problem. One of the benefits is you'll always have someone there for you."—Allasyn, thirteen, six siblings

"I like having people to play with. There is always something to do!" —Haleigh, nine, six siblings.

"I like having a lot of sisters and brothers. I love them so much. They don't always want to play, but when they do, I love to play."—Owen, four, six siblings.

"One of the best things about living in a big family is that if there's something that needs to be done, there's usually someone who can do it. We don't have a lot of little kids in our family like a lot of large families do, so I don't know how it is for them. But in my family if someone wants their bike fixed, they go to one brother. If they want to know if their clothes match, they ask one of the girls. If they want someone to write something for them, they come to me. Of course, there's always things no one can do, like build a house, but the benefit to having so many people with many different interests is that usually when there's some odd job that needs to be done, there's usually someone that knows how to do it."—Tessa, sixteen, ten siblings.

The Not-So-Good

"Sometimes we fight, and sometimes I don't like to share my stuff!"
—Kaitlyn, six, six siblings.

"When we go out together as a family, people usually stare at us. They ask us if we are a school or something like that, and my mom or dad says, 'No, these are my kids.' They just keep on asking more and more questions, which gets annoying."—Anna, fourteen, ten siblings.

"When you want your privacy, someone comes and bugs you!"
—Haleigh, nine, six siblings.

"I don't like sharing my toys, especially my tractors and Lightning McQueen stuff!"—Braxton, two, six siblings.

It's hard being the oldest; sometimes the little ones don't like to listen to you if you tell them to do something."—Allasyn, thirteen, six siblings.

"I think one of the worst things is the noise. Most of the people in our house probably make less noise than normal teenagers, but multiply it by twelve, and it makes for a very noisy house. For one thing, our house has pretty thin walls that let noise carry really far, so even if I'm in my bedroom with the door closed I can hear if someone's taking a shower, washing the dishes, arguing in their bedroom, and sometimes all of those and more. But even if our house had good soundproof walls, the sound would still be annoying at times. I don't know how many times I've been woken up by two girls laughing and talking loudly not too far outside my door, or the boys yelling at each other to get their room cleaned up. The noise continues throughout the day, too, from arguments to dogs barking

at strangers, to girls screaming at insects, etc. It's become a long standing joke around here that something strange is going on if everyone's quiet."
—Tessa, sixteen, 10 siblings.

Table for Eight Moms Talk

Now that we've let the kids have their say, what do parents think? Here, four notable moms of many dish about everything from staying sane in a busy household to raising lots of kids in a big city.

Developing "Momfidence"

Paula Spencer, mom of four, author of *Momfidence: An Oreo Never Killed Anybody and Other Secrets of Happier Parenting* (Three Rivers Press) and "Momfidence" columnist in *Woman's Day* magazine, shares with us some of her thoughts on raising a Table for Eight family:

Did you always plan to have a big family?

No! I always imagined I would have children—always plural, my mother was an only child and found it lonely—but never how many. I had one and thought, "This is great!" And then another, and another, and another, all planned because we were enjoying it so. The last one was born just before I turned 40, and although I was sorely tempted to have one more, suddenly I was just too tired.

Everyone who knew me pre-kids is surprised I have four: I was definitely "Least Likely to Wear a Snugli" among my friends. Then again, I didn't realize four was the new six or seven until I was deep into it and still hanging out at the pee-wee pool while all my friends' kids had graduated to the big pool.

Do you think you're a different kind of parent to four kids than you were to one or two?

I think I'm more mellow and less quick to intervene. With just one or two, you think you have to be regulating everything, but then with a bunch you see they are very effective at regulating and negotiating all by themselves.

Another example: when my son was a toddler, he was a very picky eater, and I went through all kinds of machinations to get him to eat—I mean for years. The youngest is only slightly better, but I never made a big deal out of it. By then I guess I had learned that she wouldn't starve or develop scurvy and it would be a better use of my energies at mealtime to get her to sit up straight and say "please" and "thank you."

I also used to call the doctor every time the first two had a fever and learned by the last two when I really needed help. A lot of how I am a different parent has to do with just climbing a learning curve.

School is different—with just one, I knew the names of all his preschool classmates and hung out in the room. I only knew a handful of the kids in my youngest child's preschool. It's both the result of experience—i.e., realizing there is no point to hanging out in the kids' classrooms when I could be capitalizing on this time alone—and of practicality. You can only split your attention and your body so many ways. Now I show up in the kids' classes once or twice a year and that's it, and that's just fine with everybody. They see me enough at home.

In your book Momfidence you advocate a balanced view of parenting. Do you think this kind of balance is especially important for moms with more than one or two kids?

Judging from what I hear from readers, mothers of large families seem to come by momfidence—a laid-back confidence about childrearing—more easily. I think it's because when you're responsible for a lot of little people, you, by definition, can't worry about every little insignificant thing (daily food intake, germs, etc.), or you'd go crazy. Having more than one child fracturing your focus helps you better tune into the big picture and what's really important to you, rather than what everybody else thinks. Also, of course, you gain experience with each child and that boosts your confidence.

Was it hardest for you to go from 0-1, 1-2, 2-3, or 3-4 kids? Which was the easiest transition, and why?

I think 2 to 3 is hardest because you are suddenly outnumbered (in a two-parent household) and that involves working out some new coping strategies. Three to four was easiest—the more, the merrier.

If you could go back and space your kids differently, would you?

No. I liked having them closely spaced—mine are 21 months, 32 months, and 29 months apart—because they share interests and entertainment, and they play together. And I'd much rather have spent 10 continuous years changing diapers, as I did, than to be done with diapers for a span of years and then have to start all over again.

Is there anything you used to do when you had one or two kids that you had to give up when you got to three or four? Conversely, is there anything you never did when you had a smaller family that you decided was necessary for a bigger family?

It makes it much less likely to travel anywhere by plane—that's a really big one. And much as I hate to say it, if I only had one or two, it's much more likely they would have stayed in private schools; when the third hit school age, we moved to a place with better public schools because four private educations would have been a strain, if not impossible.

We pared down to one TV so that we could better track what was being watched and all watch together as a family. Put a toy box or basket in every room the kids frequented.

How many gallons of milk does your family go through in a week?

We go through about 7 to 8 gallons a week, depending on how much spilling there is!

Birth, Twins, and After-Baby Care

Robin Elise Weiss, LCCE and author of the About.com Guide to Having a Baby is also a busy mom of seven kids, aged two to sixteen. She gave me some great advice on adding twins to an already-big family and caring for yourself after giving birth when you've got lots of other people to care for!

Tell me a little about adding twins to a family that's already got lots of kids. How were you able to care for your other children in addition to the very time-consuming task of feeding and caring for two infants?

Our twins were number five and six. It was a total surprise. We were thrilled! I think that we were a bit cocky about our ability to parent two at once. It helped us maintain our sanity during pregnancy to think, "We've done this before—we can handle two!" We were so totally overwhelmed when they came!

The twins were born on a Saturday morning just as winter break started—it was a nightmare having no real help because of the holidays. I should have planned for more help.

Breastfeeding was so helpful. I can't image having to do bottles and I know, because despite being full term, great weights, etc., my girls had trouble feeding. I pumped a lot those first few weeks. Finally around three months it all clicked and we were able to get rid of the pump and everything that went with it. It was so great to be forced to sit down, because not only did I feed the babies, but I nurtured myself and the other kids. Because even if laundry was calling, my kids had to have me and if I was sitting down I might as well color with my two-year-old or chat with the older kids, play chess, etc. It was just a neat realization, even though it took a while to piece it all together.

After giving birth so many times, did there ever come a point at which you thought … I'd really rather not do that again? How did you get past it and plan a peaceful and empowering birth experience?

Sometimes when being a doula (a caregiver who supports a woman in labor) at a birth I'd watch how hard someone was working, and I'd feel a sense of awe and worry: what did I get myself into? But watching that new mom hold her little one was always enough to turn it around for me. Homebirths were so much easier on us as a large family, even though that's not why we originally made that choice. (Originally it was to prevent interventions we didn't want for me or the babies.) I can't imagine how hard it would be to have to find someone to watch all my kids on the spur of the moment.

Tell me about the experience of having your older children at their siblings' births.

We planned to have everyone there. They were free to come and go but usually stayed away until just before a baby would arrive. They each were well prepared and had a specific job. We even let some of the kids do "big" jobs like cut the cord or announce the sex of the baby. They also liked jobs like bringing wet wash clothes or snacks to me or their dad. One of my favorite pictures from Ada's birth (#7) is of the kids all piled on my bed, peering over the edge as I sat on a stool in the corner with Kevin and the midwives. They look peaceful and happy, waiting for the new baby. They always did a great job and lovingly performed. I think it really helps with the sibling rivalry aspects.

Do you have tips for pregnant women in big families—how they can take good care of themselves when there are so many others to take care of as well, and how they can make sure their postpartum experience is as restful as possible?

I implemented a mandatory rest period. Every afternoon we'd pile in the bed and nap or read. Even working full time, I'd do it. The kids liked the extra attention and I enjoyed being off my feet.

I also take a childbirth class *every* time. It's my date night with my husband, Kevin. It helps us focus on the baby-to-be and plan ahead for the birth.

Postpartum, we have little family help, so we actually use some paid postpartum help in addition to Kevin taking several weeks off. We used a postpartum doula. She came over a couple of periods of time, like 3-4 hours 2-3 days a week. She would do a load of laundry, tidy the kitchen, make dinner and entertain anyone who would let her. She also had a good sense of when I needed help to pump or needed a snack—or a bath alone. I didn't have to say a word to her, she knew what to do. It was amazing, and a great gift idea for the mom-to-be, no matter what her family size.

Which was the most challenging transition for you as far as adding new member(s) to your family? Which was the easiest?

Timing is an issue. I've found I'm more likely to get postpartum depression if I give birth in late fall/winter, simply because it's hard to get out. We don't always have great control over that but it helps! Other than that I think the hardest part is the same no matter how many kids—going back to car seats and diapers, the sleep deprivation, etc.

In talking to families who don't have as many children, they think I've got the big secret that makes it all easy. The big secret is that I don't.

I'm not well-organized, I struggle with that every day. I don't have extra patience—just ask the kids. Don't think I have a larger than average maternal instinct. I put one foot in front of the other just like everyone else. The only difference is that my pot for oatmeal holds more than most.

What's the dumbest or rudest thing anyone's ever said about your family's size, and how did you respond?

This is where the title of my blog came from: "Don't you know what causes that?" I have a lot of zingers for the answer, though my personal favorites are: "My husband is a mathematician and he loves to multiply!" "Of course I do, I have a degree in it," and "Yes we do—and we like it!"

How I feel about questions and comments depends on how I predict the person is asking or meaning it. A generic stranger smiling is one thing with a passing question. It's the people who stop and grill you on costs of raising kids, global warming (it's large families' faults don't you know!), what kind of car do we drive?, do we have cable TV? (yes, that's where we learned *how* to do it), and all of the other questions.

I take exception to some of the large family stereotypes. I don't home school. I'm not (insert religion here). Having a large family was just something that happened, we didn't plan to have this many kids and yet we planned every single one (well, one of the twins was a surprise, but we don't know which one).

I don't stay home all day. My kids aren't overly sheltered. I'm not a strict disciplinarian, nor am I permissive as a parent. The apron strings are cut when appropriate per kid, and each child is an individual.

What food does your family eat the most of? How much do you go through in a week?

We eat kosher, so there's no meat in the house. We run through beans and brown rice. In a week, I'd say we use 5 lbs of brown rice!

One Big, Diverse Family

Mary Ostyn is a writer and mother of eight kids, four of whom came to her family through international adoption. Mary keeps two popular blogs, both of which can be found through her website: www.maryostyn.com.

Here, Mary tells us about her experiences with international adoption and how raising a very large family has changed her as a parent.

You came from a big family. How did that play into your decision to have a big family yourself?

As a child I always adored babies. But as a teen I swore I'd never have more than four children. At 15 I cringed to be seen in the grocery store with all my siblings—I hated all the attention we got. But even back then when I was wishing my family was more "traditional," I couldn't imagine who we could do without. Each person contributes so much.

When John and I got married, we thought we'd have three or four kids. After our fourth child we had a couple years where we thought we were actually done; we even took "permanent" measures. But when he was three, our eyes were opened to the orphans in the world, and we realized that adoption would be the perfect way to add to our family. Some people think of adoption as second best, but having experienced both, I can truthfully say that adoption is just as wonderful a way to build your family.

Did you adopt your children in or out of birth order (or a mix of both)? Was this a conscious decision?

Our four oldest are ours biologically, and our youngest four arrived through adoption. We adopted them all in birth order. We plan to adopt again, and may adopt out of birth order at some point, especially if we end up adopting a sibling group. I know lots of people who have adopted out of birth order and it has worked fine. But there's a lot to be said for adopting kids one at a time, and letting kids each have a time to be the youngest in the family. I think it makes it less stressful on everyone.

I'd like to hear about some of the challenges involved in adding to an already-large family through international adoption. A few things that come to mind immediately: associated costs, all the travel involved, and caring for children who may have emotional issues or attachment problems when you've already got a lot of kids. Have any of those been issues for your family during your adoption journey?

Of course money is an issue when you're talking about international adoption. Our adoptions all cost in the range of $13,000-$15,000. Twice we refinanced our house. Another time we got an unexpected inheritance. For our most recent adoption my husband sold a large piece of equipment.

One thing many people aren't aware of is the $11,000 adoption tax credit that helps people get their money back after they adopt. And many big companies offer adoption benefits as well. My husband's employer offers a $2,000 adoption benefit; we keep joking that if they decide to get rid of that particular benefit, it will be because of how often we use it.

Sure, adoption is expensive. But how many people do you know who have car loans? Or credit card debt? It is about priorities, and deciding what you value most. Chances are you can find a $3,000 car that would work almost as well as a $30,000 car. Heck, my husband recently found a nice little commuting car for $650. It has 86,000 miles and gets 40 mpg.

You asked about the adoption travel. Several countries, including Korea and Ethiopia, don't even require that you travel to get your children. But personally, I love travel. To me it's a benefit of adoption. Because of our adoptions, all three of our teenagers have already traveled internationally. Visiting another country is an eye-opening experience. We hope to travel internationally with all our children eventually.

As far as the emotional issues that can be involved in adoption—as is possible with any child, there can be issues. Adoptive parents should read all they can and be prepared. Some kids will have issues and some won't. We did have one child who took a few months to settle in, which was challenging that first year. But he is doing great now.

I think it is wise not to add too many children too rapidly. Let the new kids settle in well before you talk about more. Also, it's a good idea to prepare your other children … let them know that, even if the new child isn't a newborn on homecoming, he'll be taking up a bunch of mom's time for a while at first.

Which transition has been the hardest for you (going from 0-1, 1-2, etc.)? Which has been the easiest? Why?

Going from two to three was hardest for us. At that point we were outnumbered. When our third child was born, our first was three years old and our second was 20 months. I had kids on my lap constantly for 6 months. It didn't help that our third child was a high needs baby. He literally had to be held constantly for months.

It was then that my husband started making breakfast every morning he was home, and that helped me so much. I am not a morning person, and just knowing that breakfast is taken care of is really nice.

Subsequent arrivals were not quite as hard because by then I had big kids who were willing and able to help out. Really, #7 and #8 were some of our easiest adjustments. They are both mellow, cheery little kids, and at that point I had so many capable big kids to zip through the daily chores that I was free to cuddle the new baby and chat with the bigger ones, and really savor the time.

Name one practical challenge of having a mega-family and how you overcame it.

We've overcome various challenges over the years. When we were expecting our seventh child we really needed a fifth bedroom for our teenaged boys, but we didn't want to go into debt for some big addition to our house. We were able to carve a small bedroom into one corner of an upstairs family room. And I mean small—it measures 7 by 16 feet and part of that has a slanting-down attic-style ceiling. But it is absolutely awesome.

My husband made the boys captain-style beds with 6-drawer under-dressers for their clothes, so they don't need separate dressers. Those beds are at opposite ends of the room, with the foot of each bed tucked under the lowest slant of the ceiling. There's more storage behind the knee walls at the foot of each bed. In the middle of the room, directly opposite the doorway, there's a dormer window with a window seat and an awesome view. The empty floor space in the room totals 7 by 8 feet, but it's just big enough. They love it. Thanks to my dad helping us out, the whole room only cost us $2,000 to build. I feel happy every time I walk into that room—it is a charming, cozy space, and was just the perfect solution for our situation.

Do you think you are a different parent now that you have a big family than you were when you had one or two kids?

Yes, I think I'm gradually becoming more patient. I haven't "arrived"—at the rate I'm going, I figure I'll have my temper licked by the time I'm 70 or so. But I'm learning to expect the little frustrations. Someone is going to spill their drink at mealtime once a day at least. Someone else is going to drag seven coats out of the closet and leave them strung everywhere. Inevitably the barn boots will be left right where I'll trip over them on the way to the van. And always, always, someone is going to have to go potty when I'm at that back corner of Wal-Mart farthest from the bathrooms. I think what I'm getting better at is just sighing and dealing with it.

I also definitely have more tricks up my sleeve, more ways to deal with common problems. I've faced a lot of issues and I've figured out what's effective. I know how to teach a seven year old to read, a two year old to use the potty, and a 10 year old to clean the bathroom. Of course each kid is a little different, and I have to adapt my tactics to fit the child. But experience helps, definitely.

How many loaves of bread does your family go through in a week?

We buy bread buy the dozen, every couple weeks. Plus we go through a lot of hamburger buns and do homemade biscuits and rolls. We also go through at least 4 dozen eggs, and a couple dozen bananas. Every Sunday after church we have a tradition of hamburgers and home fries. For that meal we cook a dozen burgers and roast 8 or 10 potatoes.

Big City, Big Career

Amanda Foreman is an accomplished British historian and author. Her award-winning book *Georgiana, Duchess of Devonshire*, was a #1 bestseller. Amanda currently lives and writes in New York City with her husband, three children, and soon, baby twins! Here, Amanda tells us about her transition from childless career woman to mother of many.

Can you tell me a little about how having lots of kids has (and still is) changing the way you approach your work life?

The biggest change is how I have to combine three jobs—that is writer, wife, and mother—into just 24 hours. Before I married I used to start work at 7:30 A.M. and finish writing late into the night. Now, I am extremely lucky if I can write for three hours at a stretch. I have learned how to concentrate without any props. If I have only 20 minutes for writing, then I write for those twenty minutes. I have learned not to be upset or resentful when my work life takes a backseat to the demands of others. My view is that having such small children is temporary and that in a few years time I will be able to put in more hours for my work.

Tell me about living in a big city with a big family.

What is great about living in a big city is that everything is within walking distance—the park, school, extra-curricular activities, friends. But getting around is hard. Subways don't accommodate double strollers, taxis only take four people, that kind of thing. People are shocked when they hear we are going to have five children. Three is considered a lot—four huge. Five is simply a freak show, but also seems to indicate unimaginable wealth. The assumption seems to be that each child would naturally have its own bedroom, whereas in fact we have three in one and the twins will go in the other.

As a historian, you write about times when it was likely more common to have big families than it is today. Nowadays, critics of big families say that big families are unfair to kids—that there's less time, money, and so forth for each one. What do you think?

Studies show that women actually spend more time with their children than they did forty years ago. I think that attitudes have changed and we are much more child-centered. It is true that in big families there is much less money to go around, and children in large families have to share more. But there is a tremendous feeling of community and companion-ship that comes with having a large family. I also believe that there is less pressure from parents on their children to be perfect, high achievers.

Tell me about the reaction you get when you tell people that you—already a mom of three kids—are expecting twins. What do you say in response?

The reaction varies from "are the twins a mistake?" to "how lucky you are." Some ask whether it is difficult to manage so many children. And a few don't understand why I want so many children, particularly at the cost of possible harm to my career.

How many loads of laundry does your family wash in a week?

The washing machine never stops.